DESIGNING THE SCHOOL CURRICULUM

DESIGNING THE SCHOOL CURRICULUM

PETER S. HLEBOWITSH
University of Iowa

Boston ■ New York ■ San Francisco
Mexico City ■ Montreal ■ Toronto ■ London ■ Madrid ■ Munich ■ Paris
Hong Kong ■ Singapore ■ Tokyo ■ Cape Town ■ Sydney

Series Editor: *Traci Mueller*
Series Editorial Assistant: *Janice Hackenberg*
Senior Marketing Manager: *Krista Groshong*
Senior Production Editor: *Annette Pagliaro*
Editorial Production: *Marty Tenney, Modern Graphics, Inc.*
Composition Buyer: *Linda Cox*
Manufacturing Buyer: *Andrew Turso*
Cover Administrator: *Kristina Mose-Libon*
Text Composition: *Modern Graphics, Inc.*

For related titles and support materials, visit our online catalog at www.ablongman.com.

Between the time Website information is gathered and then published, it is not unusual for some sites to have closed. Also, the transcription of URLs can result in unintended typographical errors. The publisher would appreciate notification where these errors occur so that they may be corrected in subsequent editions.

Library of Congress Cataloging-in-Publication Data

Hlebowitsh, Peter S.
    Designing the school curriculum / Peter S. Hlebowitsh.
        p. cm.
    Includes bibliographical references and index.
    ISBN 0-205-39139-7
        1. Curriculum planning. I. Title.

LB2806.15.H56 2005
375'.001—dc22

                                                            2004049795

Printed in the United States of America

10 9 8 7 6 5 4 3   09 08 07 06 05

For Daniel Tanner

CONTENTS

CHAPTER FOUR
Defining Purposes   87

CHAPTER FIVE
Organizing the Macrocurriculum   125

CHAPTER SIX
Instruction and Pedagogy   159

CHAPTER SEVEN
Evaluation   181

CHAPTER EIGHT
Implementation   217

When my wife and I packed our oldest daughter off to school for the first time in 1993, we walked together up the hill from our home to Horn Elementary School. The name of the school had a familiar ring to it for me because, as I would later learn, it was named after Ernest Horn, a curriculum professor of some significance who dedicated many years of service to the University of Iowa. Known for his work in social studies education and spelling instruction, Ernest Horn very much fit in the style of the practical professor interested in school concerns. And his legacy is memorialized in something no less important than a neighborhood public school. That same year, when I found myself on the campus of ACT, which is located in the northeast corner of Iowa City, I noticed that one of the buildings was named after Ralph Tyler, a curriculum professor whose influence on the American school curriculum in the twentieth century is largely unmatched. I'll be making more than a few references to Tyler in these pages. But my point is that Horn and Tyler were curriculum professors who made a practical difference in the world and who are remembered not as theoreticians or critics, but as practical reformers and facilitators of the school experience.

Historically speaking, the methods of curriculum professors have followed in a line of concerns for the practical and the institutional. Progressive curricularists, especially those working out of the experimentalist views of John Dewey, provided unique insight into the process of curriculum development by focusing on approaches that used the school for the maintenance and improvement of the public interest. Practical proposals for school improvement flowed freely from these progressive curricularists. William Kilpatrick, for instance, articulated the Project Method, Jesse Newlon tested "life situations" curricula in the Denver schools, Harold Rugg wrote a series of provocative social studies texts, Ralph Tyler formulated his famous rationale in the context of the Eight Year Study and laboratory schools across the nation—often led by directors schooled in curriculum development—tested the practical vigor of various new ideas. For a short period of time, even John Dewey was involved in the operation of a laboratory school. The essential purpose of curriculum theory in such instances was curriculum development.

The sad reality today, however, is that few curriculum scholars have any interest in curriculum development concerns. But the need for curriculum development is not going to go away. The curriculum will either be influenced by curricularists or not. If curricularists decide to shift their focus away from curriculum development, they will likely give more influence to other determinants less informed by knowledge of schooling, teaching, or learning. So, here is a book that goes to school, as it were, and that makes its case on the point of the practical. It is for those of us who want to roll up our sleeves and get involved in the work of helping schools to rethink their design and their operations.

Chapter One is an introduction to the idea of curriculum design. We start with the basics because considerable confusion exists over just what comprises the act of curriculum development. Does it, for instance, script instructional methods for teachers? Does it have to be aligned to standards and standardized tests? And what about objectives? Isn't there a particular language that must be used and a particular level of specificity that must be met for an objective to be useful in the curriculum? The chapter explores the nature and main functions of curriculum development by making a separation between macrocurricular and microcurricular processes, the former focusing on school-wide concerns and the latter on classroom-based concerns. I also discuss the relation between the curriculum and the discretionary judgment of teachers in the context of practical classroom problems, such as the increasing pressure to "teach to the test."

Chapters Two and Three discuss the theoretical foundations for curriculum development. They outline the leading ideas that give early shape and meaning to the more procedural decisions in the curriculum development process. Because one has to make determinations about the purposes of the school, the content of the curriculum, the nature of the learning experiences, and the ways to engage an evaluative strategy, one needs a good theoretical foundation to make these determinations wisely. In this regard, I argue that the moving force of curriculum theory is essentially reducible to three main concerns: (1) the nature of the learner; (2) the aims and values of the society; and (3) some sense of worthy and organized subject matter or knowledge. But no one can work effectively in these three domains without exercising some philosophical sensibilities. The discussion of philosophy in Chapter Three targets the ways that different philosophical orientations broach the three essential elements of curriculum theory.

Chapter Four is the initiating chapter for the procedural features of curriculum development. The act of curriculum development should be, one way or another, influenced by a sense of mission or purpose. The design of the curriculum has to take this task quite seriously because curriculum purposes give justification to most instructional decisions. So, I articulate just what it means to get serious about the design of a school mission and what the conceptual boundaries are for the use of aims, goals, and objectives in the curriculum. The general idea is to give the curriculum a sense of identity without imposing an instructional will in the school. This is mostly accomplished by opting for generality in the formation of purposes and by seeing the organization of purposes as a two-dimensional undertaking that requires the curriculum worker to articulate the skills and values desired in the curriculum in company with an identifiable sense of content or subject matter.

The design of purposes leads directly to questions about how such purposes will be attained in the experience of the school. To tackle such questions, a general outline for the curriculum has to be undertaken. I explain this task in Chapter Five. Historically, the school can be seen as organized along two main fronts. The first, known as *general education*, could be interpreted as the core of experiences used in the education of all youth for the purposes of providing some common universe of understanding and discourse. General education coursework is conducted in mixed-ability settings with the intention of fulfilling largely normative (common) learning goals. The second organizing function, which I call *specialized education*, has an individualizing role in the curriculum, aiming to assist with individual exploratory, enrichment, and remedial needs. In most cases, the curriculum developer will have to find a way to organize experiences so that both common experiences and specializing experiences are secured in the curriculum. These dual macro-functions in the school curriculum are explored in the action of the elementary, middle, and secondary school.

Chapter Six defines a kind of moment of truth for the curriculum developer. It focuses on the acts of instruction and pedagogy, both of which are the essence of the school curriculum experience. The difference between instruction and pedagogy is explained as a distinction between planned and emergent elements of good teaching. A strong curriculum needs both elements to fulfill its commitments to school children. I also dedicate space to the question of how one selects good instructional routines for the classroom. When is a cooperative strategy, for instance, preferred over a more expository method? When is a demonstration technique viewed as more appropriate than skill drill? Such questions underscore the importance of offering a good variety of activities in the classroom. Variance, in fact, is the key to good instruction; the deeper the reservoir of instructional insight, the greater the possibilities of finding an adequate instructional approach suited to particular curriculum objectives. But the curriculum developer must also understand the special power of pedagogy. The discretionary power of the teacher resides in pedagogy, in the ability to account for the unique factors of the classroom and the changing dimensions of a learning situation.

Chapter Seven broaches the often neglected topic of evaluation in the curriculum. When we seek to teach something, we must eventually ask how successfully it has been taught. This gets us into the formulation of strategies that evaluate the attainment of the school's core educational purposes. These data could be taken from paper and pencil tests, from observational accounts, or from other relevant sources. Evaluation, in fact, should not put a single value or weight on any one particular technique or outcome, and should be prepared to bring a wide instrumentality of approaches to the task of determining whether key purposes have been attained in the experience of the school. I also discuss the methods by which the curriculum can be revised, targeting ways to appraise purposes, structural features of the curriculum, instruction and pedagogy, and the appraisal approaches themselves.

Finally, the curriculum developer must understand that the best intentions and predesigned plans for the curriculum can be easily scuttled if attention is not paid to important implementational concerns. The curriculum will likely have little influence in the experience of children unless teachers (and other important involvement groups) have some ownership of it. In Chapter Eight, I examine the nature of the planning process from the standpoint of the people who need to be involved in it. Good implementation is always served when the curriculum is responsive to emergent problems in the school community. To this end, I also designed several different scenarios that require the student to diagnose curriculum problems and to attend to them with multiple working solutions. The purpose here is to see the curriculum beyond its "paper" connotation and to understand the role curriculum thinking plays in the examination of school policies.

Because much of the work completed here is rooted, in one way or another, in conversations and experiences with a few good friends and colleagues, I would like to thank them properly. Since 1995, Gregory Hamot and I have been involved in several large-scale curriculum development projects. With U.S. State Department grants, we have taken on the reconstruction of various civic education curricula in three post-Soviet societies: the Czech Republic, the Republic of Armenia, and the Republic of Bulgaria. The scale of our work in each country varied, but the common charge was to redesign the way civic education is taught in the public schools in the light of the Soviet regime's collapse and the attendant awakening and embrace of democratic processes. The projects were all complicated by linguistic, cultural, and administrative factors, but the problem we had to solve was not unlike that of schools and curriculum developers everywhere: how to design a school experience that fulfills a clear and wise expectation of purpose in a way that is responsive to the learner and to the society, and that allows us to understand its effects on student behavior and student knowledge. Hamot has always had wisdom to offer on this point and has helped me to cultivate my own sense of what it means to do curriculum work. I have also been lucky to be able to dial-up William Wraga whenever I needed to talk or to think through an idea. This has been going on for about ten years now and he still tolerates it. No one, however, has had a greater influence on my thinking than Daniel Tanner, who taught me long ago that the school curriculum needs to be deliberately and consciously conceived to fulfill a comprehensive mandate that represents an ideal for living a good life in a good society. Although I didn't know it at the time, this book was started twenty years ago in Professor Tanner's seminars.

The author is grateful to the following reviewers for their thoughtful critiques: Dennis Buss, Rider University; Ann Ingman, Canyon College; Rachel

Ragland, Lake Forest College; Gerald F. Day, University of Maryland Eastern Shore; Joyce Mackey, Texas State University—Houston; and Alan W. Garrett, Eastern New Mexico University.

And lastly, as usual, I am grateful to my family, without whom nothing good in my life would be possible—to Margaret, Paul, Nadia, Nikolai, and of course, Erica.

DESIGNING THE SCHOOL CURRICULUM

CHAPTER ONE

INTRODUCTION TO CURRICULUM DESIGN

The first office of the social organ we call the school is
to provide a simplified environment
—John Dewey

Most people associate the term curriculum with the design and operation of the school experience. But the term has quite a bit of flexibility to it and its usage in our language sometimes reaches into circles outside of the school. Some of the references are surprising. I once overheard a group of athletes refer to the exercise or training regimen they follow as their curriculum, a reference that equates the idea of curriculum to a program of predetermined exercises to complete. And the athletes, I think, have it partly right. The idea of curriculum I will be discussing in this book is very much involved in outlining some purposeful sense of experience in the school. Saying it is a regimen to follow is going too far because good curriculum design is not at all a matter of creating a program of predetermined exercises. It is much more crafty and nuanced than that. If, however, we intend regimen to mean the forming of some structure and regularity to the school experience, it is fittingly curricular.

When we begin to think about the curriculum as a strictly professional and school-based term, a number of different interpretive slants on what comprises the curriculum come into play. One of the more popular ones equates the curriculum with the subject matter of schooling. The result is that the curriculum is viewed as a kind of registry for what is taught, often organized along content lines that rarely stray too far from the subject matter boundaries found in the traditional academic disciplines. Our expectations from the curriculum under these terms are modest, chiefly reduced to ensuring an exposure to content knowledge in English, mathematics, science, history, the foreign languages, and so forth. Such a view has its greatest following in high school settings, where specialized academic subjects still reign. But it could also be found in elementary schools, which continue to organize instruction, even in self-contained classrooms, by discipline-centered content areas. We improve the curriculum, under theses circumstances, by simply changing what gets taught. The bias inherent in the characterization of curriculum as subject matter is underscored by the fact that we often use the term *curriculum* in relation to the term *instruction*, implying at least some analytical separation between what is taught (the curriculum) and how it is taught (instruction). The distinction, however, does not hold up very well because, as we will learn, any determination about how to teach has to be made in relation to what gets taught.

Fortunately, professional efforts to give meaning to the curriculum commonly speak to broader issues than content, and depending on the perspective, call attention to a process that we could begin to identify as curriculum design or curriculum development. Eisner (1994), for instance, observed that "the curriculum of a school or a course or a classroom can be conceived of as a series of planned events intended to have educational consequences for one or more students" (p. 31). Eisner's view of the curriculum carries many of the conventional components of design: a planning component, a regard for an educational effect, an effort to see learning in the totality of the school experience, and an implied understanding that different students might require different experiences. Hilda Taba (1962) was even more specific in speaking directly to the point of design, stating that "all curricula, no matter what their particular design, are composed of certain elements" (p. 10). "A curriculum," she continued, "usually contains a statement of aims and of specific objectives; it indicates some selection and organization of content; it either implies or manifests patterns of learning and teaching. . . . Finally it includes a program of evaluation of the outcomes" (Taba, 1962, p. 10). Taba's definition reflects a procedural view of the curriculum that has had resiliency in the field of curriculum studies for many years. Ralph Tyler (1949) was the first to advise curricularists to see their work moving along the continuum Taba described—from the formation of purposes (aims and objectives), to the organization of experiences based on the purposes, to the eventual evaluation of effects attributable to the experiences. We will return to this model as we begin to sharpen our curriculum development tools.

Definitions offered by other curriculum development specialists have placed less focus on the curriculum as a planning process and more on what they see as the main effects of the school curriculum experience. Daniel and Laurel Tanner (1995), for instance, see the curriculum as "that reconstruction of knowledge and experience that enables the learner to grow in exercising intelligent control of subsequent knowledge and experience" (p. 189). The Tanners' intention is to make a case for a school experience that will produce a certain account of knowledgeable learners. Their emphasis on the reconstruction of experience and knowledge is taken directly from Dewey's (1916) position that education is "that reconstruction or reorganization of experience which adds to the meaning of experience, and which increases ability to direct the course of subsequent experiences" (p. 76), all of which underscores the school's responsibility to connect knowledge to life events and to educate individuals for intelligent participation in society. Ronald Doll (1996) describes curriculum a bit more neutrally than the Tanners, by depicting it as "the formal and informal content and process by which learners gain knowledge and understanding, develop skills and alter attitudes, appreciations and values under the auspices of the school" (p. 15).

Unconventional meaning of curriculum can also be found in the curriculum field. The reader might be surprised to learn that many of today's curriculum scholars have broadened the meaning (and the use) of the term *curriculum* in a way that leaves it with virtually no connection to schools. Pinar and others (1995), for instance, believe that curriculum needs to be understood as a symbolic representation, which in their words, refers to the institutional and discursive practices, structures, images and experiences that can be identified and analyzed in various ways" (p. 16). Such an unusual characterization of the curriculum makes it difficult to understand what it is we do when we do curriculum work. When the term is stretched so broadly, what anyone means when they use it becomes a relatively open question.

We can say, however, that one consequence of a view of curriculum that distances itself from schooling is the loss of concern for the process of curriculum development. In fact, the very idea of curriculum design has been rejected as an oppressive and imperialistic construct by a good share of scholars in the curriculum field. Pinar and others (1995) have led the charge in waging battle against the idea of curriculum development, proclaiming it to be no longer relevant to the work of the curriculum scholar. The problem, as they see it, is that the act of curriculum development is tied to an administrative (and patriarchal) impulse to impose unreasonable control and authority on schoolteachers and school children. Pinar and others (1995) have argued that the work of the curricularist should get out of the business of telling teachers what to do and move instead into more active theoretical realms unencumbered by practical institutional concerns.

Such thinking, however, misunderstands the act of curriculum development. First, one must acknowledge the fact that design can be built on principle, not program. This is essentially the difference between giving teachers principled direction and focus in the curriculum and telling teachers what to do. Second, the design of a school curriculum is the fundamental way to communicate what a school is and what a school does. When we design the school curriculum, we help to determine what knowledge, experiences, and values are most worthwhile in the education of youth over a schedule of time and place. So, in this sense, curriculum design is not imminently immobilizing to teachers, but is instead crucial to channeling the release of teacher intelligence and creativity in a way that serves a particular mandate.

And should we ever discard our commitment to curriculum design, we will have taken the first steps toward disassembling the core character of the institution of public schooling. Because the mission of the public school converges with the public interest, the school curriculum has some obligation to create experiences that will fulfill objectives tied to the public interest. Learning a common language, common sets of skills, a common value system, and a common foundation of knowledge might be among them. If we forsake the work of design, we essentially forsake our commitment to the normative experience of the school. And that could spell trouble for all of us.

So in the interests of providing some center of gravity for this book, let me say from the onset that the curriculum we will be discussing has everything to do with schooling and with various matters affecting it. The curriculum development strategies presented here, especially the more procedural mechanisms, can be transferred to other settings, but the analytical focus of this book is first and foremost on the school.

FUNCTIONS OF CURRICULUM DESIGN

The Latin derivative of the term curriculum is *currere*, which is associated with the idea of running a racecourse. The reader might find this derivative odd. How, for instance, can we begin to see a connection between our current usage (or application) of curriculum and the idea of a racecourse? But if we think about a racecourse as a metaphor, it is helpful in describing what the school is like today. Using the metaphor, we could imagine students running on a planned course, completing the requirements of the race, and receiving some certificate of participation—one that might include some judgment of or even reward for distinguished or meritorious participation. Along the way, professionally trained personnel assist the participants with the development of the skills needed to perform on the course, coaching and prodding their students to meet its demands, sometimes with success and sometimes not. Those personally staked in the race, including parents and members of the community, make their own observations and in most cases do their best to assist as well. The race, after all, is an ongoing one, with very clear effects in the life destinies of the participants. The metaphor is, of course, imprecise. It puts too much emphasis on the idea of competing and fails to apprehend one of the more fundamental processes of schooling, which is to learn to cooperate and to build common associations around common problems, common knowledge, and common values.

But in its present-day form, the term *course* has kept its place in the school setting. One takes a course or is enrolled in a course with a teacher, running through it, as it were, according to the rules and regulations set down by the teacher and other curriculum leaders. A course of studies represents a set of conditions that identifies what students should learn and in what sequence, as well as ideas on how students will be evaluated for the purpose of certifying their competence, or lack of it. When one thinks about the school curriculum, one is immediately brought to the question of what course (or course of action) best embodies the societal (or institutional) agenda to enlighten and inform the upcoming generation of youth. What knowledge is most worthwhile for all youth? What behaviors are most desirable? What forms of experience produce the kinds of effects wanted in the education of youth? How does one know whether such effects were secured? The school curriculum becomes, for lack of a better descriptor, the course for society's youth—the public educational experience needed to build the kind of society we desire.

So how does one begin to define the curricularist's job under the conditions just described? I think the answer has something to do with three important functions: (1) the setting of boundaries or limits in the curriculum; (2) the identification of the educational experience in the curriculum; and (3) the extension of curriculum concerns beyond the classroom (Fig. 1.1). Those involved in curriculum design must understand that they are engaged in the process of deliberately and consciously conceiving of a total school experience that is simplified, confined by time and space demands, and purposeful in producing an educative or educational effect. And these are precisely the main ingredients that go into our own working definition of curriculum development, which is, *the deliberate and conscious design of the totality of the school experience in the interests of producing an educational effect.* The definition, although a little clumsy, makes it clear that when one does curriculum design work, three very important functions necessarily apply.

Setting Boundaries

No curriculum design can proceed without understanding that the act of curriculum design is the act of setting boundaries. Everything under the sun cannot (and should not) be included in the school experience. In fact, curriculum designers should understand that decisions regarding the inclusion of some experiences necessarily come at the cost of excluding other experiences.

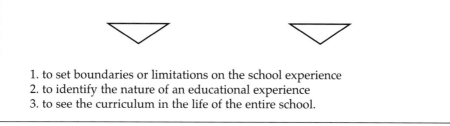

If curriculum design is "the deliberate and conscious effort to design the totality of the school experience in the interests of producing an educational effect," then curricularists confront three basic functions:

1. to set boundaries or limitations on the school experience
2. to identify the nature of an educational experience
3. to see the curriculum in the life of the entire school.

FIGURE 1.1   **The Definition and the Functions of Curriculum Design**

Much of the boundary setting inherent in curriculum development work emerges from what we call the normative agenda of the school. We know, for instance, that schools need to teach children to read and that we cannot rely on any institution but the school to fulfill this task. The skill of reading is normative. If the school does not teach it, it may not be learned. Along these same lines, schools might seek to teach school children something about core democratic values and attitudes. Or they might seek to inculcate a common foundation of knowledge in school children in order to help build a common culture, realizing again that such opportunities cannot be left exclusively to families, places of worship, or neighborhoods. So, all the things we say schools must do, irrespective of local demands, are the things we view as the normative agenda of the school.

This puts the act of curriculum development alongside the act of social planning and social control. Boundary setting is actually all about social control and no less of figure of democracy than John Dewey supported its place in the school. In *Democracy and Education*, he described social control as a vital organizing force for a culture or a society. Dewey (1916) observed that "the natural or native impulses of the young do not agree with the life-customs of the group into which they are born. Consequently, they have to be directed or guided. This control is not the same thing as physical compulsion; it consists in centering the impulses acting at any one time upon some specific end and introducing an order of continuity into the sequence of acts" (p. 39).

Some readers might be surprised to note that John Dewey, arguably the most profound American voice on the relation between schooling and democracy, saw the idea of social control as a necessary condition of democratic schooling. How could it be that social control, a tool widely associated with oppressors, emerges as a vital feature of democracy? Did the modernist rage for order and efficiency get the better of even one of our most distinguished and progressive educational voices? Some scholars might think so, but in reality social control is highly complementary to the actions of democracy. What we are talking about, however, is a particular form of social control that upholds and strengthens the attitudes and the skills necessary to conduct an enlightened life in a democracy. These skills and attitudes cannot be optional in the education of youth. Try to imagine, for instance, the possibilities of life without controls. Consider even a mundane scenario, such the conditions of driving a car. Technically speaking, a traffic light at a busy cross section is a kind of imposition (a control) on the driver who, one could argue, is only really free if allowed to motor about the streets at his or her own will. But the red light (the control) regulates the freedom of the driver and saves him from the paralytic and dangerous conditions that would surely prevail if we were all free to drive according to our felt passions. Control, in this sense, contributes to our freedom by creating a more conducive environment for living a good life. Our lives, of course, are full of controls. Various laws make it clear to us that we have removed a wide range of freedoms in the interests of securing a better life condition.

The task of setting boundaries not only helps to frame the normative but it also forces the question of time and resource allocations in the curriculum. Curriculum development is a zero sum game, dictated largely by time and resource limitations. A new inclusion into an existing curriculum likely means that something has to be excised to make space for the new addition. So, if computer literacy, for instance, prevails as an important skill in the curriculum, some thought has to go into determining its place in the organization of the curriculum, weighing the investment it will require in terms of time and resources, and considering the effects it might have on pushing something else out of the curriculum. These are all delimiting considerations.

Dewey (1916) asserted that "the first office of the school . . . is to provide a simplified environment" (p. 20). By this, he did not mean a simplistic environment. What he meant was that the first principle to the organization of the school curriculum was to focus and channel the school experience in order to ensure that the skills, values, and knowledge we most prize are not lost and are properly integrated into the design of the school. Just last year, I heard a professor at a conference talk about the need to complicate the school experience for children. By complicate, he meant to create alternative viewpoints in the classroom that might produce the kind of cognitive dissonance in learning that gets children to think deeply about the world. But to complicate the school experience along these lines requires us to simplify the school experience, which is to say, to design the curriculum in a way that will deliberately and assuredly produce the kinds of experiences we most value.

To understand the importance of setting purposes (and boundaries) for the school curriculum is one thing, but to understand how to convert these purposes into educational experiences is quite another. Thus, we must identify some ideal or criterion that gives us comfort in saying that the experiences we desire are especially good and suitable for school children. This brings us to our second function.

Identifying the Educational Experience

The second guiding function we confront has to do with identifying the character of an educational experience. What we decide to do through the curriculum must be educational. And this is not as simple-minded or obvious as it might sound because one is likely to get into quite a debate over the question of what is educational. As a result, curriculum designers have to be ready to make their own case on the point.

Fortunately, the history of the curriculum field has yielded important insights on this matter. As a starting point, we could say that all educational experiences need to pass at least a three-part test: that they are by design (and by operation, and ultimately by effect) responsive to the nature of the learner, to the values of the society, and to some framework of useful and empowering knowledge. This is another way of saying that an educational experience must be calculated in relation to the developmental, experiential, and psychological dimensions of the learner, to the axiological foundations of democracy, and to the teaching of usable and empowering knowledge. Consequently, curriculum designers should think about this theoretical triad (the learner, the society, and the subject matter) in all their deliberations. As is discussed in the next chapter, the configuration of the three elements in the curriculum is not arbitrary. It is based on John Dewey's original conception of what he called the *educative process*, an idea that has had an ongoing presence in many of the leading curriculum documents of our time.

By using the three factors in the educative process, we can begin to ask important questions about our design. We might ask how effectively responsive our curriculum is to the nature of the learner. Is it attuned to the developmental or maturation level of the student? Does it account for the learner's life experience and interests? We might also scrutinize our curriculum according to the values of society, asking ourselves if we know whether our curriculum encourages behaviors and skills considered essential for informed participation in a democracy. Part of the educative process also demands that the learner encounter a base of intellectual and useful knowledge, so again we could ask questions on this point, ensuring that our design fulfills our obligations to each of the three features of the educational process. The purpose is to make a rational or defensible demonstration of responsiveness to the key factors in the educative process.

I should add that it is a mistake to accept only one version of what it means to be deferential to the educative process. The use of the three factors allows room for argument and the exercise of philosophical prejudices. A behaviorist perspective on the nature of the learner is quite different from a nonbehaviorist perspective, and the determination of just what are good democratic values and usable knowledge could get into a thicket of political and philosophical debate. We could disagree on our interpretation of the educative process, without compromising its importance to the curriculum development process.

Designing the Totality of the School

Finally, one must understand that the work of the curriculum relates to virtually everything that affects the school. I hedge at the use of the term *extracurricular* because it implies that some things in the school operate outside of the curriculum. Every experience had under the auspices of the school is curricular; curriculum work is not limited to the classroom, the development of instructional units, or the formation of general school policy, but suffuses the totality of the school experience. Thus, extra-classroom experiences, which might be rationalized through sports, clubs, student government, community outreach, music, art and theatre activities, and various other outlets, are part and parcel of the overall calculation of the school. Like classroom experiences, they are curricular and are put under the same analytical microscope.

LEVELS OF CURRICULUM DESIGN

At least two major levels of educational activity have to be acknowledged in the design of the curriculum (Fig. 1.2). The first, which we'll refer to as the *macrocurriculum*, embraces the design of the all-school experience and concerns itself with building-level design factors, including the organization of courses across and within grade levels, school-wide mission features, and school-wide (extra-classroom) experiences. The other is a subset of the macrocurriculum, known logically as the *microcurriculum*. The principal focus of the microcurriculum is the development and operation of classroom-based activities. Curriculum development in the microcurriculum is conducted through an articulation between classroom actions and macro purposes, and includes any number of dealings pertaining to the classroom, such as the development of classroom units, the design of lessons, the application of various teaching models, and the design of classroom-based assessments. Because classroom activity is the touchstone of the curriculum (the main point of contact between teachers and students and the place where the curriculum is given instructional life), the microcurriculum deserves and often gets the lion's share of the curricularist's attention. Macrocurricular concerns, in fact, are largely relevant to the extent that they influence teacher behavior in the classroom.

MACROCURRICULUM (General School-wide Organization)

School-wide policy, services, and organizational priorities, including the organization of school-wide purposes and curriculum content, coursework within and between grade levels, school-wide extra-classroom experiences (such as sports programs, student government, club activities, and theater and art programs), and services (including counseling and health, community outreach, and library services).

MICROCURRICULUM (Particular Classroom-based Practice)

Classroom-based judgments, including the planning and execution of classroom instructional, pedagogical, and assessment decisions.

FIGURE 1.2 **Two Levels of Curriculum Planning**

The Macrocurriculum

Let us discuss the concept of the macrocurriculum first. When we make reference to the macrocurriculum, our thinking turns to the organizational framework of the entire school experience. This means that the macrocurriculum concerns itself mostly with the organization of the coursework across and within the grade levels of the school as well as with the organization of out-of-class activities, such as guidance and counseling services, community outreach initiatives, and other essential school services, including library, recreational, and health functions. Remember we are interested in the totality of the school experience.

As the overall framework for the school curriculum, the macrocurriculum serves two main purposes: (1) general education, which refers to the educational experiences common to all youth in the school; and (2) specialized education, which refers to individualized educational experiences in the school.

In general education, we think about how to encourage common insight and common understandings. We might think about cultural literacy issues and the idea of common knowledge, which might lead to designing and organizing courses that offer common content in government, history, science, and mathematical studies. We might also think about the importance of commonly held skills and ask ourselves if and how we should design and organize courses that encourage the development of these skills. The focus of such courses could include the teaching of common communication skills (such as persuasive writing), common inquiry skills (such as conducting library research and understanding the difference between reliable and unreliable evidence) and common thinking skills (such as the ability to evaluate, analyze, and synthesize data). The effort to define a common learning experience might also aim at some expression of or support for common values, resulting in coursework that emphasizes, say, the exercise of Constitutional values or the examination of common cultural values, such as tolerance of certain differences. The way to think about general education is to think about what is best for all students, whether bound for college or not, in relation to their common participation in and understanding of democracy. As Tanner and Tanner (1995) put it, "general education is designed to provide for a common universe of discourse, understanding and competence. In essence, general education is intended to develop autonomously thinking, socially responsible citizens in a free society" (p. 352).

General education can be construed as common courses in the school, or as common experiences in the school. There is a difference. To say that four years of English is required for graduation might speak to common courses and to common subject matter, but not necessarily to common experiences. Four years of required English coursework offered in a tracked (or between-class-ability-grouped) setting will not likely deliver common experiences. Everyone might be required to enroll in four years of English, but the differences in the experiences across the tracks could be substantial. This distinction is not fully understood by schools that offer "general education" courses in highly stratified tracked settings.

Self-contained elementary school classrooms continue to be our best example of general education as a common experience, although we have also witnessed increasing between-class grouping even in elementary school, especially in reading and math education. But in most (not all) elementary schools, much of the instructional time is still conducted in common (mixed ability) undertakings, resulting in the same exposure to the salient content and skills of the curriculum.

The design of general education in the macrocurriculum must, of course, be balanced against the design of specialized educational experiences. Once we admit the need to respond to individual differences, to account for certain student aptitudes, to consider differences in student interest and student backgrounds, and to attempt remediation and special instructional assistance, we necessarily move into the realm of specialized education. Specialized education itself encompasses several subfunctions, including what we traditionally label as exploratory education (educational experiences that respond and broaden the individual interest levels of students), enrichment education (educational experiences that respond to high aptitude, achievement, and interest levels), remedial education (educational experiences designed to assist with lower performing students) and career education (educational experiences, such as vocational education, designed to fulfill particular career needs). In each case, the intention is to provide a special set of experiences attuned to the interests, aptitudes, achievements, needs, or career choices of the individual. At the macrocurriculum level, this could result in a particular set of elective courses (exploratory), the development of accelerated coursework for high aptitude students (enrichment), or the design of a school-wide student assistance center offering ongoing, including after-school, help to students needing extra instructional support (remediation).

The functions of general education and specialized education work together to encompass the comprehensive mandate of the school. We expect the school to provide a common basis for informed participation in society, a project that entails the development of common knowledge, values, and skills. But we also expect it to advance the individualized education of children, strengthening and giving application to their innate talents, remediating their weaknesses, and responding to as well as broadening their interests and awareness levels.

The Microcurriculum

The design of the macrocurriculum very much affects the design and operation of our other level of curriculum design, the microcurriculum. As mentioned, the macrocurriculum derives much of its meaning from its influence on the microcurriculum. This should remind us that whatever happens to children in school is largely the result of what teachers do, and most teachers find their points of contact with children in the classroom, which is the domain of the microcurriculum. As Eisner (1998) observed, "in a sense, one could have a curriculum only after it is experienced by a child" (p. 26). The microcurriculum inherits school-wide purposes and other broad influences from the macro structure of the school. But because its realm is in the classroom, its analytical concern is instructional and pedagogical. No curriculum has validity except to the extent that it influences the engagement between teachers and students. The microcurriculum is the place where we can witness and judge this engagement. So, in the microcurriculum we ask questions about the connection between purposes and instruction, about the effectiveness of various instructional approaches, about the educative powers of pedagogy, and about various issues pertaining to classroom assessment.

CURRICULUM DESIGN AND DISCRETIONARY SPACE

Among the many difficulties facing curriculum developers is achieving some balance between framing the curriculum experience and allowing for the exercise of teacher authority in the school. In other words, how does one begin to design the school experience in a way that does not suppress or otherwise deny the emergent professional judgments of teachers?

Curriculum developers know a lot about the problem—it has plagued the field for many years. Many of the earliest efforts in the field of curriculum development showed very little regard for the teacher and in fact, many curriculum designers often viewed themselves as a source of protection against presumed teacher incompetence. One does not necessarily have to go by eighty years to the founding of the curriculum field to find this style of curriculum development. During the competency-based movement of the 1970s, a popular method of curriculum development proudly yielded "teacher-proof" curriculum materials. The intention was to design the curriculum in a way that reduced the teacher to the role of a functionary in the school, carrying out the specifications of the curriculum according to the orders laid down by curriculum planners. Here curriculum objectives, lesson designs, practice activities, and even student tests were prefashioned, given to the teacher to follow uncritically. In some cases, actual language was scripted for teachers to utter during their lessons with students. Most of us who have taught school probably remember being given teachers manuals that contained redlined instructional language ("The teacher will say . . . .") that we were supposed to use in our lessons.

The curriculum can bind the teacher into obediently yielding to external prescriptions like those offered in teachers' guides and other prepackaged curriculum materials. But this is bad design practice. The idea, to use Eisner's (1998) characterization, rests on the erroneous assumption that teachers are best viewed as subservient to the curriculum and that learning itself follows some linear assembly-line process. We know that attempts to apply formulaic approaches to teaching contradict the complex nature of the classroom and result in reducing the teacher's role to its most routine and rudimentary (and unprofessional) elements.

The reality is that it takes creativity and intelligence to plan and implement educative engagements in the classroom. Such engagements can only be realized if the teacher has some room to conceptualize the classroom (and its curriculum) according to some professional rationale.

At the same time, the curriculum developer should understand that no good teacher judgment in the classroom could operate outside of a curriculum. Channeling, focusing, and professionalizing teacher judgment, rather than scripting or prescribing it, is the key to good curriculum design. As Eisner (1998) observed, "one function of well-designed curriculum materials is to free the teacher to teach, with ingenuity, flexibility and confidence" (p. 373).

So, before we take our first steps toward the design of a curriculum, we have to understand the sense of balance that needs to be achieved between the design of the curriculum and the discretionary space of the teacher. We start with understanding that the purpose of curriculum design is to help frame the overall nature of the school experience—to normalize it, as it were—and to do it in a way that empowers teacher judgment rather than cuts away at it. As Dewey (1904) observed, "teachers should be given to understand that they are not only permitted to act on their own initiative, but that they are expected to do so, and that their ability to take on a situation for themselves would be more important in judging them than their following any particular set method or scheme" (pp. 27–28). Dewey's words should be encouraging to the curriculum developer because the design of a curriculum should not mandate or otherwise establish a "particular set scheme or method" of teaching. It should, however, give teachers some sense of what should be taught, and why it should be taught, leaving the question of how it should be taught up to the teachers as they calculate it in relation to the student population at hand and to certain professional elements we will discuss later.

Critics of curriculum development sometimes forget that the framing of the normative experience in the curriculum is also central to fundamental equity issues in the education of children. If, for instance, the school mandate includes teaching children how to read, solve mathematical equations, or strengthen their critical thinking and persuasive writing skills, then the school curriculum has an obligation to ensure that all children gain an equal opportunity to learn these skills. No amount of teacher freedom can be accepted as a rationalization against these skills. So, it is clear that teachers must accept some direction from the curriculum.

But what if the school curriculum mandates something that teachers simply cannot bear or crosses over into the realm of scripting teacher actions? This is actually less of a problem with design than it is with poor design. Aspects of the curriculum are always up for debate and teachers do have the right to question features that they believe work against the educative process. We probably have known some teachers who have had to make the best of a less-than-ideal curriculum situation. Teachers can and should supplement or modify the curriculum in ways that are within professional lines and that have a professional justification—a point that I will elaborate on throughout the book.

Testing Issues

Among the more salient issues featured in the tension between design and discretionary space is the topic of testing. Interestingly, the prominence of testing in the school experience has disrupted the manner in which curriculum development is typically conceived. And the effect for teachers has not been positive. Commonly, we view testing in either formative or summative terms, meaning that the curriculum and the students experiencing the curriculum are tested during and after selected experiences or learning opportunities. But the pressure to lift test scores has resulted in a strange inversion of the instructional and evaluative sides of the curriculum. Where we once thought of "the test of the curriculum," we now have something like the "curriculum of the test." The sheer force of these high stakes tests (meaning tests that have some clear or even profound effect on the life destiny of the student or even of the teacher or the principal) reduces the discretionary space of the teacher and trivializes teaching to covering items on an exam.

Since the early part of the 1980s, standardized testing in public education has gained widespread popularity and authority in the school curriculum. The penchant for testing has shaped virtually all facets of the school, affecting grade promotion decisions, admission into gifted and talented programs, assignments into special education programs and various curriculum tracks and even, in some cases, actual graduation from high school. In some schools, tests have stood as the key criterion for assessing a teacher's performance in the classroom and for judging the overall educational value of a school.

The mandate to teach to the test emerges in the life of a classroom in various ways. School principals and district-level administrators have a decisive role in creating and managing the problem. With the public image of the school at stake, administrators are under considerable pressure to ensure favorable examination outcomes. To get a sense of how serious the public stakes truly are, consider the fact that real estate agencies often use local test scores as a selling point for homes in particular neighborhoods. Under these conditions, the very quality of a school (and by extension the quality of the teacher) is often measured strictly by student performance outcomes on high stakes tests. In other words, a good teacher is someone who can generate high student performance outcomes on standardized exams. The school principal, of course, knows that she falls within the same narrow markers of quality, that her longevity will be also tied to test scores. But support for teaching to the test can also emerge from the teachers themselves, who reasonably observe that if student destinies are being dictated by examination results, then educators (like it or not) must do their utmost to boost these all-important scores. This kind of thinking is naturally encouraged when schools set policies that intensify the significance of standardized test scores. The embrace of grade retention policies that only allow students to be promoted to the next grade if they perform at or above some minimal cut score on a standardized exam set is an example of this. Grade retention obviously has a dramatic effect on a student's life and aggregate grade promotion rates have considerable public relations currency. The stakes are indeed high when such policies are in place, compelling teachers to think first and foremost about how to teach in ways that lift standardized exam scores.

But the problem is not simply what gets taught; it is also a matter of how it gets taught. Teachers who are most openly committed to teaching to the test are likely going to be most overtly reliant on teacher manuals and other imitative contrivances. Teachers most inclined to teach directly to the exam will be most broadly committed to low-level and mechanical instructional procedures. Where teaching to the test occurs, one is likely to find fewer possibilities for instructional innovation and less evidence of the kind of independence of thought that inspires teachers to develop creative and stimulating learning experiences for children.

The pressure to teach to the test is a pressure on the discretionary space of the teacher. The core purposes of the curriculum that are supposed to produce a flow of wide-ranging experiences in the school are often lost and forgotten by teachers who are preoccupied with testing priorities. Teachers get the signal that whatever is not tested is also not instructionally worthy.

But anyone who has taught in schools knows that much of what is most important in the education of youth is not and often cannot be tested. I do not want to get sentimental about attitudinal features in schooling, but the fact is that teaching children to love school, to love learning, and to be socially conscious and intellectually curious are all pretty important but are rarely, if ever, part of any school testing program. In a high stakes testing climate, if such attitudinal objectives are not tested, they are ipso facto not important. Most educators would also say that general skills such as inquiry skills that allow students to understand evidence and data, or communication skills that encourage the development of good expository writing or other communicative proficiencies are also quite important. But such skills again are not typically tested. They are, at best, given short shrift in a high stakes climate or, at worst, ignored. Teachers must have the intellectual liberty to fulfill the comprehensive purposes of the curriculum without the fear of being viewed as less adequate than those who do little more than teach to the test. In the design of the school curriculum, tests should not be an imposition on the teachers but should instead serve as tools that help them understand whether certain experiences have helped to attain certain purposes. Putting the test before the curriculum is very much like putting the cart before the horse.

But the issue of testing and discretionary space can be tricky business because all teachers are required, in some way, to teach what is tested. No test used in the curriculum could otherwise be considered valid. The very definition of achievement implies having learned what was taught. So, how does one reconcile this requirement with the expressed limitations that accompany teaching to the test?

The answer resides in the design of the curriculum and the assurance that the school curriculum promotes experiences that properly flow from core purposes, not from test items. There is an indisputable connection between teaching and testing. But in the design of the curriculum, a sense of directionality has to be understood. As curriculum developers, we work with the idea of testing what is taught, not the reverse. Using the test to evaluate the experience is the proper direction of our work. This should give us some confidence that the tests are valid (that is, connected to the curriculum) and that the curriculum has not become just a laundry list of test items. We will explore this important sense of directionality between teaching and testing in Chapter 7.

Curriculum Standards

Issues related to teacher liberty in the curriculum also arise when the topic of curriculum standards is raised. In many cases, curriculum standards turn out to be little more than content standards that help define what teachers and schools should be trying to accomplish. Their purpose is to assist with the general coordination of the school curriculum by ensuring that all students receive the opportunity to learn a core of subject matter or knowledge. Supporters of content standards believe that there is indeed a set of skills and knowledge appropriate for the education of all American youth, and that anyone denied access to this core of skills and knowledge suffers an inequity. Some people see the need for these standards to be set at the national level, others at the state level, and yet others at the local level. Those supporting standards say that teachers could use content standards to plan their lessons and to otherwise provide some content focus to the classroom without feeling the loss of professional decision making. In fact, we should be reminded that teachers are generally not free to design the content of the curriculum, although they do have certain liberties with it.

Ravitch (1995), among others, has emphasized the need for curriculum standards to be tied to tests. She believes that this will result in unifying the school curriculum and will ultimately give teachers an unambiguous sense of what is important to teach. She also makes it clear that standards should not be constructed in a manner that implies or requires some standardization or uniformity of instructional practice. For such an outcome to occur, however, the standards must avoid reducing themselves to test items on high stakes exams that will, far from liberating teacher intelligence, only result in producing a teaching-to-the-test mentality. So, the real mischief-maker here is still the test. If we link our tests to only standards, we run the risk of creating a curriculum experience that is not fully attentive to the widest purposes of the school. A better or more enriching way of ensuring the same connection is to integrate our standards into our purposes. This should give rise to experiences congruent to our purposes, which will ultimately be evaluated with, among other things, tests. Curriculum developers are also advised to think about formulating and using standards set at a generalizable level, which takes the pressure off of making direct and specific linkages to test items. We will discuss this task in more detail in Chapter 4.

Instructional Issues

Some of the problems with discretionary space also have to do with the instructional side of the curriculum. Sometimes the source of pressure arises not so much from the content or even testing mechanisms, but from instructional procedures held to be universally applicable and appealing. Think for a moment about the manner in which teacher effectiveness has been framed over the years. Historically speaking, the determination of effectiveness has been closely tied to purely instructional behaviors, to the "how" of teaching and to the management of established techniques or methodologies. The result is that a teacher's sense of worth becomes associated with an ability to engage certain instructional manipulations. This might include techniques on, say, gaining the class's attention, or informing the class of the lesson's objective, or eliciting the so-called "desired behavior" of the lesson. Questions pertaining to the appropriateness of the objective or to the fundamental educative character of the experience are of secondary importance.

One of the insights emerging from the teacher effectiveness literature illustrates this point. For many years now, researchers have been touting the importance of the principle of *time on task* in the classroom. It is, at its most superficial level, an unremarkable idea that espouses the need for teachers to keep learners engaged in classroom activities. Obviously engagement is a requisite condition for learning. But when such a principle stands at the forefront of how one views good teaching, potential problems can occur. To put it simply, all forms of engagement are not necessarily educative. Because the time-on-task dictum does nothing to highlight or underscore the qualitative character of the task, it is of limited value. Thus, a teacher might achieve high grades from supervisors in keeping children on task, but if the task itself is not educationally worthwhile, the level of student engagement is not even an issue. Time on task is clearly an idea that is rooted in exclusive instructional and managerial concerns.

Another manifestation of the same problem emerges from the *teacher effects* research, which has identified and promoted the value of what purports to be universally effective instructional practices. Findings of this research indicate (to name a few generalizations) that so-called effective teachers have high expectations for performance, that they convey enthusiasm in their teaching, and that they are vigilant about monitoring student work. But one needs to be able to show the criteria by which the term *effective* is being defined. The term is theoretically neutral. One could be an effective thief or an effective ax murderer. In the context of the effective teaching literature, the use of the term is related to how well certain practices raise standardized test scores. The problem is that what one might do to raise test scores may not always lead to enlightened teaching. For instance, one teacher effectiveness researcher stated that effective teachers of disadvantaged pupils: (1) ask low-level questions; (2) tend not to amplify, discuss, or use pupil answers; (3) do not encourage pupil-initiated questions; and (4) give little feedback on pupil questions (Medley, 1979). A preoccupation with asking low-level questions might raise test scores on some basic skills exam (and is therefore judged to be effective teaching), but it comes at the expense of a vital and dynamic cognitive experience. To advise teachers against providing substantive feedback in the name of effectiveness signifies the extent of the instructional myopia that results from this type of research.

In-service training programs have sometimes shown the same preoccupation with instructional technique. The Hunter (1980) approach is perhaps best known. Hunter's program, often referred to as the "Seven-Step Lesson" or the "Elements of Effective Instruction," was one of the most enduring features on the educational landscape during the 1980s and 1990s. It dominated teacher in-service programs throughout American schools, affecting the thinking and behavior of thousands of teachers. Some school districts even went so far as to adopt the Hunter model as their choice for assessing teacher performance and staked it into promotion and salary decisions.

The Hunter approach lists various structural elements of a lesson (anticipatory set, statement of objectives, careful monitoring for understanding, guided and independent practice, and a sense of closure) as the foundation for effective pedagogy. The seven steps to the lesson design are:

1. *Anticipatory Set*. This phase of the seven-step lesson is designed primarily to get students' attention. One of the problems Hunter noticed as she developed her lesson design is that some teachers began to teach before they had the students' attention. The anticipatory set helps to focus the learners on what is going to be taught. It is designed to "grab" the students' attention.
2. *Objective and Purpose*. Once the students are attentive, the teacher, in clear and concise language, states what the students will be expected to learn and why.
3. *Input*. This is the phase in which the teacher provides the information that students need to meet the lesson's objective. A teacher, for instance, might help his students understand how to add fractions by performing examples on the board, asking for strategies that students might have in performing certain manipulations with fractions, or providing visual or hands-on demonstrations.
4. *Modeling*. The teacher models or shows students the process, skill, or knowledge that is being taught. The teacher might, for example, anticipate the errors students may make and model how students can correct their own errors.
5. *Checking for Understanding*. In this phase, the teacher attempts to discover how many students understand the lesson's objective, and to what degree. Hunter included this phase because she noticed that many teachers would call only on students who knew the answer, or worse, simply ask if there were any questions, and move on.
6. *Guided Practice*. Students practice the lesson objective under the guidance of the teacher. For example, teachers may put a practice problem on the board and help the class solve it together. They might also put a problem on the

board and ask a student to work on it independently while they circulate around the room, checking students' work.

7. *Independent Practice.* This is the phase of the lesson in which students work on exercises associated with the lesson's objective or objectives independently. In high school classes, independent practice is often used as homework. In elementary school, teachers are more likely to allow students to complete their independent practice in school.

As one instructional method, the Hunter model is certainly worthy. But if used as an exclusive instructional method, the Hunter model runs the risk of saying that a good teacher is someone who follows the seven-step lesson design, irrespective of the nature of the activity justified by or operated through the design. The instructional elements of the lesson become the ends of a teacher's performance rather than the vital means toward securing an educative learning environment. Here the discretionary space of the teacher is affected by an often misguided conviction that certain instructional procedures are inherently worthwhile and deserve to be equated with what it means to be a good teacher. The reality, of course, is that the curriculum development process demands instructional variance, a conclusion largely at odds with those who accuse it of shutting down teacher judgment.

A CONTINUUM FOR CURRICULUM DEVELOPMENT

Before concluding the chapter, I would like to give the reader a thumbnail sketch of the model we will be using to coordinate our ideas on curriculum design. Because of the need to give teachers discretionary latitude in the classroom, the curriculum development strategy used here focuses on key processes. Using Ralph Tyler's well-known rationale, I will construct an approach to curriculum development that moves across a continuum of concerns that speaks to school purposes, school experiences, and school evaluation (Fig. 1.3, p. 20). Tyler (1949) used four questions to outline this continuum:

1. What educational purposes should the school seek to attain?
2. What educational experiences can be provided that are likely to attain these purposes?
3. How can these educational experiences be effectively organized?
4. How can we determine whether these purposes are being attained?

We will use this framework to organize our thoughts on curriculum design, remembering that Tyler's rationale was originally conceived as a strategy to help teachers analyze and interpret the curricula they developed in experimental high schools. And although the questions imply a linear structure of moving from question 1 to question 4, one should note that in the context of the school, the act of cur-

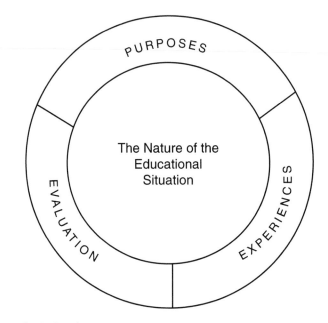

FIGURE 1.3   Tyler's Continuum

riculum development could start along any point of the continuum. In fact, the problems identified in an existing school experience dictate the point of entry. Thus, poor evaluation results (question 4) could be the starting point for the renegotiation of instructional methods used, or even for the reconsideration of the purposes themselves. The lack of available resources needed to provide the kind of experiences necessary to fulfill key purposes (question 3) might also be an entry point for rethinking the purposes. In another situation, a new outlook on the mission of the school (question 1) could and likely would call for a new evaluative strategy.

Purposes

The idea that the school curriculum is moved by purposes cannot be stated strongly enough. To put our emphasis on the mission of the school prevents us from falling prey to a teaching-to-the-test mentality and protects us from the overreaching effects of instructional prescriptions. The framing of purposes sets the course for the curriculum and allows us to exercise our philosophical hopes for the education of youth.

But even the setting of purposes is not a free for all. As we shall discuss in the next chapter, a certain theoretical structure is required to circumscribe the ambitions of the curriculum so that we can retain a focus on the educational and on the kind of learning experiences that are in the best interests of the learner and the society. The formation of the school's purposes, in other words, is not an arbitrary or idiosyncratic affair. In fact, when curriculum developers help to set purposes for the school curriculum, they must shoulder the weight of a normative mandate while also attending to the local wishes and judgments of the school community. They must also understand the psychosocial and philosophical rationale justifying the formation of purposes and examine it against strategic design factors (which will be discussed in the next chapter).

Curriculum developers must additionally acknowledge the fact that the nature of the school's purposes and the actual manner in which they are described and organized will have dramatic effects on the practice of the school curriculum itself. For example, some curriculum workers believe that purposes should be detailed into a list of highly specific and particularized learning objectives, so that no ambiguity exists in determining just what is expected of the teacher. The danger in this arrangement, of course, is that there is little interest and little opportunity for the expression of individual visions of teaching and emergent judgment. Moreover, where the purposes of the curriculum result in the incorporation of thousands of detailed objectives, we commonly find that, by virtue of the commitment to specificity, the curriculum suffers from a low cognitive orientation. Only relatively simple tasks can be so easily described.

To combat the problem of specificity in the framing of school purposes, Tyler (1949) made repeated efforts to draw attention to the need for the school to retain a strong sense of generalizability in its design, thus giving the school experience some flexibility and some discretionary space for teacher judgment. Tyler believed in the authority of general content and key generalizable skills. To learn something as specific as, say, addition facts (which are indisputably important) helps learners in some obvious ways, but generalizable skills, such as how to solve problems and how to communicate effectively, obviously have a wider and more influential place in a learner's future. Tyler advised that in setting purposes one should look at the development of generalizable objectives, a point addressed in Chapter 4. And to the extent that a school's purposes are general and clear, the curriculum has the amplitude it requires to take full advantage of professional judgment.

The management of purposes in the curriculum is not as simple as it might seem. The difficulty is finding a way to balance everything the schools need and want to do. Determining what knowledge or content to include is not the only concern. Various skills, values, and attitudes also have to be integrated into an organizational matrix. And once these various elements are understood, the organization of the purposes must take on a form that will allow the next stage of curriculum development to proceed, so that the school can begin to securely develop a logical sequence and progression of experiences.

Experiences

What educators decide to do in the school curriculum is naturally a function of our defining sense of mission or purpose. At the macro level, we have to decide on the nature of the coursework within and across the grade levels. For example, can the purposes of the curriculum justify a high school course on comparative religion? Should keyboarding skills be taught to students beginning in third grade? Can we justify the inclusion of a required vocational education course dealing with the everyday skills associated with home ownership? And, when will these courses be offered and in what sequence? Should they be required, exist as an option on a required menu of choices, or should they be freely elected? And what in the extra-classroom experience has sanction in the school's purposes? Student government and student newspapers are probably safe bets, as are various sports programs and club activities dealing with special interests in math, science, or language, but should community outreach or even service learning experiences be part of the picture too? These are all macrocurricular decisions made in the context of the school's purposes.

Making decisions related to the kinds of experiences had in the microcurriculum is essentially what teachers get paid to do. Here the talk is about instruction and pedagogy. Instruction speaks directly to the notion of formulating a lesson design or lesson strategy that aims to fulfill some key purpose or purposes in the curriculum. For this reason, no single instructional strategy ever has rule or superiority over all others. Instructional decisions (such as using cooperative learning, skill-drill methods, demonstration techniques, or an expository lecture method) have validity and use mostly to the extent that they can offer an experience that will fulfill some purpose or purposes in the mission of the school. There are a few other things to consider, which I will discuss in the next chapter. But one key principle prevails: that instructional variety is required in the microcurriculum, not because variety is intrinsically virtuous, but because the more instructional options teachers have at their fingertips, the better the odds they will use one well suited for a particular purpose. The job of the curriculum developer is to provide a working framework that makes it easy for a teacher to make instructional decisions in the context of purposes.

The other thread that runs through the formation of experience is something known as pedagogy. Many decisions made in the classroom are not a function of some predetermined objectives. They occur naturally, spontaneously, and emergently from the student-teacher interaction. Dealing with student questions and student misbehavior, for instance, calls for on-the-spot decisions. Teachers' style of language, the gestures they use to convey various points, the behaviors they display in various contexts, and the attitudes promoted by what they say and do all are part of this phenomenon we call pedagogy. The influence of pedagogy on the curriculum is enormous because it allows the curriculum to go in a direction that the teacher determines is best, using what Eisner (1998) calls expressive outcomes in the curriculum. Such outcomes are the result of judgments that have no precise or explicit sanction in the curriculum but nevertheless emerge from experience, moved by decisions that the teacher makes in the best interests of the child. As Eisner (1998) observed, "purposes need not precede activities; they can be formulated in the process of the action itself" (p. 119). We rely on good pedagogy for these types of judgments.

Evaluation

Many educators do not understand that evaluation is an essential component to the act of curriculum development. This is partly understandable, given the high priority placed on testing as an end in and of itself. But no design of evaluation can be understood outside of its moorings in the curriculum. Educators evaluate in order to understand whether they have reached the purposes they explicitly sought. And notice I used the term *evaluate*, not *test*.

The difference between the two terms is significant. All tests represent some form of evaluation, meaning they make some contribution to our knowledge of whether certain purposes have been attained. But all evaluation does not represent some form of testing. Tyler (1949) showed us that evaluation, a term he originally coined in the context of schooling, need not be reducible to a pencil-and-paper testing affair, but should instead be approached as an evidence collection process, requiring innovative thinking about ways to demonstrate whether core purposes in the curriculum have been fulfilled. This means that tests could and should be part of the evaluation tool box, but so much more should be there too, including (potentially) interview data, survey data, samples of student work, observational notes taken in the classroom, photographic documentation of student projects, writing samples, and even electronic portfolios. Which tools to use depends, of course, on what needs to be evaluated.

The evaluative component of curriculum development is obviously the one way we can determine where changes might be in order for the curriculum. If achievement test scores are lower than expected or than can be tolerated, then the school might look for solutions in the instructional component of the curriculum. If the evaluation shows that many students hate school, dislike learning, rarely read a book on their own, and rarely use a library, the school might redesign its purposes to strengthen the commitment to the realization of certain positive attitudes and appreciations in learning. If the evaluation demonstrates racist, sexist, or homophobic attitudes in the school, again some curriculum response is in order. And in all the examples mentioned, we can see these evaluations (and the subsequent decisions they influence) emerging from either the classroom (microcurricular) or the entire school (macrocurricular).

SUMMARY

Curriculum development is all about the design of the school experience. Although precautions should be taken to ensure that the curriculum does not bind the intelligence and creativity of the teacher, curriculum developers should not withdraw from the fact that the curriculum aims to outline the normative project of the school. Such an outline shows—to teachers and parents and others interested parties—exactly what the school has decided to privilege in the time it has with its charges. Curriculum design frames the purpose of the school, and helps to organize the means used to bring these purposes to life in the educational encounter between teachers and students. Curriculum designers also concern themselves with finding ways to evaluate the worth of these experiences against stated purposes. Determinations made in the macrocurriculum reside mostly in the hands of a curriculum leader who looks at all the component parts of the school and pulls together a coherent program that includes decisions related to the organization of coursework across and within grades, and to the organization of various school-wide services and extra-classroom activities.

The teacher, however, is the main curriculum worker at the microcurriculum, taking her lead from various factors conceived in the macrocurriculum and making instructional judgments from the widest perspective of the school's purposes and from a sense of teacher professionalism. Ideally, the discretionary judgment of the teacher is empowered in such a situation because it is given direction and purpose. But prudence is in order here. The design of the curriculum must be careful to not be too heavy-handed in the microcurriculum. Teachers must be free to pursue instructional actions that are not only consonant with the curriculum but also responsive to the particularities of the educational situation. Thus, we must be conscious of anything in the design of the curriculum that results in unduly restricting the teacher. Pressures to teach to the test, to use only one type of instructional model (or approach) in the classroom, or to be allegiant to highly specific predetermined objectives, are all unhealthy invasions of the teacher's discretionary space.

DISCUSSION QUESTIONS AND SUGGESTED ACTIVITIES

1. Solicit educators for their definitions of curriculum and analyze them according to the principles discussed in the chapter. Do they focus on processes or effects? Do they give us a sharp sense of a curriculum developer's job responsibilities? Compare these definitions to ones drawn from the literature or the ones shared in the beginning of the chapter.

2. What are some of the factors that play into the process of setting boundaries in the curriculum? Interview teachers and ask them what they might do if they encounter a requirement in the curriculum that they strongly believe is miseducative.

3. When Dewey suggested that the first function of the curriculum is to provide a simplified environment, what was the main principle he was advancing? Did this mean that all complexity has to be eliminated from schooling? Why put such an emphasis on the simplification of the school environment?

4. How might we begin to argue that one type of curriculum design is actually better suited to produce educational experiences than another?

5. Do you agree that what goes on in music choir, on the football field, or in student government is as much a curricular concern as what transpires in the English classroom? Why or why not?

6. Explain the difference between the macrocurriculum and the microcurriculum. Provide an example of how the design of the macrocurriculum in the high school setting affects decisions in the microcurriculum.

7. Explain the difference between general education and specialized education and discuss how each affects the design of the macrocurriculum.

8. What is Eisner's point when he writes that "one could only have a curriculum after it is experienced by a child."

9. Some critics have argued that design is an unprofessional imposition on the teacher. Describe the ways that curriculum design could impose on teachers' professionalism and ways that design could help and empower them.

10. Why is there so much criticism about teaching to the test, when no test can be considered valid unless its general contents are taught? What is the way out of this logical dilemma?

11. What is the greatest potential danger posed on the discretionary space of teacher judgment by content standards?

12. Survey a few teachers, asking them if their principal or school district imposes any strict instructional regulations on their teaching? In other words, are they required to follow any particular method or lesson approach? Does the school have an instructional program that they must follow? Describe the teachers' attitudes and reactions to such programs.

13. Imagine curriculum development moving along a continuum from purposes, to experience, to evaluation. Does this mean that all curriculum development work must begin with the formulation of purposes?

14. What is the difference between instruction and pedagogy?

15. What is the difference between evaluation and testing?

NOTES

Dewey, J. (1902). *The child and the curriculum*. Chicago: University of Chicago Press.

Dewey, J. (1904). The relation of theory to practice in education. In the Society for the Study of Education 3rd Yearbook, Part 1, *The relation of theory to practice in the education of teachers*. Bloomington, IL: Public School Publishing.

Dewey, J. (1916). *Democracy and education*. New York: Macmillan Co.

Doll, R. (1996). *Curriculum improvement: Decision making and process*. Boston: Allyn and Bacon.

Eisner, E. (1998). *The educational imagination*. New York: Macmillan Co.

Hunter, M. (1980). *Teach more—faster*. El Segundo, CA: TIP Publications.

Medley, D. (1979). The effectiveness of teachers. In P.L. Peterson & H.L. Walberg (Eds.), *Research on teaching: Concept, findings and implications*. Berkeley, CA: McCutchen.

Pinar, W.F., Reynolds, W.M., Slattery, P. & Taubman, P.M. (1995). *Understanding curriculum*. New York: Peter Lang.

Ravitch, D. (1995). *National standards in American education*. Washington, DC: The Brookings Institution.

Taba, H. (1962). *Curriculum development: Theory and practice*. New York: Harcourt, Brace and Jovanovich.

Tanner, D. & Tanner, L. (1995). *Curriculum development*. New York: Macmillan Co.

Tyler, R. (1949). *Basic principles of curriculum and instruction*. Chicago: University of Chicago Press.

CHAPTER TWO

THEORY
AND DESIGN

Curriculum development without curriculum theory is tragic;
curriculum theory without curriculum development denies
the essential purpose of the theory
—Ralph Tyler

Because the development of the school curriculum is not a freewheeling affair, some theoretical structure is needed to assure us that what we are doing is in the best interests of school children. So, we turn to the theoretical threads that bind the curriculum to better understand our decisions and to face head-on what we mean when we speak of educational school experiences. Understanding the caveats mentioned in the earlier chapter about the dangers of imposing too much will on the curriculum, we look to a theoretical framework for the curriculum that provides the school with direction without resorting to prescription.

THE IDEA OF THEORY

The first step in moving toward a theory of design is to understand the limitations of theory in the context of practice. Theory cannot and does not have prescriptive powers in the school. It cannot sanction or sustain universal rules about good teaching or give support to invariant instructional methods, such as fixed lesson-planning structures and plug-in teaching models. Designers who fail to understand these limitations to theory run the risk of imposing one method of conduct on the teacher, one way of characterizing and approving of the interaction between the teacher and the student.

Unfortunately, this is precisely the problem often witnessed in schools. The status of reading education in the schools is a good example. Because of the importance of reading instruction in the elementary school curriculum, teachers often find themselves under the influence of a school-wide theory of reading education that touts the application of a particular methodology. Thus, a theory of reading instruction that highlights, say, the importance of whole language learning implies that whole language instruction is best for all, no matter the child or the particularities of the educational situation. At the same time, another school might be interested in a different reading theory (say, for analytical purposes, phonics learning), resulting in an instructional norm that urges a phonetical approach to teaching reading. Reading education specialists have found themselves involved in exactly this dispute, debating whether whole language or phonics-based instruction should command the language arts elementary school curriculum. Even the federal government has gotten into the act, with No Child Left Behind legislation suggesting the use of phonics instruction as the only scientifically valid approach to reading education.

But here is a case where theory overreaches its capacity, creating a false debate over whether one method of instruction is better than the other. The debate is false because only the teacher, in interaction with the child and working in a school context imbued with a variety of purposes, can really decide which method is best. Such decisions depend on the nature of the child, available resources, the defined purposes in the curriculum, the evaluative evidence, and on a raft of other variables residing in the educational situation.

A similar problem arises when theory gets entangled with political ideology. Many curriculum theorists make no distinction between theory and politics, believing that you cannot have one without the other. The result is that theory sometimes becomes the building block for a politicized school experience. So-called postmodernists thinkers are the best examples. Rejecting the place of overt objectives in the curriculum as an oppressive mechanism, postmodernist thinkers see themselves as guardians against the hegemony of the dominant culture. They openly state that they are protecting the school from the harmful influences of Western, upper-class, European, male ways of thinking. Yet their theory seeks to install a curriculum that imposes a different worldview, one which they are convinced is better. As a result, the school experience includes an overt commitment to a politicized experience at odds with the Western canon and with what one might interpret as traditional values.

As Schwab (1969) observed, "theories cannot be applied, as principles, to the solutions of problems concerning what to do for real individuals, small groups, or real institutions located in time and space—the subjects and clients of schooling and schools" (p. 287). Curriculum developers, whose bottom line is practice, should be humble in the face of theory, understanding that it provides important epistemological boundaries on the school experience, but no automatic, ipso facto responses. The fact of the matter is that theory should allow for multitudinous ways of teaching children, but it should also send strong qualitative signals about learning experiences it deems worthy.

Beauchamp (1975) observed that curriculum theory "gives meaning to a school curriculum by pointing up the relationships among its elements and by directing its development, its use and its evaluation" (p. 58). Theory, under this description, is still a dynamic construct, but with obvious limitations. Curricularists should see theory as directing rather than dictating experience and as giving meaning rather than an exact method or subject matter to the school.

What then are the theoretical lines that bind the curriculum, that direct and give meaning to the school experience? The answer resides in the precedential work of the curriculum field. We can point to a few sources and influences on the school curriculum that have transcended school reform and school change efforts over the years. Daniel and Laurel Tanner (1995), in fact, make their case for a theoretical center of gravity for curriculum design by pointing to the centrality of Dewey's fundamental factors in the educative process. Dewey's described three key factors: (1) the nature of the learner; (2) the values and aims of society; and (3) the world of knowledge and subject matter. The Tanners argue that prominent historical efforts at curriculum innovation have followed the pathway of these three concerns, resulting in a theoretical tradition that demands that the curriculum be responsive to the learner, to the society, and to some sense of subject matter.

THE EMERGENCE OF THREE FACTORS
FOR CURRICULUM DESIGN

The formal identification of the curriculum field and of the emergence of the curriculum expert can be traced to the early parts of the twentieth century. Interest in the growing development of the public school brought forth several thinkers who wanted to offer their own version of what might constitute a good public education. The absence of federal authority in the formation of school policy and practice, and the American tradition of keeping the conduct of the public school close to the hands of the people, opened the debate up to virtually all comers. Various thinkers freely offered their own versions of how the public school curriculum should be designed and operationalized. The questions guiding the debate were profound: What knowledge should the school sanction? What objectives should the school seek to attain? What teaching methods were most appropriate? These were the kind of early queries that gave birth to a field dedicated to the development of the school curriculum.

The initial response to these questions emerged from the work of cultural conservatives, who brought attention to the role of the liberal arts in the education of youth, arguing that true learning is located in an interaction between the learner and the subject matter of a few essential disciplines. Exposure to these disciplines, they asserted, not only exercised the mind in a way that increased the potential for more intelligent action, but it also delivered the native wisdom of Western culture to the student. Because the civilizing effects of our humanity were believed to be inherent in the categorical boundaries of the academic disciplines, the school curriculum had an obligation to carry this weight. The result was a school curriculum conceived in sharply subject-centered terms. And, contrary to popular perception, the purpose of the curriculum was not intended to serve only a few academically inclined students, but to act as the main method of learning for the masses—the one sure way to bring about some measure of cultural and intellectual training for all. This was, in fact, the essential message promoted in the Committee of Ten report (National Education Association, 1898), which offered the first blueprint for the American high school curriculum. This conservative perspective on the curriculum very much prevailed in the school and by the turn of the twentieth century it was clear that the source of subject matter had become well established in the calculation of the curriculum.

But discord was in the air. The emerging pattern of subject-centeredness in the early coursework of the school was a troubling development to a number of more progressive-minded thinkers. The problem, as they saw it, was that the school was working with the wrong variable in setting the course for its experiences. To focus on the subject matter in a way that resulted in a uniform and undifferentiated academic curriculum was, by their account, an open violation of what was best for children. Led by new European child-centered theories, a countermovement in school reform took hold. Its aim was to recalculate the curriculum, not from the standpoint of the subject matter, but from the standpoint of the child. The new argument encouraged the school to be openly responsive to the nature of the learner, to acknowledge the learner's experiences and interests in school, to take the idea of individual differences more seriously in the curriculum, and to break from the traditions of a mentalistic education in favor of an experiential education. It also helped to launch something known as the child study movement in America, which openly sought to learn more about children in ways that could directly assist the effort to teach them.

But child-centeredness reached too far in the direction of the child, creating schools openly dedicated to the romantic-naturalist view of permitting and endorsing anything that struck a child's whim and fancy. By finding their way as a palliating force against traditional subject-centered extremes, child-centered thinkers created their own counterextremes. Still, the lingering effect was that the child had become part of the emerging thinking of the curriculum. It became a force with no less authority in the curriculum than the subject matter.

The problem facing school reformers, however, was that the consideration of the child in the curriculum was framed as a variable antagonistic to subject-centered thinking. Thus, the struggle for identification and influence in the school curriculum at the turn of the century was largely a struggle between subject-centered and child-centered schools of thought. This was an untenable dualism that ensnared many curriculum thinkers. Advocates lined up on either side of the debate. Dewey (1902) described the situation:

The emphasis is put upon the logical subdivisions and consecutions of the subject matter. The problems of instruction are problems of procuring texts giving logical parts and sequences, and of presenting these portions in class in a similar definite and graded way. The subject matter furnishes the end and determines method. . . . Not so, says the other sect. The child is the starting point, the center and the end. His development, his growth, is the ideal. It alone furnishes the standard. To the growth of the child all studies are subservient. (p. 8)

Not surprisingly, a third response emerged from a group that rejected the party-line loyalties that the dualism encouraged. Largely orchestrated by John Dewey, the new response was synthesizing because it claimed that the school should be both child-centered and subject-centered, and that another factor, attesting to the school's vital place in the development of democracy, also had to be considered. The debate between subject-centered and child-centered ideological positions now faced some resolution in an antidote that combined both ingredients with a third one. And so we arrive at John Dewey's claim that school formulations should be attuned to three fundamental factors: (1) the nature of the learner; (2) the values and aims of the society; and (3) the reflective consideration of the subject matter. The construction of this new trinity in educational thinking provided unique insight into the process of curriculum development.

Over time, the three factors have evolved into a historical framework for guiding school practice. They have surfaced, time and time again, in the work of various curriculum reform efforts (Tanner and Tanner, 1995). Taken together, they continue to represent a working theoretical framework for decisions made in the curriculum, from the planning of purposes to the actual design and implementation of educational events. Their potency is very real in practice. They have the effect of forcing educators to weigh their decisions in the light of the learners' interests and developmental needs, in the spirit of the ethical foundations of democratic living, and in the context of worthy knowledge.

THE NATURE OF THE LEARNER

Few debate the centrality of the nature of the learner in curriculum decision making. Most of us, in fact, would think it wise for an educator to try to see the world as the students themselves might see or experience it, and to attempt to otherwise connect the life of the school to the life of the learner. Moreover, knowledge of learners could help us decide the best time to teach a particular set of skills and the best way to sequence and organize instruction. Such knowledge could give us insight into readiness and pacing and provide us with the instructional advantage of knowing individual strengths and weaknesses. Understanding the nature of the learner also reminds us of a vital instructional principle, which is that no two individuals develop in exactly the same way, and that intellectual capacity as well as social, emotional, and physical maturity are unevenly distributed across the student population and are all set to different biological clocks. Because curriculum designers are, one way or another, entangled in decisions influencing the formation of school purposes, the choice of content and instructional technique, and the ways to assess learning effects, they need to be conscious of the learner's nature.

But we need practical guidelines to systematically approach this key variable in the curriculum and to integrate it into our planning and deliberations. Because we are saying that no educative learning experiences can materialize in the school unless they account for the nature of the learner, we need to be clear about what we mean.

As a starting point let us say the nature of the learner has for four main factors: (1) developmental issues in learning; (2) individual aptitudes and deficiencies; (3) home and community cultures; and (4) individual interest levels. These four factors allow us to take a more finely grained approach to the learner. To understand learners means to have a sense of their developmental maturity and needs, and to be familiar with how various cognitive, social, and emotional factors affect their ways of thinking and behaving. It also means to be responsive to what children can do best and to know the advantages that nature and experience might have granted to them, while also acknowledging individual deficiencies and points for remediation and improvement. And finally, to understand learners means to have some association with their home and community environments, to appreciate family-based factors related to race, ethnicity, income, and even religion, and to be on familiar terms with pervading community issues as well as individual interest levels. The net effect of accounting for all these factors is a school experience that has some meaningful placement in student lives, that deals with age-appropriate issues and problems, and that works with individual strengths and weaknesses.

Developmental Issues

An important proviso is in order before we examine developmental factors in learning. Despite the fact that considerable work has been done to give some coherence to the developmental literature on the cognitive, affective, moral, social, and emotional growth of school-aged children, quite a bit of debate also exists. Thus, when one speaks of the developmental nature of the learner, one is not necessarily speaking without controversy or disagreement. The nature of the learner to someone who is working out of a behaviorist learning tradition, for instance, will likely be quite different from someone who is working out of a field-psychology approach. So, there is room for argument regarding the developmental nature of the learner. What we are calling for here is not a singular construction of the developmental nature of the learner, but a deliberate and fully formed notion of child development that informs the thinking of the curriculum designer.

Furthermore, when we discuss the nature of the learner we are not looking at the variable as a sole source or influence on the curriculum, but as one factor in a combination of factors. Thus, keeping Dewey's educative process in mind, our view of the learner is one that aims to be responsive to democratic values and some sense of useful knowledge. Thus, a behaviorist position on learning, which tends to characterize learners as conditioned organisms, might not be the best learning theory to embrace in a school that holds itself up to a democratic standard of behavior. The behaviorist embrace of the conditioned response and its heavy reliance on external controls could be interpreted as contradictory to the democratic ideal of an autonomously thinking, critically minded and socially responsible learner. However, we need to be reminded again that theory does not give us hard and fast prescriptions in the actions of the school, and that at the instructional level, some behaviorist approaches might very well prove to be helpful in teaching children critically useful skills.

Cognitive Development.   Most educators probably understand that there are qualitative differences between the way children think and the way adults think, as well as qualitative differences in the nature of children's thinking at different ages. The initiated reader will of course recognize this to be a familiar Piagetian notion. It came to Piaget's attention when he examined the wrong answers children gave on an IQ test and noted a trend in the nature of the wrong answers given by children of a certain age. The children all seemed to always give the same type of wrong answer (Pine, 1999). Piaget subsequently pursued a research agenda to identify the nature of these differences in thinking and eventually organized them into a stage theory of cognitive development (Piaget, 1950).

It is not our purpose here to reproduce a complete exposition of Piaget's work. But looking at the main features of his stage theory is instructive in its potential to affect curriculum design.

Because we are interested in the design of the public school curriculum, we could start with *preoperational* development. This cognitive stage—loosely ranging from ages 2 to 6—is marked by the early development of symbolic functioning, which includes the use of language to mark symbols and objects. The egocentrism of children at this stage does not allow them to make any distinction between the words they use to mark an object and the actual object. They simply lack awareness of the perspective of others. Thus, a child playing with a ball might refer to it as a *plaything*, and believe that the referent *plaything* is enough information to convey the object. All four-legged animals might be known as *cat*, all buildings as *house*. Children at this stage also have trouble understanding the relation between two dimensions of stimuli at the same time. Piaget discovered this when he conducted an experiment that asked children to count the number of marbles used to create two separate figures. The marbles associated with each figure were exactly the same in number and were identical in their arrangement. Piaget then spread out the marbles associated with one of the figure, while keeping the marbles associated with the other intact. Children at this stage were convinced that more marbles now existed with the figure where the marbles were spread out than where they were not. They could not simultaneously hold one dimension of the stimuli constant while dealing with change in the other. They could not conserve, or hold constant, the number of objects once their place in an arrangement was changed. Knowledge of such cognitive structures could very much assist with questions related to whether (and how) to teach various literacy and numeracy skills.

The *concrete operational* stage is representative of what we typically see among children between the ages of 6 and 11. Formal instruction in literary and numeracy could proceed more smoothly at this point because children at this stage of development are able to deal with more than one feature of their environment at one time. Thinking, however, is limited to concrete things and generally speaking, children cannot make any distinction between their thoughts and their experiences. The idea of the abstract—an interpretation of reality as opposed to actual reality— is really not possible. Hence, the tendency is to rely on concrete objects in the learning situation. To prefer the mentalistic over the experiential (or over the concrete) with this group of learners could prove to be especially costly to their education.

Finally, the stage of *formal operations*, generally 11 years old and onward, gives some clearance to the school curriculum to focus on more abstract ideas, and to encourage hypotheses testing, logical thinking, and problem-solving techniques. Not surprisingly, schooling for preadolescents is marked by these kinds of experiences. Middle school instruction, which is manifestly designed for preadolescents, sees the introduction of reasoning and abstract possibilities to be among its key features.

The point here is not to advocate for a Piagetian perspective on learning. Some critics point to the possibility that Piaget's stage theory is much more influenced by environmental factors than Piaget appreciated. They also claim that the nature of the task could profoundly affect a child's developmental status, allowing some children to be in different stages for different tasks. And others even claim that the age ranges associated with the stages are fundamentally inaccurate (Pine, 1999).

The purpose here is to show that recognizing the learner's developmental condition contributes to an instructional argument. The justification for stimulating hypothetical thinking in the adolescent is certainly on stronger ground than it might be if we sought to do it with kindergarteners. Concrete operations in teaching, which call for a reliance on objects and senses, could be viewed as essential to the education of elementary-school-aged children. Practical examples of how we might make good use of Piaget's insights include being sure that formal operations are in place before relying too heavily on lecture methods of instruction and generally trying to individualize instruction in accordance to a student's place along the developmental continuum.

Developmental factors related to cognitive growth could also be viewed as reaching into sociocultural realms. The Soviet psychologist, Lev Vygotsky (1978), offered important new insight on this front by introducing a theory of cognitive development that accounted for the effect that social interactions have on the development of thought. Because Cold War hostilities between the United States and the Soviet Union lasted for nearly half a century, Vygotsky's work came late to United States (translations were offered in the late 1970s). Today, however, Vygotsky's work has central relevance to any discussion of cognition and learning.

To Vygotsky, intellectual development is rooted in language development, which itself is ultimately formed in social interactions. Vygotsky's contention was that children learn to think by developing their inner speech, which he viewed as a kind of internal guidepost for thinking. Thus, Vygotsky put great analytical attention on the development of language. But language itself is most manifest and has its main purpose in the social world; it is the vehicle for socialization and for the building of culture. So, Vygotsky's concern for language took him into the social realm, where adults are obviously involved in assisting children with social functions and social interactions—all of which, contended Vygotsky, have a profound influence on the metacognitive structure of a child's internal speech. Because thought is transmitted to the child by means of words, language becomes the main instrument in determining how the child will learn how to think. The responsiveness of the social world to children is the key to their language development, just as their language development is the key to their cognitive growth.

Vygotsky's regard for the social environment led him to speak directly to ways that educators could manage a child's education. According to Vygotsky, cognitive growth resulted when the learning environment was kept within a range of tasks that children could only do with the assistance of adults, within what he referred to as the *zone of proximate development* (tasks that were in between what children could complete independently and what they might find impossible to complete). In the zone of proximate development, children benefit from the prompts, hints, cues, and general assistance provided by adults.

Practical and usable approaches in the classroom followed Vygotsky's work. Included among them is the instructional idea of scaffolding, which suggests that teachers provide only enough support to accomplish learning tasks. They continuously recalculate the amount of support required as the child grows more independent and as the task moves out of the zone of proximate development (McCormick and Pressley, 1997). Elementary school teachers, for instance, often use this very concept to regulate the teaching of reading, by encouraging children to read books that are neither too easy nor too hard, but on the edge of being challenging enough to require some assistance. Vygotsky's ideas also teach us the primacy of language in learning and the importance of using rich linguistic engagements to help children build upon their own descriptions (and hence understandings) of the world. An expansion of language is an expansion of thinking. Vygotsky also pointed to the importance of individualization in the curriculum. Where direct group instruction is the norm, for instance, it is likely that the underlying instructional task will be out of the zone of proximate development of several children, denying them the possibility for further cognitive development. Finally, and most significantly, the zone of proximate development insists that learning become a social process; social engagement is required in the zone of proximate development. To Vygotsky, cognitive processes operate best when children are interacting with people in their environment and the opportunities for language usage are at their height, building inner speech and inner thought.

Personal and Social Identity.   Developmental factors can also be viewed in terms of personal and social identity. Thus, we move away from our concerns about the cognitive into concerns about social and psychological adjustment. Erik Erikson's stage theory of psychosocial development argued that individuals pass though different developmental stages of self-identity, each of which highlights what he called an *identity conflict* (Erikson, 1950). The resolution of these conflicts is crucial to the well-being of the person because, according to Erikson, the stages represent one-time chances for healthy ego development. If the conflicts are not properly resolved in each stage, the timetable of development moves on with the residual effect of unresolved identity.

For elementary-school-aged children, the main identity conflict is represented by what Erickson identified as a struggle between industry and inferiority—that is, a struggle to either achieve mastery of the tasks expected of the child in society (industry) or to suffer the inferiority that failure brings. Because the main expectations of a child's performance at this age are often linked to the school, healthy ego identity is wrapped up with the achievement of academic tasks. To achieve in school gives the child a social identity, the approval of society, and a sense of capability. So, one implication of Erikson's theory is the importance of giving children good opportunities for mastery and to minimize the outward signs of failure. Thus, grading schemes that include language or symbols of failure, or learning experiences tipped too far in the direction of challenging the student could be especially problematic for children in this stage. In fact, using Erikson's theory, we could say that healthy ego development in the elementary school years could be undermined by all sorts of things, including, to name a few, the failure of the teacher to give outward signals of approval for work well done, the use of marginalizing categorical student labels (such as the term *learning disabled*), the elimination of social promotion policies, or even the use of letter grades on report cards.

The identity struggle becomes arguably more intense during the period of adolescence. To make this point, Erikson characterizes the struggle during this period as strictly an identity struggle, a conflict between identity and identity confusion. Identity becomes a front-and-center concern during adolescence because of obvious physiological changes, the appearance of sexual needs and the surfacing of formal operations. And with formal operations taking hold, the teenager can gain an abstracted sense of self, which leads to self-reflections over matters such as sexual orientation, philosophy of life, religious viewpoints, career objectives, and intellectual interests. For adolescents, Erikson argues that self-identity has two main conditions to fulfill: a sense of individual identity and a sense of a social identity. The road to identity has to lead to a definable sense of who one is and what one does for society. Hence, self-actualization needs (individual identity) should make their way into the curriculum during this period. We could ask, for instance, does the curriculum help students develop a philosophy of life? Does it give them opportunities to realistically assess their own skills and limitations, to accept responsibility for their own decisions, and to cultivate artistic, vocational, and avocational interests? Similarly, we can ask if social identity skills are being served in the curriculum. Are the students given opportunities to learn to communicate effectively in groups, to develop a commitment to the values of our democracy, and to learn the action skills needed to take on political and community causes?

The practical consequences of Erikson's theory on the curriculum of the middle school or the high school can also lead to important content decisions in the macrocurriculum, including a focus on pre-occupational courses and courses tied to the public welfare and civic causes (social identity), as well as a place for electives and choices and more personal engagements dedicated to self-actualization issues (individual identity).

Moral Development.   Developmental issues can also be understood from the standpoint of moral behavior, a concern obviously relevant to the educational mission of the school. Because moral functioning is a basic component of humanity and serves the purpose of maintaining social control, it is a key feature of all school education. To the extent that schools affect the behaviors and values of children, they are likely involved in some form of moral education.

Lawrence Kohlberg (1981) recognized the importance of moral thinking in the education of children and developed a stage theory of development that outlined a progression of moral reasoning. Kohlberg asked children to respond to various moral dilemmas he presented to children in the form of stories. The dilemmas typically took the form of forcing the children to choose between two culturally unacceptable alternatives: for instance, either steal from others to pay for the medical treatment of a loved one or decide not to steal and allow the serious ailment to have its way. Kohlberg was less interested in the answers the children provided to the dilemmas than in the reasons or justifications they gave for their answers.

Kohlberg formulated his stage theory from an analysis of the reasons provided by the children to his moral dilemmas. He observed three major levels of moral reasoning in the student responses. The first level, known as *preconventional moral reasoning*, demonstrates minimal ability and is moved by an egocentric point of view. It is reducible to equating moral decisions to obeying authority (and fearing punishment) and satisfying self-interests (and accumulating rewards). At the second level, *conventional moral reasoning,* the individual acts in conformance with the rules of society and a general sense of the majority, with a desire to please others and with an eye toward the expressed standards or mores of society. Finally, at the third level, *postconventional reasoning,* moral decisions are moved by principled views, by an understanding that rules can be broken if higher principles are involved.

Criticism of Kohlberg's stage theory includes the contention that no sense of moral reasoning can be captured through the use of hypothetical and abstract situations. Moral reasoning is ultimately tested in concrete situations, in moral behaviors, so Kohlberg's emphasis on abstract reasoning can theoretically result in higher moral reasoning scores for poorly behaved children than for well-behaved children. Criticisms have also prevailed over Kohlberg's lack of both gender-based and class-based perspectives of moral reasoning.

So, what can curriculum developers do with Kohlberg's theory? We should be reminded that Kohlberg's theory of moral reasoning is a stage theory. The implication is that everyone goes through the stages sequentially without skipping any stage, but that movement through these stages, although influenced by maturational factors (such as formal operations), is not automatic. As Kohlberg put it, "you have to be cognitively mature to reason at the level of principled morality, but you can be smart and never reason morally" (p. 262, quoted in Sprinthall and Sprinthall, 1977). Kohlberg believed that movement through the stages of development was affected by dissonance, or in this case, by an understanding of one's dissatisfaction with how a moral dilemma is handled. Therefore, according to Kohlberg, we would do well to present moral arguments one stage ahead of a person's present level of reasoning to stimulate movement to higher stages. Those responsible for the design of the school curriculum might find a place for such explorations in the general education phases of the curriculum, looking to introduce moral reasoning as a component part of common learnings, especially as they might relate to the study of the social sciences.

Hierarchical Needs.   Accounting for developmental concerns also means being conscious of meeting a hierarchy of basic needs. Abraham Maslow (1962), described the hierarchy, arguing that the most fundamental needs were physiological ones (e.g., sleep shelter, clothing, and food), followed by a succession of needs that included, in hierarchical order, safety, love, acceptance, self-esteem, and self-actualization. The hierarchical pattern of the needs testified to their relative importance; those placed lower in the hierarchy had to be fulfilled before the higher-placed needs could be met. So, children who come to school tired or hungry will likely not be able to learn, as their most basic needs would fail to be realized. Using the hierarchy, we could understand that children who attend school where safety is an issue might find their education completely compromised. Similarly, children who have to deal with some form of dislocation in the home (e.g., an impending divorce or family illness), or who live in homes where love and acceptance are in short supply, or who are rejected or ridiculed by their peers will not be poised to succeed in school. The curriculum and the teacher, of course, have a role in regulating these factors.

Aptitudes and Deficiencies.   To say that the school curriculum needs to be attendant to the range of strengths and weaknesses that children exhibit in school is not exactly new. The school has long recognized the need to differentiate the curriculum so as to meet both enrichment and remediation needs. This has been especially true in the core instructional areas of reading and mathematics, where the use of ability grouping, curriculum tracks, and resource assistance in the form of special education (including gifted and talented education) is relatively common. Consciousness of student aptitude should be part of every curricular encounter for it is central to the integration of the learner into the teaching-learning equation.

The term *aptitude* is used here to denote the innate abilities that individuals might demonstrate with a particular cognitive skill or set of cognitive skills. We might find children with notable innate abilities (aptitudes) to, say, memorize information, play musical instruments, learn a foreign language, manipulate mathematical ideas, build three-dimensional objects, act, dance, or draw. High aptitude obviously correlates with high achievement, while deficiencies, on the other hand, correlate with lack of achievement. Deficiencies might be rooted in an aptitude concern, or they might have something to do with any number of environmental factors, such as poor student study skills, less-than-supportive home conditions, or even shoddy teaching. Educators have some obligation to recognize student aptitudes and remediate student deficiencies.

We will not get much of a debate from anyone on the importance of attending to student aptitudes and student weaknesses, but there is plenty of disagreement on the kinds of aptitudes and weaknesses that qualify for the attention of the school. In most cases, the idea of aptitude in school is reducible to demonstrated verbal and mathematical skills. Early efforts to design general intelligence (IQ) tests, in fact, dramatized this prejudice. The IQ tests focused almost entirely on verbal and mathematical expressions of intelligence and sent a strong signal to the curriculum about what was instructionally important. To this day, schools tend to see reading and mathematics as their core instructional concerns and the achievement tests used in schools usually reflect this priority.

But for the curriculum designer, the idea of aptitude must be broadened to make it more within the true domain of the learner. The only way to be responsive to the learner is to be responsive to the whole learner. To this end, Howard Gardner's (1983) work on human intelligence has made it clear that intelligence cannot be reduced, as it has been for years, to purely verbal and quantitative manipulations. Gardner identified several categories of intelligence, including linguistic intelligence, musical intelligence, logic-mathematical intelligence, spacial intelligence, body-kinesthetic intelligence, interpersonal, and intrapersonal intelligence. The categories are posited as aptitudes. Thus, to Gardner, it makes little sense to define intelligence in general terms, and much more sense to see it as a reflection of different iterations of aptitude.

The categories Gardner formulated can help justify more learning experiences expressly dedicated to forms of intelligence often forgotten or at least relegated in the school experience. The macrocurriculum would certainly have a different profile if each of the intelligences highlighted by Gardner had equal standing in the core purposes of the school. Imagine the difference in the make-up of the school's coursework if we took seriously the idea of putting all the intelligences outlined by Gardner on an equal footing. The microcurriculum (classroom-based curriculum decisions) would be no less affected if teachers calculated their instructional decisions along these more pluralistic lines of intelligence.

Gardner's work is also just a short conceptual step away from the work done on learning styles, which refers to the preferences students exhibit in their learning. Some children might be what is known as field-dependent learners, who benefit from more interactive and social models of teaching, while others are field independent and learn best in more formalistic, lecture-based settings, often working alone. We have probably all known friends or peers who work or study under conditions that we might find impossible for ourselves. The point, at least at the microcurricular level, is to become familiar with these divergencies and to craft a school experience responsive to the variety of learning patterns we witness in children.

The school curriculum, of course, must also be attuned to students who suffer from any number of disabilities. Federal law in the United States mandates that these children be taught in the least restrictive environment, that is, in the most inclusive setting possible with the fewest number of special placements. As a result, children with disabilities have a presence in the regular classroom today that they did not have in the past. Most children with a documented disability in school are labeled as learning disabled (LD), a condition that is due to a range of factors. LD students could have trouble listening, speaking, reading, writing, reasoning, and doing mathematics. Such children are also taught by special education teachers who help keep the regular classroom experience responsive to the particularities of the student's disability through the use of an individualized educational program (IEP).

One should also remember that children whose school achievement is low are not necessarily suffering from a disability. Poor academic performance might simply be a matter of low motivation, short attention span, low self-esteem, limited opportunities to learn, difficulties at home, truancy, anxiety disorders, lack of sleep, poor eating habits, or just a poor attitude, none of which is necessarily considered a disability. Almost everyone needs a little extra help with something, which is why remediation and attention to underachievement are basic to the nature of learning.

Home and Community Environment.   The influence of family and community life on the school achievement is obvious. In America, families and communities often come together in a unique interplay of ethnic, linguistic, racial, and even class-based flavors, all of which become factors in the nature of the learner. If we believe that schooling should have some meaningful role in a student's life, then we certainly cannot ignore home and community life.

Being aware of the problems and issues that prevail outside the school lives of children is obviously the first step in making the important connection to the home and community environment. The behavior that students exhibit outside of school very much influences the kinds of experiences rationalized in school. If a community, for instance, believes that many middle school students are experimenting with cigarette smoking, the school should address the problem in the curriculum. An investigation of the students' school and neighborhood life might help with the effort to teach about the dangers of smoking. We might find that certain advertising gimmicks are preying on preadolescent social pressures, or that peer pressures are exerting a strong pull, or that the children who are smoking have parents who smoke. The resultant curriculum plan might include learning about the tactics of Madison Avenue advertisers. It might use teaching strategies that stress peer pressure scenarios and group projects that involve the participation of parents, smokers, and nonsmokers alike.

Poverty in the family and the neighborhood very much affects the school lives of children. Over 12 million children live in poverty in the nation. For young children, home literacy experiences (which include activities such as being read to, being told a story, being taught letters, words, and numbers, and visiting the library with family members) all occur significantly less frequently in families living in poverty than in those living above the poverty line. School readiness skills, which include recognizing letters, counting to twenty or higher, writing one's name, and reading or pretending to read a storybook are, on the average, all less developed among children living below the poverty line than among those living above it. Homebound resources for school success, such as access to computers, are also dramatically affected by poverty conditions. Parent involvement in school activities, such as monitoring and assisting with homework, participating in various school-based activities, providing extended enrichment activities and offering critical feedback to the school regarding the child's growth and development, are also negatively associated with low income families. The anxieties and real deprivations of living in poor, under-resourced neighborhoods also have their effect. Drug use, membership in crime gangs, and high dropout rates all provide negative working models of behavior in the neighborhoods. Community-based social capital, what Putnam (2000) calls the norms of reciprocity and trustworthiness that arise from the social networks in the community, is often weakly established in poor communities.

Knowing all this, as it might be demonstrated at the local level, is helpful to educators in making the curriculum more responsive to the learner. In neighborhoods marked by poverty, the macrocurriculum of the school could invest heavily in after-school activities (in order to provide a place for children to go to get help with homework or to simply engage in recreational play). It could put an emphasis on technology resources, knowing that they are in short supply at home, and actively seek creative ways to encourage parental involvement in the mandate of the school.

Ethnic differences in the classroom should be similarly approached. Although part of the school agenda is to help amalgamate the student population into an American community, a diversifying factor is at play as well. Understanding that ethnicity intersects with and is confounded by other key variables, most notably income, the curricularist must nevertheless make connections with the culture of students and show some sensitivity to uniquenesses of religious faith, music, art, and language.

Some researchers report learning style differences between ethnic groups or even racial groups. But if such differences exist, they are best discerned at the local level, largely because it is difficult to generalize about how black or white children learn, or how Hispanic or Asian children learn without experiencing significant confounding effects related to income, parent education levels, and homebound resources for learning. Having said this, I acknowledge that the achievement of minority children in the United States is decidedly low when compared to majority white children, so it is not as if the issue can be ignored. Any number of factors related to family structure, language, and even neighborhood culture could affect achievement or success in school in a way that is particular to children of a certain race or ethnicity.

For instance, understanding the disproportionate representation of certain ethnic groups in the dropout population might require some knowledge of ethnic traditions. Hispanic students are at much more risk of dropping out of school than any other identifiable ethnic subgroup and one explanation might be cultural. Young Hispanics who live in financially strapped families are frequently culturally compelled to leave school in order to supplement their parents' wages. Hispanic students apparently venture the risk of dishonoring their family if they do not drop out to take employment that could assist the family. Yet in other ethnic cultures the opposite holds true. Asian-American students, for instance, might tend to stay in school, even in the face of financial hardship, because dropping out would dishonor the family. One educator who has worked with the problem of school dropouts in the San Francisco area stated the cultural problem clearly: "What motivates the Latino to drop out of school to contribute to the general welfare of the family is love. What motivates the Asian to stay in school is also love for family. It's just a different view of the world by two different cultures" (Celis, 1992).

Student Interest.   Student interest in school activities has an undeniably important place in the formulation of curriculum. Much of what we do in schools is designed to respond to healthy interests. Elementary school teachers, for example, have long recognized the importance of using interest inventories in the classroom, which is a procedure that helps the teacher catalogue key interests in a child's life. The inventories are used as a means for the curriculum to reach out to students, to not only reflect what a child might like to do, but to try to capture the overall dimensions of a child's life (interests, problems, issues) in the curriculum. To know that certain children like to read comics, are Civil War buffs, enjoy writing poetry, have an active interest in government and politics, watch certain TV shows, or are aficionados of William Shakespeare's plays, is to know something important about how to teach them.

But the curriculum worker should realize that taking advantage of preexisting student interests, although undoubtedly important, is not itself enough. Healthy student interests not only need to be understood and reinforced but they also need to be widened. It might not be in the students' interest to devote all of their time to one area of interest during the course of an academic year. Students who only work on the computer or who only read to themselves all the time need to be encouraged, if not required, to widen their bases of participation. Thus, the curriculum should build in objectives and experiences that develop new interests and awaken positive attitudes toward various skills, knowledge areas, and even the act of learning itself.

The idea of student interest is also central to the development of student motivation. Rather than seeing motivation as something that needs to be created or compelled in school, the curriculum planner might look to ways that make motivation inherent to the nature of the learning experience. The difference between compelling motivation versus making it a seamless part of experience is fundamental. The former is appended to the experience and is, to paraphrase Dewey (1902, p. 29), held in contrast to an alternate negative experience, such as receiving a scolding, being held up to ridicule, staying after school, or receiving low marks. The latter is umbilically tied, again to paraphrase Dewey, to the consciousness of the child, to his or her own interests. From this perspective, motivation involves making an effort to construct learning experiences that are intrinsically appealing to youth.

THE VALUES AND AIMS OF SOCIETY

The school is, by all accounts, a democratizing institution. It is designed to carry the public mandate of the society and offer a normative experience that contributes to improving each child's chance of leading an informed and satisfying life. The family, of course, plays a role here too, but the school is deliberately conceived to fulfill a democratizing agenda. Thus, unlike family-based experiences, which tend to be parochial, the school experience has to reach across a wide range of concerns, and teach children all sorts of important skills, including how to read, think, communicate, inquire, study, and ultimately to behave in a way that embodies the best values of the society. If the school fails to teach these things, no other institution necessarily will or even can fill the void.

Skills and Competencies for Democratic Participation

The American promise of "government by the consent of the governed" presupposes the wide education of the citizenry. The shibboleth of America—*e pluribus unum*—underscores a profound idea. Unlike virtually any other nation in the world, America draws its common strength and insight from its differences. Even the very identity of an American is forged from many different religions, ethnicities, races, and political outlooks. As the world's oldest (and arguably most mature) democracy, America represents principles attesting to the importance of justice, equality, fairness, and community. The foundation of American democracy depends on virtues such as freedom of choice, openness to new ideas, respect for individuals, protection of minority rights, and a wide assembly of constitutionally protected freedoms, including the freedom of press, freedom of religion, and freedom to speak one's mind. But upholding these ideals requires an educated and actualized citizenry. And that is where the school curriculum comes into play.

Democracy begins in the school. All teachers, irrespective of their academic domain or discipline, make some contribution to the overall democratizing effect in the school. The social studies teacher will naturally have the most prominent role in the democratizing stage because the subject matter of social studies partly overlaps with what we might view as traditional civic knowledge (knowledge of government, current political events, and concerns). But the skills and competencies of democracy are part and parcel of virtually every instructional engagement in the school curriculum. We typically do not think of them this way, but literacy skills, for instance, are at their very core democratizing skills. To read with full comprehension is a requisite skill for citizenship, but to read with a critical eye (to discern the emotive and the bias in the narrative and to consider the logic inherent in the written argument) goes beyond what we conventionally see as reading or language arts education. Critical reading, in fact, has no less relevance in the language arts classroom than in the social studies or science classrooms. Likewise, when educators aim to teach children communication, thinking, or inquiry skills, they contribute to the development of a good citizen. Students who write well, express themselves clearly, think cogently, insist on the presentation of persuasive evidence, and are capable of inquiring or researching into problems, are undoubtedly better equipped for citizenship than students who cannot do such things well.

Thus, we can say that all teachers, in all public school settings, irrespective of their subject matter obligations (whether it is to teach algebra, or biology or kindergarten) should understand that the inherent theoretical design of the curriculum insists that all school experiences make some effort to reflect the skills and competencies of democracy.

So, what are these pervasive skills? I can make a case for any number of possibilities, including communication-related skills such as the ability to debate or dramatize ideas, or even inquiry skills such as knowing how to use the full complement of resources available in a library. The curriculum designer, of course, should help formulate a list of democratizing skills that relate to the mission of the school as they emerge from deliberative engagements with key school personnel. One needs simply to think about the kinds of skills that cut across the curriculum and that have a direct hand in the development of a good citizen. Adjustments naturally need to be made to account for the nature of the learner and for certain subject matter demands at different ages and grade levels.

Here is an example of one set of skills, fashioned at the highest level of generality, for middle and secondary school. I chose to focus on thinking skills, because they are indisputably important to our democracy and they cut across all subject phases of the curriculum. I itemized thinking and problem-solving skills to include the ability to

- Compare and contrast data
- Judge the quality of the evidence
- Seek reliable sources of information and identify authentic information
- Use qualitative and quantitative methods of reasoning and understanding
- Understand cause and effect relations
- Demonstrate independent and persuasively conveyed thought
- Detect propaganda, and
- Synthesize and evaluate information and interpretations.

The list could be longer and more specific, but here it is adequate because it gives us a sense of how thinking skills are constituent skills of democracy that have relevance across the landscape of the school curriculum.

But someone might ask that if these skills cut across the curriculum, what does, say, the math teacher have to do with teaching the skill of detecting propaganda? The answer depends on the school situation. One answer is to say that propaganda has a lot to do with mathematics, which puts the priority on the designer to help make the connection between the two. The use of mathematical manipulations to deceive is not exactly an unfamiliar concept. Numbers *can* lie. But another curriculum design might expect little from the high school math teacher in this skill area, not because detecting propaganda doesn't match up well with math but because a choice might be made, at the macrocurricular level: to emphasize such a skill in other areas of study, such as literature, history, social studies, and even science class. Instead, the math teacher might pay more attention to other thinking skills better emphasized in mathematics classes. This mixing and matching of skills within grade levels and across the coursework and subject areas of the macrocurriculum, is known as horizontal articulation. Curriculum designers want to know the manner in which a course or set of experiences within a grade level articulates or relates to other courses or experiences, so that unproductive redundancy is avoided and full and complete coverage of key skill areas is ensured. We will revisit articulation issues in the curriculum in Chapter 5.

Other civic or social skills should also make their way into curriculum deliberations. A curriculum that finds a place for communication skills that cultivate debate and negotiation, or that encourage students to express persuasively conveyed views, is responsive to the source of society. Moreover, inquiry skills, such as distinguishing between fact and opinion, judging the authenticity of evidence, and knowing where to turn to further explore an idea or problem, are precisely the kinds of skills we aspire to achieve with a curriculum actualized by the values and aims of democracy. We should also mention the importance of democratic skills more directly linked to civic knowledge, such as civic writing (to politicians and newspaper editors) and political action skills (campaigning for a candidate, formulating a petition, or organizing a protest assembly).

The curriculum looks to the values and aims of society for theoretical guidance. And I do not mean that all curricula have a responsibility to teach civic knowledge—that is typically the reserve of the social studies teacher. But we should understand that many skills we value in our society are ones that should find their way into all phases of the curriculum. The construction and use of pervasive skills will be explored in more detail in Chapter 4.

Democratic Processes and Values

If the public school is an agency of democracy, its responsibilities include teaching youth about the core values and attitudes of democratic living. This is a matter slightly different from the teaching of democratizing skills, but it should be viewed as no less pervasive across the curriculum. In other words, all curriculum design must consider the importance of democratic values and processes.

Dewey (1916) referred to the school environment as an embryonic democracy. It was his way of saying that the school is not a fully formed democratic body and that we have to accept the fact that the operation of the school often requires the exercise of superordinate (adult) authority. An embryonic democracy is in the formative stages of growth and development, requiring a level of care reserved for the young and immature. But democracy, even in its least advanced form, relies on democratic processes for growth. This means that the curriculum, in order to be responsive to the values and aims of society, must embody democratic processes and values in its general operations.

Democratic processes refer to the actual conduct of the teacher and the students in the interactive circles of the classroom. Doing things democratically and highlighting activities that reinforce democratic values are the main ways to model democratic processes. The curriculum designer asks if the curriculum is producing experiences that encourage children to work together and get along, or is it producing experiences that encourage children to follow orders and egoistically pursue only individual objectives? Is it creating circles of social interaction that produce trustworthiness, respect for difference, and a concern for the well-being of others, or is it reinforcing values of authority and subordination? Are debate, conversation, and civility highlighted in the classroom or are they stifled? If teachers need to scream and yell to get things done in the classroom or if they make constant references to punishment, threats, bribes, or other forms of coercion to maintain discipline and order, can their classrooms pass the democracy test?

What exactly are the democratic values that we prize in the school curriculum? Learning how to engage others in a way that results in satisfying relations based on respect, trust, cooperation, and caring is key. As Goodlad (1997) wrote, "the arts of mutual accommodation, of communal ties, and the common good are teachable. . . . They represent and define a large part of what education is: a deliberate, systematic and sustained effort to develop and refine human sensibilities and sensitivities" (p. 33). Does this mean we need to specifically develop lessons dedicated to fostering mutual accommodation and communal ties?

The answer is best found by returning to our distinction between instruction and pedagogy. Consciousness of democratic values in our design obviously affects the kinds of instructional methodologies used in the curriculum. Active methodologies that encourage social interaction, discussion, and problem-focused inquiry are generally the kind of instructional styles that could easily find a place in a curriculum that upholds democratic values and processes. Such styles are instructional insofar as they serve to achieve a planned lesson's objectives. But they can also be much more than just instructional tools. The integration of democratic values and attitudes into the school experience is also a matter of good pedagogy: the emergent judgment of the teacher moving in the design of the curriculum. The way a teacher handles student questions or acts of student incivility, for example, very much determines the quality of the democratic processes in the classroom. And the extent to which the social interaction between teacher and student is built on mutual respect and trustworthiness also speaks to the life of democratic values in the classroom. These are largely pedagogical actions, meaning actions made by teachers in emergent interactions with students. Other examples, such as developing critical appreciations for cultural differences, for the values of liberty, and for the idea of the common good (to name a few worthy democratic causes), all rely on a working commitment to uphold the importance of such causes in the school experience. These values could manifest instructionally, as part of a pre-planned lesson, and pedagogically, in the process of teachers' interactions with children.

The school curriculum, as mentioned in the preceding chapter, must always be deliberately conceived, but its effects are not always easy to harness or to understand, and its educative action, as it were, often goes beyond its manifest design. Every teaching-learning engagement in the school, no matter its purpose or design, operates on two planes—the manifest and the latent. If our manifest objectives are to intentionally teach some particular set of skills and knowledge, we must acknowledge that, when such things are taught, we are simultaneously involved in the latent teaching of certain values and attitudes, although we may not always know it. We sometimes refer to this aspect of the curriculum as the latent or hidden curriculum, or what Dewey characterized as *collateral learning*. If an instruction plan that manifestly intends to develop important mathematical problem-solving skills also results in personal interactions between students that strengthen the communal ties of the classroom, then one can say that the intended plan did more than was expected. The latent effect (community building) was achieved by a lesson dedicated to teaching mathematical problem solving. The point is that understanding the relationship of the school curriculum to the values of society is to acknowledge the role that all experiences play in shaping attitudes, appreciations, and values. The more we are aware of this fact, the better the odds that positive attitudes and values will be bred in the school experience. As Damon (2001) put it, "the moral atmosphere that students experience in their schools—the manners of their teachers, the integrity of the school codes, the quality of the peer relations that they form—has more influence on character growth than academic programs."

One of the main effects of a school that shows sensitivity to the values and processes of democracy is *social capital*. Recently popularized in Robert Putnam's book, *Bowling Alone*, social capital refers to the norms and social networks of engagement witnessed in a community that supports trustworthiness, good will, and a strong sense of social mutuality or reciprocity. Putnam believes that social capital is at the center of all healthy communities, including schools, and that greater attention should be paid to its influence in the lives of children. Schools are better in communities rich in social capital, where community members trust and help each other, where they work toward a sense of public good, and where sympathy and fellowship toward each other are in large supply. Drawing from Putman's work, curriculum designers could think in terms that encourage community organizational life, engagement in political affairs, community volunteerism, and informal sociability. The idea is to teach a student population to take community and democratic life seriously.

The decision to incorporate democratic values in the school experience is not always made without controversy. You will probably get into a good argument, for instance, if you want to find a place for patriotism in the school curriculum. Part of the problem is that patriotism, as a value, can be manipulated in a way that contradicts other important democratic values. If teaching patriotism meant encouraging an unquestioned love of country or some kind of national chauvinism, we might have serious misgivings about it. At the same time, it does not seem reasonable to altogether leave it out of the curriculum. Patriotism is fundamental to building the kind of emotional attachments needed to move citizens to work in the best interest of their society (Damon, 2001). Thus, when dealing with values in the curriculum, the issue of balance is crucial. A democratic construction of patriotism teaches children to be both critical and loving toward their country.

KNOWLEDGE AND SUBJECT MATTER

The question of what content or knowledge is most worthwhile in the experience of the school has been an enduring one for educators. Students, after all, need to be taught something and selectively choosing just what to teach in the school is not an easy task. For instance, does Shakespeare deserve all the attention he typically gets in high school English classrooms? Should AIDS be discussed in elementary school health classes? Should the horrors of certain events (such as the Holocaust, the Bombing of Nagasaki, and the Rape of Nanking) be included in the teaching of World War II? If so, do we include content taken from different societal perspectives of these events? The curriculum developer must face these types of questions and have some process for determining what shall be taught.

Such decisions start with understanding that inclusions of certain content or subject matter in the curriculum are *privileging actions.* When we say that *x* is worthy of the time and energy dedicated to studying it, we are also saying that we value *x* because we believe that our school children will be served by knowing it. And because the world of knowledge is so vast, each new inclusion in the curriculum displaces something else, making it all that more important that our selections are careful.

Empowerment and Knowledge

To say that the curriculum supports the place of content or knowledge in the school experience requires us to be a little more definitive about what we mean by *content.* The definition of content used here is those ideas, concepts, generalizations, definitions, and facts that hold together as a discipline, a category of inquiry, or as some other well-delineated form of representation.

When the curriculum is responsive to the source of subject matter it conveys a world of knowledge to the student—and brings useful ideas, concepts, generalizations, definitions, and facts to the school experience. Tyler (1949) emphasized the need for curriculum designers to seek the contribution of subject specialists in making curricular decisions. He asked, "What can your subject contribute to the education of young people who are not going to specialize in your field; what can your subject contribute to the layman, the garden variety of citizen?" (p. 26). These questions remind us that we are looking for content relevant to the lives of school children living in a democracy.

Cliché as it seems, knowledge is power. What we know has much to do with how we behave and with how successful we become at directing and controlling our lives. Knowledge, in fact, is only knowledge to the extent that it induces intelligent action and results in an informed sense of meaning in the world—an evolving perspective on how best to go forward in life. For example, to know that smoking cigarettes dramatically increases one's odds of contracting a serious illness is empowering—it can inform behavior. To continue to smoke in the face of the facts is to deny the power of knowledge, to reduce it to something better classified as information or simply fact. To know is to be given the capacity to do.

The need for knowledge or subject matter in the school curriculum is undeniable. Although the schools have historically encountered child-centered efforts that have eased the influence of content on the curriculum, the general framework of the school curriculum has always held subject matter in relatively high esteem. Today most high schools are still organized by subject disciplines, high school teachers are still certified by content areas, and graduation requirements are still itemized as credit hours achieved in various subjects. Even the block scheduling pattern used in self-contained elementary school classrooms tends to be carved up as planned experiences in various subject areas—language arts and mathematics in the morning hours, science and social studies in the afternoon, for instance. School children tend to see the world of knowledge in terms of traditional subject matter categories.

This is not to say, however, that all school experiences are connected to subject matter. I have personally witnessed teachers implement lessons dedicated to the development of certain sets of skills or values that were fundamentally without any connection to content. I have seen thinking skills, for instance, taught through so-called thinking workbooks, which were little more than puzzle-solving activities, requiring students to solve spatial dilemma problems and logical conundrums. Similarly, I have observed stand-alone character education programs that touted role-playing activities as a way to broach ethical dilemmas and to tout the virtues of various character traits. In each case, the experience was essentially content-less, meaning it was without any clear bridge to an identifiable discipline or to some set of principles, concepts, or facts. I will not pass further judgment on these activities except to say that thinking skills and character education need not be taught without some substantive involvement of subject matter. Thinking skills are elemental to every content area in the curriculum and character education obviously runs through the disciplines of literature and the social sciences. In curriculum design, one rule of thumb is to find an instructional point of coalescence between skill and content as well as between values and content: to seek applications for the development of skills and values in a body of worthy knowledge.

Despite the privileged place disciplinary knowledge seems to have in the school experience, some evidence indicates that American students are deficient in their knowledge of fundamental mathematics, history, literature, and science. The National Assessment of Educational Progress (NAEP) data on history, for instance, are rife with examples of student deficiencies. One third of all 17-year-olds could not identify Abraham Lincoln as the author of the Emancipation Proclamation. Almost half of all 17-year-olds could not identify Joseph Stalin as the leader of the Soviet Union during the Second World War II and more than half could not identify the nature of the controversy surrounding Senator Joseph McCarthy (Ravitch and Finn, 1989). Test results in literature and science were similarly unimpressive.

It would be easy to say that the NAEP history test does little more than assess trivial knowledge and that the students' documented failures to recall historical facts may not be troubling at all, especially if we can show that such failures are the result of aiming at higher objectives (such as the teaching of concepts, principles, and higher-ordered skills). But failures to recall key facts cannot be so easily dismissed. To know the key facts of history, literature, and science may not be a striking achievement, but to *not* know them likely points to deep problems. To know that Abraham Lincoln signed the Emancipation Proclamation is obviously not all that impressive, but to *not* know it likely means that the students know little more about Lincoln's presidency or about the broader historical events that occurred during his term in office.

The inevitable question, then, is what knowledge is most worthy or most empowering? To start, content is obligated to be connected to the nature of the learner and the values and aims of society. In other words, knowledge or content sanctioned in school must be age-appropriate and within the democratic mission of the school; there are limits as to what can be taught to children at different stages of development and maturity. At the microcurricular level, factors related to home environment and community also play a role in the content selection process. When teachers consider the content of a lesson, they think about the logical organization of subject matter (the rational organization of key principles, propositions, facts, and concepts) in relation to what Dewey (1902) called the *psychological organization* of subject matter, which takes it basis in the learner's life. To psychologize the subject matter is to screen it through the experiences, interests, capacities, and life conditions of the learner—the learner's psychological location in time and space, as Zais (1976) put it. The starting point for the teaching of simple mathematical operations (logical organization) might be in connection to real world problem-solving needs such as the operation of a classroom store, the calculation of survey data dealing with problems (or issues) in the school or community, or some statistical depiction of other social phenomena. Teachers see the logical as it applies to the psychological, making the logical organization of subject matter crucial to learning situations.

The question of what content is included in the curriculum also turns on important cultural considerations. The decision, for instance, to teach English high school classes through literature drawn mostly from the Western canon reflects an overt enfranchisement of one set of writings over another and even the concomitant privileging of one cultural perspective over another. These are decisions that curriculum designers cannot be bashful about making. Can we say then that if we give Shakespeare a prominent place in the English curriculum that we are sending a message to school children about the important of white, male, European voices? It is something to think about. The school curriculum, especially the content of the curriculum, carries cultural weight. But part of the normative enterprise of the school is to transmit cultural knowledge, and given our nation's Western heritage, Shakespeare has an indisputable place at the nation's cultural table. The question becomes how important is it to the school to invite a diverse audience of writers into the English classroom? To what extent is the school prepared to see the teaching of English as a phenomenon that expresses cultural priorities? How important is it to screen or select the readings used in high school English class by noting and accounting for the gender, skin color, cultural background, and even social class status of the authors?

The reason we think so hard about content in the first place has to do with an ongoing belief that the knowledge represented in the school experience reflects the accumulated wisdom of our humanity. Many believe that what we have learned, as a civilization and as a nation, must be transmitted to youth in a way that helps us avoid any repetition of past mistakes. This familiar argument still stands as one of the main pillars supporting the primacy of content in the school curriculum. Children are expected to know and to use the accumulated wisdom or knowledge inherent in the sciences, mathematics, history, social studies, and literature. Such knowledge is an inheritance from the past, a way of teaching youth the lessons learned by their elders.

At the same time, content is also at the very core of building a common culture for the society. The mechanism of commonality is crucial to the building of community. To have a common culture, one needs a common language, common values, and a common cultural vocabulary. On the latter, the content of the curriculum makes an especially profound contribution. Our common vocabulary is forged by what we learn in school. Hirsch (1987) refers to this body of knowledge as cultural literacy. The purpose behind cultural literacy is to facilitate a common discourse of social exchange and social understanding; it is a way to build units of community and social mutuality with shared bases of knowledge. Thus, the selection of content in the school curriculum is partly influenced by a normative project that defines and cultivates a national sense of literacy, "something every American needs to know" as Hirsch (1987) phrased it.

Directives and Content Standards

Content inclusions in the curriculum often fall under the province and dominion of state and local directives. Because, as indicated, the content of the curriculum is a normative concern, states often exercise some authority in setting forth content requirements for the schools. These requirements typically take the form of content standards, which are little more than goals that stipulate what should be taught. They do not address how they should be taught or where in the fabric of the school experience they should be integrated. Content standards denote standardization in what is taught but no real standardization beyond it, except to the extent that the organization of the standards themselves might influence the organization of knowledge and even of coursework in the curriculum.

Content standards are helpful in the curriculum if they supply guidance to the teacher on what should be taught. They are especially valuable as a coordinating function in the curriculum if they are clearly and unambiguously stated. To reformers like Hirsch content standards represent precisely the kind of solution he has in mind to the failures of cultural literacy. Through standards designed by national agencies, states could insist on the teaching of a certain identifiable body of content believed to be most critical to the development of a national sense of cultural literacy. As Ravitch (1995, p. xxv) once put it, "there is no such thing as Nevada science, New Jersey mathematics, and Illinois English."

SUMMARY

The role of theory in the practice of the curriculum is important but limited. Theory should not be used to impose one's political will on the school curriculum or to demand that only one instructional approach be used in the classroom. Theory directs, but does not dictate the curriculum. It speaks more to the meaning and purpose of the school than to any particular method or even particular content. Nevertheless, the school curriculum has certain boundaries that are largely defined by its normative commitments and by historically sanctioned theoretical factors related to the learner, the society, and the subject matter. The three factors tell us that a school curriculum must account for some formulation of learners, some vision of a democratic society, and some identifiable sense of content or subject matter. I detailed what this means in practical terms by showing the linkage of each factor to the practical question of curriculum design.

DISCUSSION QUESTIONS AND SUGGESTED ACTIVITIES

1. What are the general limits we put on theory in the context of curriculum development?

2. Provide an example of how theory can be misused in instruction or result in a highly politicized vision of the curriculum.

3. Describe the general history linked to the emergence of the three factors used to direct curriculum development.

4. How can consideration for the nature of the learner contribute to designing a successful curriculum?

5. What are the practical implications for the curriculum worker of Piaget's and Vygotsky's work on cognitive development?

6. How can one usefully account for home and community culture in developing a curriculum? What are the limitations to such a process?

7. How does Howard Gardener's exposition on multiple intelligences completely alter the traditional configuration of what we value in the school curriculum?

8. How can learning to read be viewed as a democratizing skill?

9. What is the difference between the manifest and the latent curriculum and how is the distinction important to understanding the role the school plays in teaching values and attitudes?

10. How is the idea of horizontal articulation linked to the teaching of democratizing skills?

11. Would you support the teaching of patriotism in the curriculum? If so, how might you go about teaching it?

12. NAEP data suggest that many students in the United States do not possess very impressive proficiencies of knowledge in the academic disciplines. Do you see this as a problem? How might the curriculum begin to address it?

13. Provide an example from your experience of contentless teaching. Did you find the experience to be educational to the students?

14. What point is Diane Ravitch making when she claims that "there is no such thing as Nevada science, New Jersey mathematics, and Illinois English?"

15. Do you believe that the normative agenda of the public school should include some effort to identify a body of knowledge that every American should know?

NOTES

Beauchamp, G.A. (1975). *Curriculum theory* (3rd ed.). Wilmette, Illinois: Kagg Press.

Celis, W. (1992). Hispanic dropout rates stay high, since children work. *New York Times*, 14 October: B9.

Damon, W. (2001). To not fade away: Restoring civil identity among the young. In D. Ravtich & J.P Viteritti. (Eds.), *Making good citizens: Education and civil society.* New Haven: Yale University Press.

Dewey, J. (1902). *Child and the curriculum/School and the society.* Chicago: University of Chicago Press.

Dewey, J. (1916). *Democracy and education.* New York: Free Press.

Erikson, E. (1950). *Childhood and society.* New York: W.W Norton.

Hirsch, E.D. (1987). *Cultural literacy: What every American needs to know.* Boston: Houghton Mifflin.

Gardner, H. (1983). *Frames of mind: The theory of multiple intelligences.* New York: Basic Books.

Goodlad, J. (1997). *In praise of education.* New York: Teachers College Press.

Kincheloe, J.L., Slattery, P. & Steinberg, S.R. (2000). *Contextualizing teaching: Introduction to education and educational foundations.* New York: Longman.

Kohlberg, L. (1981). *The philosophy of moral development.* San Francisco: Harper and Row.

Maslow, A. (1970). *Motivation and personality.* New York: Harper.

McCormick, C.B. & Pressley, M. (1997). *Educational psychology: Learning, instruction, assessment.* New York: Longman.

National Center for Education Statistics. (2000). *Trends in educational equity of girls and women.* Washington, DC: U.S. Department of Education.

National Education Association. (1898). *Report of the Committee of Ten on secondary school studies.* Washington, DC: NEA.

Piaget, J. (1950). *The psychology of intelligence.* New York: Harcourt.

Pine, K. (1999). Theories of cognitive development. In D. Messer, & S. Millar (Eds.), *Exploring development psychology: From infancy to adolescence.* London: Arnold.

Putnam, R.D. (2000). *Bowling alone: The collapse and revival of American community.* New York: Simon and Schuster.

Ravitch, D. (1995). *National standards in American education: A citizen's guide.* Washington, DC: The Brookings Institution.

Ravitch, D. & Finn, C. (1987). *What do our 17-year-olds know?* New York: Harper and Row.

Schwab, J.J. (1969). The practical: A language for curriculum. (originally in *School Review* 78(1):1–23). In I. Westbury, & N. Wilkof (Eds.). (1978). *Science, curriculum and liberal education.* Chicago: University of Chicago Press.

Sprinthall, R.C. & Sprinthall, N.A. (1977). *Educational psychology: A developmental approach* (2nd ed.). Menlo Park, CA: Addison Wesley.

Taba, H. (1962). *Curriculum development: theory and practice.* New York: Harcourt, Brace and World.

Tanner, D. & Tanner, L.N. (1995). *Curriculum development* (2nd ed.). New York: Macmillan.

Tyler, R.W. (1949). *Basic principles of curriculum and instruction.* Chicago: University of Chicago Press.

Vygotsky, L.S. (1978). *Mind and society.* Cambridge: Harvard University Press.

Zais, R.S. (1976). *Curriculum: Principles and foundations.* New York: Crowell.

CHAPTER THREE

PHILOSOPHY AND DESIGN

If we are willing to conceive of education as the process of forming fundamental dispositions, intellectual and emotional, toward nature and fellow man, philosophy may even be defined as the general theory of education

—John Dewey

The design of the school curriculum must be free to be influenced by the hopes and the wisdom of the school community and the school leadership. Part of the responsibility of the school leadership, which obviously includes teachers, is to articulate some vision and ambition for the school. And although theory and philosophy can be mishandled and used programmatically, it is important to understand that curriculum development is not a mechanical or objectively neutral process. It is an undertaking that uses a base of values to direct the nature of the experience in the school. John Dewey understood the influence of these values in our thinking and believed that to the extent that such biases represented a coherent philosophy, they also represented a theory of education—a way to begin to make distinctions between what is important and what is less important in the school experience. The theoretical foundations discussed in the preceding chapter help us understand and evaluate the philosophical dimensions of the curriculum by pointing an analytical finger at just how the learner, the society, and the subject matter are constructed in the school curriculum. I will use these three factors to bring some clarity to the place of philosophy in the curriculum development process.

THE SCREEN OF PHILOSOPHY

Tyler (1949) likened the role of philosophy in the curriculum to a screen through which ideas are filtered. The screen of philosophy helps to crystallize and focus the teacher's purposes and objectives of the classroom. Because a philosophy is tied to wider epistemological questions, such as what it means to lead a good life in a good society, it will have a defined perspective on what is worth knowing and doing.

There are certain restrictions, however, that limit the possibilities for the expression of philosophy in the curriculum. One is that a philosophy is only valid in the curriculum if it is responsive to the three sources discussed earlier (the learner, society, and subject matter). A fascist school philosophy, say, cannot be justified when educating youth for participation in a democracy. This would be considered a violation of the "society" factor, which demands that the values and aims of the society are honored in the school. Naturally, people will use various arguments to justify whether certain actions and experiences in the school are responsive to democracy, but an overtly antidemocratic philosophy cannot stand. A philosophy also has to have some linkage to the learner. No philosophical justification will be accepted for experiences that are not age-appropriate or that are viewed, in any way, as harmful to the mental, emotional, and physical well-being of the child. A teacher, for example, who has an earnest philosophical commitment to bringing the hard realities of the life experience to the classroom has to be careful not to overstep certain boundaries—one must not teach children that fire burns by putting their hands into the flames.

Thus, these philosophical considerations must lie at the center of the curriculum development process. The curriculum developer must ask, what is the conception of the learner supported by a particular philosophical point of view? What is the ideal of an educated citizen? What knowledge (subject matter) is most worth knowing and how should it be organized and taught? Each of these points of departure leaves room for the expression of a different philosophical position and the formation of different school purposes and school practices.

SCHOOLING IN THE CONSERVATIVE TRADITION

The conservative philosophical position on the school curriculum is essentially a subject-centered one. It holds that teaching is largely a matter of maneuvering through the considerable amount of wisdom embodied in organized knowledge. The purpose of the school is primarily a matter of cultural transmission, the conveying and the preservation of common cultural knowledge. Students are believed to be well served because schools expose them to the essential dimensions of civilization. Among young children, the focus of education is devoted to the teaching of the basic skills needed for later mastery of the subject matter. This general orientation is viewed as conservative because it is committed to the conservation of humanity's wisdom, as it is believed to be found in particular academic disciplines.

Perennialism

From a perennialist perspective, the value of learning is unalterably tied to the subject matter. Learning is primarily a matter of immersion in a set of subjects believed to be endowed with the verities and virtues of Western civilization. Grammar, reading, rhetoric, logic, mathematics, and great literature (the historic core of the liberal arts) have long stood as the main columns of content for perennialists. Hutchins (1936) referred to them as the *permanent studies*. The choice of this term is revealing because it reflects the assumption that the educating powers of these studies persist over time. In other words, the studies are perennial—everlasting through time. This is the strongest way of saying that the subject matter itself and the powers that transfer from it represent the main ends of education. Learning arises from the activities generated by the subject matter. Teachers might seek ways to guide, stimulate, and assist it, but the subject matter is the true teacher. And where teachers might focus on basic skills instruction (rather than content), especially with younger children, the rationale justifying their actions is that such skills are required to access the subject matter in a way that will allow the student to eventually benefit from its mind-training possibilities. Believing that these subjects represent a kind of repository for the knowledge and wisdom of western humanity, perennialists are confident that a well-managed and carefully supervised exposure to the permanent studies will produce the kind of rational, enlightened, and intellectually stimulated person that democracy demands.

A perennialist maintains that one must have a wholly exclusive experience in the permanent studies to be educated. Thus, there is a kind of one-size-fits-all mentality to the perennialist, a belief in posing one uniform curriculum experience to all students in virtually all places and all times. This insistence comes from a desire to expose all youth, not just the elite, to a form of education believed to be essential to democracy. Thus, all youth not only benefit intellectually from experiences that discipline the mind, but they also receive their cultural inheritance from their studies. Through the eternal truths and virtues of perennial studies, the new generation can share a bond with previous generations and carry with it the common outlook it will need to advance itself. As Hutchins (1972) stated, "the primary aim of the educational system in a democratic country is to draw out the common humanity of those committed to its charge" (p. 209). To Hutchins and other perennialists, this common humanity dwells in the permanent studies.

The commitment to the mind is justified by the doctrine of mental discipline and is so intense that other areas of study in the school that seem to have less of a claim to the mind (including vocational and elective studies, physical education, the performing arts) are often viewed as anti-intellectual frivolities. Vocational education in particular has no place in the school, in the eyes of a perennialist. It is seen as taking time and resources away from the central cause of developing one's mind and character. During the 1980s, Mortimer Adler, who has been a long-time proponent of the perennialist position in the schooling, argued for the elimination of all electives in the upper six years of schooling (with the exception of a choice of a second language) and the elimination of all specialized job training throughout. "The kind of vocational training that now goes on in schools is worse than useless" observed Adler (1988), "it is undemocratic in the extreme" (p. 281). Adler could see no value in job training when the important task of mind training was before the school. Vocational education took time away from the intimate tutoring that Adler believed each student needed in order to be brought through the canons of high western thought. This privileging of matters pertaining to the mind over matters pertaining to the body leaves a mentalistic mark on the schooling experience, one that stresses a rational, contemplative, abstract, bookish, and subject-centered approach to learning. To Adler, even physical education was justified from the standpoint of its contribution to mindful learning. In 1984, he described the two purposes of physical education in the school as "to develop the knowledge and habits requisite for the care of the body throughout life, and to provide some physical relief from the taxing brain work of schooling" (p. 161).

For the elementary school teacher, the perennialist view means that serious attention will be given to the management of basic skills education, especially reading instruction. At this level of schooling, the development of the basic skills tends to take on a life of its own. It is viewed as the key needed to unlock the doors to civilization, the very skills that will enable students to eventually read and think their way through the subject matter. Thus, the instructional repertoire of the perennialist is unabashedly supportive of skill-drill strategies. As Adler (1984) observed, "often painful, usually boring, drill is necessary. . . . Students have to develop error free habits. Repeating the act (i.e., experience) is indispensable" (p. 42).

But the elementary school is also where students get their first instruction in reading and understanding the literary classics. The Great Books curriculum, the centerpiece to perennialist thinking, first takes hold here. As one perennialist phrased it, "There should be no school in which the young mind fails to receive, like seeds destined to germinate in later years, a full sowing of sentences great men have spoken" (Van Doren, 1943, p. 95). The responsibility of the teacher, from elementary school to college, is to use the Great Books to bring the meta-narrative of civilization to the student. A varied set of instructional actions could result. One role for the teacher is that of a seminar leader (Adler, 1984), one who draws out the powers of the literature through questioning techniques that "catch the mind" and promote virtue. Another is that of the coach, the vigilant tutor who pays close attention to the work of the student, offering immediate feedback, "shrewd" criticism, and hard-driving repetitions of skill.

The duty to coach or attend to the intellectual skills of the individual is often the perennialists' main argument against a more comprehensive school design. If a school tries to take on too much, they claim, the teacher cannot keep a close eye on the intellectual education of a student. Why see education as an endeavor that is, metaphorically speaking, miles wide and inches deep, the perennialist might ask, when one can focus on mindful learning with precision and depth?

And what of the fact that, until the nineteenth century, all great books were written by white European males? Adler's (1977) response is "The educational purpose of the Great Books is not to study Western civilization. Its aim is not to acquire knowledge of historical facts. It is rather to understand the great ideas" (p. xxxii). The fact that only great ideas could be had from the Great Books is unproblematic to Adler because the hand of history drew the repertoire of such books. The issue of diversity does not calculate because learning is not about diversity; it is about training the mind, the will, and the character through the permanent studies.

During the 1980s, the U.S. Secretary of Education, William J. Bennett, often displayed his perennialist colors. In 1986, for instance, he helped to author a report on elementary education in the United States, entitled *First Lessons*, which outlined general curricular conditions for reform (Bennett, 1986). The report bore an unmistakable, if not proud, resemblance to the 1895 National Education Association's *Committee of Fifteen* report. William Torrey Harris, a well-known mental disciplinarian, authored the nineteenth-century document. In framing the curriculum, Bennett referred to Harris's report, stating that "grammar, literature, arithmetic, geography and history are the five branches upon which the disciplinary work of the elementary work is concentrated" (p. 20). In 1987, Bennett published a similar report—this time on the American high school—entitled *James Madison High School*, which also championed some nineteenth-century ideas. Stating that "schooling in the full set of core academic disciplines should be central to the true purposes of American secondary education," Bennett (1987, p. 2) proposed a set of courses that looked very much like the general course requirements found in the 1893 *Committee of Ten* report, which itself featured a classic mental disciplinarian approach to high school education.

After his tenure as secretary concluded, Bennett continued to be a national presence in education as an indefatigable critic of the public school, repeatedly alleging that it has neglected basic education and failed to give due deference to the literary works of Western civilization. He also helped to popularize perennialist causes by editing the *Book of Virtues* (Bennett, 1993), a compendium of "great" essays, poems, and stories, chosen for their enduring relevance as stories of virtue.

Irrespective of what one might think, perennialism's principles (illustrated in Fig. 3.1, p. 62) certainly make a good argument for their place in the school

---

Ideal of the Learner

A disciplined mind immersed in the highest traditions, values, and wisdom of Western humanity

Ideal of the Society

A democracy moved by its Western inheritance and the eternal truths and virtues that accompany it

Ideal of the Subject Matter

A core of permanent studies, resembling the core of the liberal arts, that can discipline the mind and embody the wisdom of humanity

---

FIGURE 3.1   Conceptual Features of Perennialism

curriculum. Its most dramatic educational claims are tied to its advocacy of a well-defined sense of subject matter. It also holds to a well-developed theory of society, asserting an egalitarian position by contending that civilizing outcomes are accorded to all who are properly taught by its methods. The perennialist view has also carved out its own image of the learner, putting emphasis on the mentalistic and the intellectual. Some readers might claim that the perennialist position is at odds with any honest calculation of the learner, especially to the extent that mental discipline still prevails as a rationale for the school curriculum. Wrongheaded or not, it can stake its claim to relevancy among the three factors and thus earn its status in the curriculum.

Essentialism

Essentialists and perennialists are brothers under the same skin. They share a basic commitment to training the intellect through subject-centered knowledge. The dividing line, however, is drawn at what the most worthy form of knowledge is. The perennialists prefer the timeless intellectual virtues of our Western heritage, as reflected in the Great Books and the liberal arts, while the essentialists support a more fundamentally modern outlook on the academic disciplines. Essentialism is a more academic and disciplinary experience than that found in the humanities approach of the perennialist.

Essentialist thinking, as implied, is rooted in the learning doctrine of mental discipline. So, the focus of the school is very much subject-centered, academic, and mentalistic. A core of knowledge and skills, residing in logically organized academic disciplines (the traditional disciplinary lines that one typically sees in a high school or even college curriculum), is the headline performer in the curriculum. The general educational plan is disciplined study in language and grammar, mathematics, the sciences, history, and foreign language. An essentialist justifies the primacy of the subject matter in learning just as a perennialist might: the subject matter not only trains the mind but also provides the basis for a common universe of discourse and understanding in society. Essentialism, in this way, asserts to be on the side of democracy.

The connection to democracy is important. At the turn of the century, William Bagley (1907) took an essentialist position by arguing that school curriculum should be "a storehouse of organized race experience, conserved against the time when knowledge shall be needed in the constructive solution of new and untried problems" (p. 2). This statement touches on some of the main principles of the social theory behind the essentialist argument. Essentialism aims to provide an education in the "essentials" of our civilization, the indispensable features of our core cultural knowledge as it is organized in the academic disciplines. Bagley's reference to the race experience should be translated to mean the experience of the human race (humanity), which he believed was warehoused in the academic disciplines. This body of core knowledge is brought to the experience of learners for the purposes of cultivating the faculties of thinking and reasoning, and of promoting a common or shared culture. This is the essentialists' way of offering a general education to the population, an education in the knowledge one needs to lead an informed life in a democracy.

The heyday of essentialists, however, was less influenced by democratic factors than by nationalistic ones. During the Cold War period in America, the discipline-centered traditions of the essentialists looked to be the perfect foil against the perceived imperialistic designs of the Soviet state. The specializing dimensions of the academic education thought to be needed in the workforce (to combat nefarious Soviet intentions) fit hand and glove with the academic orientation of the essentialist curriculum. The education of engineers, scientists, and mathematicians (the main workers in the technological and space-related defense of the nation), required a highly academic disciplined-centered experience. This was a position strenuously maintained in the federal sponsorship of high school curriculum projects during the Cold War period. Intellectual training in the fundamental disciplines became the first duty of the school because it was viewed as crucial to the defense of the nation. Anything that could not find a justification within this duty was likely to be excluded from, or at least de-emphasized in, the school curriculum.

But the essentialist position would return to the idea of general education during the late 1980s, in an argument that was no longer about nationalistic concerns but about the kind of education students needed for participation in a democracy. The impetus for the refocus was a widely read and controversial book by E. D. Hirsch (1987), entitled *Cultural Literacy,* which was a kind of call-to-arms for the essentialist position. The gist of Hirsch's argument was that a spiraling decline in the shared knowledge of the citizenry was threatening the livelihood of American democracy. The concept of *cultural literacy* favored literacy in the core cultural traditions of western civilization, and Hirsch's book drew attention to the fact that much of the power of such traditions had been lost in the school. Students, Hirsch argued, did not know anything especially penetrating about their own cultural history and cultural literature. They did not benefit from insights in science and mathematics. They were simply not culturally literate. This conclusion was buoyed by NAEP data documenting embarrassingly poor student performances on history and literature-based knowledge tests (Finn and Ravitch, 1987). From the standpoint of the essentialist, two vital factors in the education of youth were being neglected. The students' minds were not being effectively trained or disciplined, but more importantly, the students were failing to gain the cultural background (the shared knowledge and shared vocabulary) they needed to forge a national identity and to participate in a common universe of understanding and insight. The antidote, of course, was to bring back the academic disciplines and place them front and center in a no-nonsense curriculum.

Hirsch has continued his quest to revitalize the tradition of the essentialist in the school and in the society. He has emerged as a critic of what he views as "contentless" teaching in the school and has made his own contribution to fill this perceived void by publishing a series of cultural-literacy dictionaries, workbooks, and tests. He has also founded the Core Knowledge Foundation, a group that offers schools insight into ways to encourage learning in the core knowledge areas.

In many ways, the American school, especially the high school, has continued to operate in the wake left by the essentialists during the Cold War, supporting discipline-centered graduation requirements, curriculum organization, and testing. And increasingly, advocates for the establishment of national standards and uniform content standards could be heard using a classic essentialist rationale: the need to give students a standard or uniform program of disciplined intellectual training in core academic areas.

The advocates of the essentialist view have a well-defined position on the school curriculum, which is featured in their insistence to bring the integrity of the subject matter back to the schools. By focusing on this point, essentialists are working with a key factor in curriculum development. But concerns over subject matter represent a broader and more important purpose, which originate in a social theory of democracy. Figure 3.2 illustrates the essentialist assertion that an intellectual and cultural core of skills and knowledge is needed to bring insight and stability to our democracy. Such an emphasis makes for a clearly essentialist curriculum, offering value judgments on the purposes and the experiences of the school.

SCHOOLING IN THE PROGRESSIVE TRADITION

To the degree that a conservative perspective on schooling aims to preserve and transmit a core culture, a progressive perspective aims to change it. The root of progressive, *progress*, implies change by critical evaluation for the sake of bet-

Ideal of the Learner

A rational mind immersed in the fundamental academic disciplines

Ideal of the Society

A democracy dependent on a common or shared core of academic knowledge

Ideal of the Subject Matter

A strictly academic and discipline-centered curriculum, attendant to the inner designs and intellectual powers of the individual disciplines

FIGURE 3.2   Conceptual Features of Essentialism

terment or improvement. This shift in focus takes the progressive vision of schooling directly into some estimation of the actual skills, attitudes, knowledge, and competencies needed to respond to and improve upon life's problems. Talk of mind training is replaced with discussion of relevance to the life experience. Because progressives do not believe that subjects carry internal mind-training capacities, the subject matter loses its exalted status in the curriculum, although it retains its importance.

Experimentalism

The experimentalist variant to the progressive perspective is embodied in the work of John Dewey. The controlling aim of the philosophy is to conceive of the school as an agency for democracy, as the place where children are taught the values, skills, attitudes, knowledge, and general competencies needed to lead a good life in a good society. Dewey was widely known as a philosopher of American democracy, one who took an unusually strong interest in schooling. Philosophers historically write about ethics, logic, religion, aesthetics, truth, and even reality, but few have addressed the topic of schooling. Dewey, however, was interested in the connection between schooling and his philosophical views, especially in relation to the concept of democracy. His interest in schooling led him to direct his own laboratory school at the University of Chicago, a rare endeavor for a philosopher indeed!

How does experimentalism begin to represent a philosophy that identifies with democracy? And why the term *experimentalism,* which seems to connote some strange association with specialized laboratory techniques? The answer to these questions starts with an understanding of what Dewey (1916) saw as the basis of all education: the "reconstruction or reorganization of experience which adds to the meaning of experience and which increases ability to direct the course of subsequent experiences" (pp. 89–90). To understand experimentalism, one must understand this idea. To simplify, "reconstruction or reorganization of experience" is another way of saying that one must learn from one's experience in a fashion that avoids repeating mistakes and that contributes to one's ability to make more informed decisions in the future. The implication is that learning is a process of experiential growth, always in the state of becoming and, if properly managed, improving, but never achieving completeness or finality. Such view of growth, however, does not emerge idiosyncratically. Some method of thinking or a process of intelligence has to be used to help regulate it.

To Dewey, this method could be scientific. A scientific method applied to learning in school has several advantages from the standpoint of an experimentalist. First, it holds all truth up to ongoing inspection, a principle running counter to the conservative belief in the eternal value and truths of the Western canon. The tentative nature of truth puts extra emphasis on the process of inquiry and the use of evidence and reasoned argumentation in decision making. Second, the scientific method is designed to be responsive to the improvement of existing conditions. It is a problem-resolution method that tests new ideas in the interests of producing improvements. This makes it an elegant method for democracy because it poses problems as opportunities for new understanding and insight. Finally, a scientific method of thinking hones the very important skills of reflective thinking, a required condition for informed participation in a democratic society. Thus Dewey's insistence in seeing education as a "reconstruction of experience" could be seen as a desire to teach students how to effectively handle their personal and pubic lives. Inculcating students in the attitudes, habits of mind, and methods of scientific inquiry could not only give students, as Dewey (1938) phrased it, "freedom from control by routine, prejudice, dogma, unexamined tradition, (and) sheer self-interest," but also "the will to inquire, to examine, to discriminate, to draw conclusions only on the basis of evidence after taking pains to gather all available evidence" (p. 31).

The practical consequence of positioning the "reconstruction of experience" in the center of the school experience is a problem-focused curriculum that highlights the importance of inquiry-based learning. This obviously calls for a very different conception of subject matter than what one might witness in a more conservative philosophy. No single body of content prevails among experimentalists, as it does with perennialists and essentialists. In fact, to the experimentalist, traditional subject matter lines are dissolved and are reconstituted topically, according to the problems and the purposes of the educational situation. Because life problems are not easily placed in disciplinary subjects, a premium is put on the interdisciplinary construction of subject matter. And the aim of knowledge (or the subject matter) is the contribution it makes not to one's mind but to one's behavior. To know that poor eating habits, for instance, increase the odds of certain illnesses can be interpreted as mindful knowledge (one could know it, but still eat poorly) or as knowledge that exists in the actions of life (one knows it and acts accordingly). The experimentalists stake their claim with the latter.

The focus on behavior is especially important, because as a philosophy of democracy, experimentalism ultimately judges the effects of schooling against some standard of betterment or progress in the life experience. This is a principle associated with the roots that experimentalism has in a broader philosophical tradition known as *pragmatism*. The pragmatist's goal is to affect the here and now, to look at life as a matter of present significance not as a matter that has some ultimate judgment at the gates of heaven or some other transcendental place. This is a way of keeping focused on experience and on the kind of intelligent conduct that will produce the prize of progress. As Dewey (1938) observed, "We always live at the time we live and not at some other time, and only by extracting at each present time the full meaning of each present experience are we prepared for doing the same thing in the future" (p. 51). Even the study of the past only has relevance as it grants understanding to the present. "The present," stated Dewey (1916), "generates the problems which lead us to search the past for suggestion, and which supplies meaning to what we find when we search" (p. 89).

Thus, we return to the primacy of experience in the school. Schooling, to paraphrase Dewey, is not a preparation for life but is life itself, and in the case of American schooling, life in a democracy. This means that the whole child must be educated, not just the mind. The curriculum, as a result, is comprehensive in its ambition, interdisciplinary in its overall organization, and activity-based in its sense of experience. And because the school is the engine of democracy, considerable emphasis is placed on the value of the shared experience and the communion of values, outlooks, and problems that help to amalgamate the nation as a people of democracy. Experimentalism's concepts are summarized in Figure 3.3.

Ideal of the Learner

A socially conscious, democratically inspired, and intellectually empowered problem-solver

Ideal of the Society

A democracy whose citizenry is engaged in a common universe of social discourse and social understanding

Ideal of the Subject Matter

A problem-focused, idea-oriented curriculum directly responsive to the personal and socio-civic experience

---

FIGURE 3.3 **Conceptual Features of Experimentalism**

Experimentalism can be used as a moving force in the curriculum. The nature of the learner and the nature of the subject matter have definitive shape in the experimentalist tradition. A curriculum's focus on social consciousness and problem solving sends strong signals as does the reconceptualization of subject matter as an interdisciplinary construct. The latter point often proves to be problematic in the school curriculum because subject matter still tends to be organized within discipline-centered lines and teachers are typically not trained to handle interdisciplinary inquiries. The implications for practice include a more experiential, democratic, and inquiry-based classroom than might otherwise be the case but also one, some critics add, that gives short shrift to key content knowledge.

Romantic Naturalism

The first signs of a progressive movement in the schools of the United States occurred at the turn of the twentieth century and were largely child-centered in orientation. Because schools were so deeply ensconced in a conservative subject-centered view of learning during the late nineteenth century, conditions were conducive for a counter-reaction that would attempt to undo the extreme of subject-centeredness. The child-centered movement in America offered a philosophy of learning unabashedly dedicated to providing children with joyful, open-ended, activity-based education. Where the subject-centered view was mentalistic, the child-centered view was active; where the subject-centered view staked its claim in a uniform, knowledge-based, and planned experience, child-centered proponents countered with an individualistic, emotional, and spontaneous experience. Where teacher-directed instruction, teacher authority, and a structured curriculum ruled in the school, child-centered advocates aimed for reforms that allowed children to direct their own learning and to determine for themselves what, how, and when they will learn.

These expressions of child-centeredness unfolded under the influence of a romantic naturalist philosophy. The story of romantic naturalism begins with the peculiar manner in which the nature of the learner is understood. Taking its philosophical leanings from Rousseau, whose disdain for institutions and adults was legendary, romantic naturalism puts forward the idea that children are best educated in a free and largely unhampered environment, with only minimal adult intervention. Professing a commitment to the innate goodness and innocence of children, romantic naturalists put little stock in the relevance of uniform experiences in the school or even in the act of curriculum or instructional planning. The philosophy believes in the child's self-educating powers, in the notion that learning is so much a matter of individual choice and individual direction that it is best approached by simply allowing it to be dictated by the preferences and pleasures of children. Nature provides the inner processes needed for producing virtuous, self-actualized human beings. Romantic naturalists believe that schools tend to ruin this natural process by imposing an "educational" agenda on children that undermines their self-educating inclinations. Thus, the teacher's role is to help create a classroom environment that facilitates individual expressions and the pursuit of individual interests. One author put it this way: "What we need to do, and all we need to do, is bring as much of the world as we can into the school and the classroom; give the children as much help and guidance as they need and ask for, listen respectfully when they feel like talking; and then get out of the way. We can trust them to do the rest" (McCracken, 1973, p. 16).

The romantic progressives sometimes represent their position by flying under the banner of "learning by doing," arguing that there is educational virtue in essentially any task that the child is committed to perform in the classroom. In short, having an experience moved by student desire or student decision is ipso facto educational. This idea drew opposition from experimentalists, who argued that all experiences (doings) were not necessarily educational and that great many were, in fact, miseducative. So, while we might learn by doing, all doing is not a form of learning (Hook, 1973). The distinction very much exemplifies the difference between experimentalist and romantic naturalist thinking.

Put in historical context, one could appreciate the early appeal of romantic naturalism. Many early progressives were keen to repudiate the assumption that children were innately evil (or ordained as originally sinful). They were attracted to any idea that opened up possibilities for the child to gain due consideration in the curriculum and that provided a foothold for active learning experiences in an institution that had long equated formal education with a stale uniformity of mental exercises and limited physical activity. Anointing the child in educational theorizing could bring activity and life to the school, freeing the student from the abstract and lifeless quality of early timeworn forms of schooling. Moreover, the progressive impulse to personalize schooling held possibilities for the outward extension of schooling, making it not a matter of elitist conceptions of high Western thought but one that resided naturally in all human beings. As Bode (1938) put it, "the emphasis of progressive education on the individual, on the sinfulness of imposition, and on the necessity of securing free play for intelligence, is a reflection of the growing demand, outside of the school, for recognition of the common man" (p. 11).

This, however, did not prevent romantic naturalism from suffering early attacks from both conservative and progressive quarters. Critics targeted several theoretical problems. First, child-centered progressives were accused of advancing a form of education that denied children the central source of all learning, which was the wisdom of adults and the extended wisdom of the race experience. To the conservatives this meant that the power of the subject matter was eviscerated from the experience, an inexcusable failing. To the experimentalists, this meant that the learning would somehow proceed in a free form without any engagement to the agenda of democracy. The combined criticisms argued that the romantic naturalists failed to offer any vision of subject matter and or society. Their abhorrence for the authority of direction and planning in the school

experience left no systematic approach to educating youth in any socially principled point of view. This not only removed the school from its historic role as
an agency for democracy, but also it set the potential conditions for a form of
antidemocratic education. Because the school program supports no social agenda,
in the interest of advantaging only individualistic endeavors, it runs the risk of
failing to teach students the skills they will need to avoid being victims of antidemocratic authoritarian forces. Bode (1938) put it another way. "If democracy
is to have a deep and inclusive human meaning, it must have also a distinctive
educational system" (p. 26).

Romantic naturalism was the by-product of progressives thinkers who were
absorbed in the concept of the individual and threatened by the boundaries implied by any social theory or mission of schooling. Although romantic naturalism sounds like a philosophy with little viable application to the realities of
schooling, it was quite popular during the early stages of its development and
later during the 1960s. The late 60s and the early 70s brought forth school reforms touting the value of open-ended experiences, self-directed learning, and
facilitative teaching. Open education and the open classroom became educationally fashionable because they encouraged a free form of teaching and learning, often in an open physical environment that resulted, in some cases, in
classrooms without walls or doors. Popular best-selling authors preached a gospel
of school renewal that portrayed emergent acts of love and compassion as the
main basis for school improvement. Free schools, alternative schools, and concepts such as deschooling society (which implied that one could receive an education simply from freely chosen experiences in the wider society) gained
popular currency. There was much criticism of public schooling that featured
images of repressive schools.

From the standpoint of the curriculum, romantic naturalism breaks some of
the rules. As indicated earlier, the theoretical foundation for curriculum development demands some view on the learner, society, and subject matter. If any of
these factors are ignored or rejected, the curriculum-development process is likely
flawed. Romantic naturalists have a clear vision of the learner. It is, in fact, the *sine
quo non* of the philosophy. The curriculum is about, for, and even by the child.
From it, all else flows. Such concepts, illustrated in Figure 3.4, leave the curriculum with no clear perspective on society, other than one that values egoistic pursuits, and no clear vision of subject matter, other than that which emerges from the
quixotic experience of the child.

Social Efficiency

Yet another group of thinkers was also intent on bringing life activity to the curriculum. However, they differed substantively from other progressive groups by
supporting a factory model of schooling that standardized experiences in the
curriculum while it also sorted and slotted the student population according to

> *Ideal of the Learner*
> A self-educating force of nature whose education is best served with only minimal adult intervention
>
> *Ideal of the Society*
> Multitudinous egoistic and individualistic pursuits
>
> *Ideal of the Subject Matter*
> A content-neutral curriculum emphasizing free activity

FIGURE 3.4 Conceptual Features of Romantic-Naturalism

their station in life. Advocates of such a view sought to use the curriculum to strike the chord of order, control, and social harmony in the school. Out of this group of thinkers arose a concept of curriculum that was management oriented, efficiency driven, and highly prescriptive in its detail. In the literature, it is commonly referred to as the tradition of social efficiency, but more contemporary formulations of it can also be seen in competency-based or mastery-learning instruction.

The commitment to social efficiency in the curriculum was historically preceded by a commitment to social efficiency in the society. During the 1900s, the business community led the way with a new efficiency strategy known as scientific management. Developed by an engineer named Frederick Taylor (1911), scientific management promised to provide a method for businesses, particularly factories, that would increase production while also lowering costs.

The key to the idea had to do with identifying and then standardizing the action of the most productive workers. The premise was that there was one best way to do any job, and that such a way could be discerned through careful study. To Taylor, if the most productive worker had an output of x, then there was no reason why all workers could not have the same output. By using various incentives, Taylor identified the very best workers, meaning those who produced the most in the least amount of time. Taylor then analyzed their actions, and tried to note, in behavioral terms, what made them so productive. After identifying what factors were central to productivity, Taylor standardized a practice by which other workers could be taught them.

The lesson that Taylor provided to businesses soon reached the schools. Applied to the curriculum, scientific management was deceptively simple: find the best practices, standardize them, and make them part of the school routine. The "best" practices under Taylor's conditions, however, were always those that managed to secure the highest productivity with the least amount of effort. But there were going to be complications if the same rationale was to prevail in the schools. It was one thing to note the productivity of an assembly line worker, but it was quite another to make similar judgments with something as complex and dynamic as the education of children. To make it work, substantive changes had to be made in the way that the curriculum was to be conceived. Generally speaking, a factory model had to be embraced for the curriculum. The idea of productivity in the school meant that actual learning outcomes needed to be identified and that measurements needed to be taken to determine whether or not they had been reached. The Taylorian regard for efficiency had in fact set the wheels in motion for a whole new science of school measurement, a numerical way of demonstrating achievement and mastery.

The implications of Taylor's work were very clear in the early curriculum design work being promoted by like-minded thinkers in the burgeoning field of curriculum studies, the most prominent being a University of Chicago professor named John Franklin Bobbitt. For the curriculum to be manageable and operative, Bobbitt believed that learning had to take on a character of specificity that it had never seen before. Many social progressives had advocated for a school experience based on generalizability, talking of the need for broadly framed objectives that were more statements of principle than specific actions to be undertaken. Bobbitt, however, thought such thinking was unrealistic and irresponsible and he wanted to change it:

> Objectives that are only vague, high-sounding hopes and aspirations are to be avoided. Examples are: "character building," "the harmonious development of the individual," "social efficiency," "general discipline," "self-realization," "culture," and the like. All of these are valid enough; but too cloud-like for guiding practical procedure. They belong to the visionary adolescence of our profession—not to its sober and somewhat disillusioned maturity. (p. 32)

Out of this demand for a new level of specificity arose a method of curriculum development known as activity analysis. An admirer of Taylor's work, Bobbitt believed that the school curriculum was best served by preparing the learner for specific activities in adult life. He wanted the school to survey all of the relevant activities in the lives of adults (as they related to occupations, family, society, and so on) and then, similar to Taylor's standardized production model, teach directly to each activity. Bobbitt (1918) expressed his theory in clear terms:

> The central theory is simple. Human life, however varied, consists in the performance of specific objectives. However numerous and diverse they may be for any social class, they can be discovered. This requires only that one go out into the world of affairs and discover the particulars of which these affairs consist. These will show the abilities, attitudes, habits, appreciations and forms of knowledge that men need. These will be the objectives of the curriculum. They will be numerous, definite and particularized. The curriculum will then be that series of ex-

periences which children and youth must have by way of attaining those objectives. (p. 42)

The intent was to be as specific as possible in the framing of activities because the job of the curriculum was to prepare the learner for specific tasks through a process of habit formation. "The most significant feature of the work of practical curriculum making today," stated Bobbitt (1921), "is the tendency first to particularize with definiteness and in detail the objectives" (p. 607). As a result, Bobbitt's curriculum was filled with thousands of specific skills and behaviors that were often fixed at rather low, mechanistic levels. Here is a list of objectives taken from a reading program designed for the Los Angeles schools (Bobbitt, 1921, p. 609):

> **YOU WILL BE READY TO UNDERTAKE A-1 READING WHEN YOU CAN DO THE FOLLOWING THINGS:**
> 1. When you are spending at least sixty minutes a day on reading and phonetics.
> 2. When you know at sight one hundred words from the list of one hundred and twenty-five on flash cards chosen from the main list.
> 3. When you can use any of the one hundred words in sentences with the following word phrases: This is, I see, I have, We have, I can, We can, Can you, Have you, I like, We like; a, the, an.
> 4. When you can read the first, second, fourth, and fifth stories in the *Free and Treadwell Primer*.
> 5. When you are able to read no less than ten pages of your Supplementary Unit primer.
> 6. When you can speak the English language well enough to understand the work of the next grade intelligently.
> 7. When you read a sentence as a whole and not word by word. If a sentence is long, you will phrase it properly.
> 8. When you can read print from the flash cards or from your books, also standard script as written on the blackboard by your teacher.
> 9. When you can read silently and interpret sentence units with our required vocabulary as "Was the cat black?" or "Can a dog fly?"
> 10. When you have read the *Jack Straw Stories* (optional).

This style of atomizing the curriculum and the instruction of the school applied to virtually every facet of the school experience, including reading, arithmetic, spelling, language, and penmanship. As Bobbitt (1924a) claimed, activity analysis is intent on discovering the specific forms of behaviors for humans to follow. "It would discover the five or ten thousand words they spell, the several mathematical operations they perform, the several hundred specific practical home activities in which they engage, the main things they do in the care of their health, the specific things involved in managing a checking account at the bank, and the like" (p. 50). The readers should note that Bobbitt worked out of a functionalist perspective, trying to prepare the student population for the performance of life's functions or activities. He did not concern himself much with the nature of the learner or with the ideals of society. He simply observed the environment and chose objectives that emerged from the common judgments of teachers and other curriculum participants. His advice to curriculum-makers was, as Jackson (1975) phrased it, "Keep your eye on behavior and particularize it" (p. 125).

Bobbitt believed that the curriculum could be reduced to a conveyor-like process that yielded a completed product. Bobbitt (1913) was not subtle about such matters. "Education," he declared, "is a shaping process as much as the manufacturing of steel rails" (p. 11). The factory metaphor captured the essence of education that Bobbitt promoted. Students were the raw products, the school was the assembly line, and the society the consumer. The world of philosophy and concerns for social reform and socio-personal growth were simply not important considerations. The charge of the school was to fit individual into a life that ensured order and stability.

To its advocates, the method of activity analysis carried certain positive results. By virtue of the method, for instance, the school curriculum was undoubtedly more closely connected to life. It was based after all on activity. This was not an insignificant claim because Bobbitt believed that activity analysis worked out the progressive regard for "learning as doing." He felt activity analysis presented a good working alternative to the tradition of mental discipline, which placed misdirected attention, to use Bobbitt's phrase, on "the memory reservoir" of students, on the idea of "subject storage" and the image of a student "as knower." Armed with activity analysis, Bobbitt could claim that he was interested in conduct, action, behavior, and the construction of the learner "as doer." Activity analysis also presumed to be better suited for teachers because it offered prefashioned and ready-made activities that did not require the teachers to think independently. "The burden of finding the best methods," stated Bobbitt, "is too large and too complicated to be laid on the shoulders of the teachers" (1913, pp. 51–52). Activity analysis also was applicable to the areas of waste elimination and institutional order by making it clear that some scale of measurement was needed for assessment purposes. Lastly, social efficiency, by aiming to teach children according to their needs and abilities, was a victory for differential experiences in the school, ones that led to different social and vocational destinies. This willingness to differentiate in the school curriculum presumably helped to secure a world where everyone could find his or her place, where the individual was adjusted to a social order that stabilized society.

Job analysis had its share of critics. No one's critical remarks, however, were more penetrating than Boyd Bode's (1927). Bode attacked Bobbitt for the manner in which Bobbitt discerned his objectives, noting how Bobbitt drew largely from adult activities. He contended that Bobbitt had set into motion a condition for education that simply served the status quo. To Bode it was clear that job analysis was little more than training for adjustment to existing social conditions. In a democracy, Bode continued, society is better served if education proceeds from the level of general training, targeting abilities that cut across particular conditions and particular problems. Individuals (and by implication, the collective society) could only grow and develop if they had the skills needed to deal with emergent problems and issues, as opposed to being adjusted to and knowledgeable of particular existing conditions. Specific activities change over time—farming, for instance, is different now from what it was decades ago. Thus, to look at specificity as the answer to the curriculum was to promote outdated training that would not likely have much currency beyond the present. Bobbitt was no progressive in Bode's estimation.

The general conceptual components (Fig. 3.5) of social efficiency can still be found today in its hybridization with behaviorist psychology. The stimulus-response connection inherent to behaviorism was friendly to the demand for specificity that the social efficiency perspective valued. The effect was the use of instructional forms that relied on finely specified objectives, such as competency-based instruction, mastery learning, and programmed instruction. Each of these curricula was designed around a sequential and hierarchical pattern of highly specific learning objectives. The purpose was to offer a tightly designed sequence of objectives integrated into instructional exercises (often in a workbook), which if followed properly, were guaranteed to result in an individual's mastery of the skills and knowledge. The presumption was that anything worth knowing was measurable and reducible to a working sequence of objectives.

Under the demands of competency-based strategies, the curriculum developer itemizes exactly what needs to be taught and eventually evaluates it for mastery. A competency-based reading program, for instance, usually represents a specific set of competencies, organized by grade level. It directs the teacher to

---

Ideal of the Learner
Individual needing to be adjusted to the tasks of adult life

Ideal of the Society
A functionalist theory advancing a harmonious and well-ordered society

Ideal of the Subject Matter
Particularized life activities required to adjust individual to life roles

---

FIGURE 3.5 **Conceptual Features of Social Efficiency**

teach each competency directly, and regulates each student's movement through the curriculum with mastery tests of each competency. The result is a highly skill-based school experience commonly marked by rather low-level activities. What cannot be effectively measured (and demonstrated as mastered) is not taught. Skills in oral communication, writing, argumentation, problem solving, cross-disciplinary insight, and research skills (to name just a few) are simply not part of the instructional picture.

The social efficiency perspective obviously does not do much to advance the professional development of educators. Most of the important judgments in the curriculum are already made for the teachers, who are left with following directions and handing out predeveloped worksheets. The idea of "teacher-proof" materials was born and came into favor in this philosophical climate. Teacher-proof materials typically comprised programmed learning workbooks, some varieties of computer-assisted instruction, and highly prescriptive learning packages that scripted what teachers should say and do. Their orientation was to find a way to protect the curriculum from the teacher.

SCHOOLING IN THE RADICAL TRADITION

Almost all of the progressive approaches in education could be characterized as radical in some way. But the radical philosophies discussed in this section are radical in a political sense, taking their pledges mostly from an overtly ideological or political way of thinking that is, more often than not, explicitly designed to revolutionize the existing system of schooling. The social reconstructionist perspective, born during hurly-burly days of the Great Depression, was largely an attempt to inject American schooling with a socialist outlook. Current radical thinking, often loosely categorized as postmodern in orientation, operates on a similar basis, although within a wider range of attendant political viewpoints.

Social Reconstructionism

To understand social reconstructionism one must understand the fundamental social class analysis that gave it its start. During the 1920s and into the 1930s, a number of scholars vented their frustration with what they perceived as rampant class-based bias in the leadership and operation of the public schools. George Counts, who would emerge as the main historical voice of social reconstructionism, had preached this message throughout the decade of the depression. His early work helped to expose some of the problems, showing, for instance, that disproportionately high numbers of student dropouts were from low-income families. He also examined school board memberships and found that the membership base mostly comprised men from the middle and upper classes. These general conditions, according to Counts (1922), encouraged the school to see its interests not in the widest public good but in the education of the wealthy and the accompanying promotion of the values of competitive and individualistic capitalism. Counts stood firm with his accusation. The school, he alleged, was systemically, even ideologically, designed to perpetuate the socio-economic status quo. It was the handmaiden of the ruling economic class, sustaining, instead of combating, the evils of extreme poverty and social inequities.

Progressive thinkers had not given class issues much standing in their philosophies. The child-centered romantics had no social theory whatsoever and the experimentalists, although concerned about socio-economic disparities, were not interested in posing an educational experience designed to remedy specific social problems. The experimentalists did, however, expect the schools to produce an enlightened citizenry that could take charge of its social problems. But they did not view the school as an instrument for dislodging or reforming a specific social ill.

So, it did not take long for the social class analysis offered by Counts and others to yield an educational philosophy that saw itself as an antidote to classism in the schools. Because the educational institution was itself accused of being deeply situated in the back pockets of business interests and socially conservative groups, some scholars had no reservation about flipping the school's ideological switch and teaching in a direction that favored radical social transformation. One had to fight ideological fire, they claimed, with ideological fire.

Thus, social reconstructionism was a philosophy openly and unapologetically dedicated to educating youth in socialist doctrine and the new social order it demanded. The duty of the teacher was to teach in a way that made a contribution to the social reconstruction of the society, which, in the view of its proponents, needed to lean heavily in the direction of a collectivist socialist society. Teachers had to understand that they were now caught in a revolutionary struggle to wrest the control of the school away from the ruling upper classes. This would call for abrupt and confrontational educational tactics. George Counts (1932) stated the matter rather bluntly. Education must

> emancipate itself from the influence of the (ruling upper classes), face squarely and courageously every social issue, come to grips with life in all of its stark reality, establish an organic relation with the community, develop a realistic and comprehensive theory of welfare ... and become less frightened than it is today at the bogeys of imposition and indoctrination. (pp. 9–10)

The educational plan was simple. Schooling must not fear indoctrination; it must use it to drive a stake through the heart of the capitalistic nature of schooling. In this way, education could become an enterprise dedicated to influencing students to accept the collectivist ideals of socialism, a position completely at odds with the experimentalist thinking of John Dewey. The social reconstructionists believed that this form of education was most suitable for democracy because their ideal of society depended on an indoctrinated citizenry prepared to defend the worthiness of a utopian social arrangement. Thus, the teacher became a kind of ideological missionary who emphasized the importance of economic equity, worker's rights, class analysis, and other collectivist ideals.

Social reconstructionism never gained much currency in the schools, but its criticism of the schools has continued to be a source of ongoing commentary. Today, the line of thinking begun by Counts continues with scholars claiming to embrace a critical theory of education. Critical theory aims to disclose all forms of injustice and inequity in schooling by revealing the interests served by the knowledge and the human action brought to bear in the school setting. Needless to say, critical theorists find that corporate ideology (capitalism) is behind the acts of injustice and inequity in schooling, although they also offer accusations of cultural hegemony or cultural imperialism, male authority, and white racism against the school. The thesis is that the main function of schools is the continued dominance of the socio-economic order (and its associated dominant groups). The school is said to offer knowledge and skills that empower the most privileged in a way that keeps social class divisions intact. Thus, the mode of analysis in this philosophy is to look closely for signs of how—not if—schools carry out the repressive mandate, because they do not openly tout it.

Critical theory is largely a theory or philosophy of protest, although some educators claim that they are involved in something known as critical pedagogy (Wink, 2000). McLaren (1989) states that critical pedagogy is about "how and why knowledge gets constructed the way it does, and how and why some constructions of reality are legitimated and celebrated by the dominant culture while others are clearly not." One could appreciate the legacy of the social reconstructionists in McLaren's statement. Concerns over dominant groups inevitably lead to a highly politicized form of teaching (Fig. 3.6) that encourages students to be more conscious of class, race, ethnic and even gender differences, and more able to see their own victimization at the hands of society, or as is the case with

---

Ideal of the Learner
Guardian of the highest principles of a collectivist doctrine

Ideal of the Society
A utopian social arrangement stressing economic and social equality

Ideal of the Subject Matter
Politicized knowledge designed to promote the utopian causes of the society

---

FIGURE 3.6   **Conceptual Features of Social Reconstructionism**

children from dominant groups, their own role as victimizers. Ideology still prevails as the main educating force in the school.

The social reconstructionist point of view has some curricular merit. It abides by a strongly worded and highly politicized view of society, which allows it to shape the natures of the learner and the subject matter accordingly. But one should keep in mind that, although social reconstructionism possesses a social theory, it is not exactly a democratic one. Its vision of society has no qualms about imposing a hard political stamp on the school curriculum, which can be interpreted as a misuse of the factor of society. The politicized nature of truth leads to a politicizing of the school experience by making hard distinctions between the politically virtuous and their enemies.

Postmodernism

Schools help create the kind of society we desire. Conservatives embrace the grand narrative of the Western canon to bring insight to this process, while experimentalists embrace a foundation of values, attitudes, and general competencies believed to be required for informed participation in a democracy. These ideals are accompanied, with varying degrees of involvement, by so-called modernist assumptions. Having faith in scientific progress, rationalist thought, the power of evidence, the reliability of social labels, and in the power of a common culture could all be viewed, at least in part, as modernist in orientation. The postmodern perspective explodes these assumptions and actively seeks to *decenter* our way of examining the world. The effort to decenter is moved by a decidedly anti-Western sentiment, by a desire to expose and undermine "the privileging of Western patriarchal culture with its representations of domination rooted in a Eurocentric conception of the world" (Aronowitz and Giroux, 1991, p. 64). In its place, the postmodernist seeks to stress the value of individual initiative, the recognition of human intention, the unmasking of political ideology in knowledge, the taming of social-control mechanisms in the school, and the general idea that society is marked by conflicting interests of class, gender, and culture.

The postmodern commitment is deeply involved in providing what one might call oppositional thought in the school experience, a pledge of negativity that helps to deny the validity of any grand claims on what is worth knowing and that also helps to preserve the dynamism of the lived experience in school, keeping the heterogeneity of the school experience intact. Thus, conventions are subjected to deep criticism. By taking up the role of criticism (or negativity), the postmodernist hopes to bring forth more self-consciousness and a better view of the plurality of thought in our experience. The school, which is perceived to be involved in transmitting established norms, becomes a place where knowledge is challenged, where its link to political ideology and sources of power and domination is shown. Such efforts are viewed as empowering because they lead to eye-opening moments that allow students to see themselves in a more authentic context. Oppositional thought also demands that the schools take an active role in revealing the interests served by the knowledge and the human action taken up by the school.

Postmodernists also believe that individuals need to escape from the forces of rationality in school. As a result, they are wary of the methods of science, believing that science is really just an ideological cloak draped over acts of oppression. One can see this, they claim, especially well in the manner in which science is used to create social categories or labels in school. For example, special education labels, which typically include Behaviorally Disordered, Emotionally Disturbed, or Learning Disabled, might be viewed by most as instructional categories designed to offer special-needs children remedial education or other educational services. To the postmodernist, however, such categories must be deconstructed because of the role they might play in the oppression of a disproportionately large number of minority and low-income children. As an instructional endeavor, special education is legitimated by a science of test sources, research findings, and other so-called objective data. But from the postmodernist perspective, special education is seen in terms of its less obvious effects, which might include acknowledging how children in such settings suffer psychological handicaps that ultimately lead to the further deterioration of their academic competencies and life skills.

Postmodernists are also very concerned about the effects of a hidden or latent curriculum. When a teacher, for instance, tells children in a low-income school that they are all "such good workers," a postmodern analysis might identify such a phrase as a latent reminder to the children that they are ordained to be workers in a class-based society. Or, when the Great Books are given to students to read, the latent message is that only the writing and thinking of white European males have a claim on greatness. When school work results in keeping children busy with drudgery and away from their heart-felt desires, the school could be interpreted as practicing a kind of breaking down of spirit in a person for the purposes of preparing them for a low-level work role in life.

Postmodernism also focuses on difference, a position decidedly at odds with conservatism and virtually all other philosophical views of the school, except romantic naturalism. Because there are different ways of knowing, experiencing, and even labeling the world, the focus of learning has to be on difference, or what is sometimes referred to as *otherness*. To postmodernists, the conservative embrace of the Great Books is a failing inspired by ethnocentrism and class bias (Aronowitz and Giroux, 1991). If the task of postmodernism is to assist with student identity, then this identity must be subjected to the full variance of experience, highlighting narratives taken from varied views of race, class, and gender. Marginalized or subordinate groups (usually women and minority groups) are especially important to the postmodern position because they represent struggles that could be used against the dominant ideology. Such groups become a potential source of subversion, opposition, and ultimately transformation. The sympathy toward so-called subordinate groups, coupled with an uncontested denial (if not hatred) of dominant thinking, has sometimes resulted in the accusation of politically correct thinking among postmodernists.

Because schools (and society in general) are believed to be heavily layered with corporate ideology, often peddled to the masses through the popular media, teachers are expected to keep an eye out for such incursions in the purposes and materials of the curriculum. Students must not be subjected to the transmission of knowledge, but should be taught to question knowledge, see the misrepresentation in it, and search for the imperialism, patriarchy, racism, and vulgar capitalism that has shaped it and that continues to sustain it.

The concepts of postmodernism (Fig. 3.7) offer an escape for the student from the social repressions inherent in knowledge and in the experience of living. Part of this freedom resides in the active questioning of everything that presumes to pass as truth or reason. But the process also asks learners to look for a more existential school experience through meditative ponder, intuition, imagination, and the active interpretation of everyday events.

The educational route is sometimes so personal that much of the school experience resembles the features of romantic naturalism. For instance, in attempting to describe how a postmodern high school might begin to conduct its own version of education, Aronowitz and Giroux (1991) grant authority to only teachers and students; none is granted to even legislative or governmental agents. "Students and teachers," they assert, should "negotiate which courses, if any, are to be required" (p. 21). Teachers discuss and "try to persuade" students into engaging in a certain regiment of courses. "The normal classroom now resembles an

---

Ideal of the Learner

An emancipated individual seeking an authentic meaning and identity in an ideologically layered world

Ideal of the Society

Emancipated individuals and subordinate groups finding identity and understanding in a repressive society

Ideal of the Subject Matter

Deconstructed knowledge, understood in relation to its link with dominant ideology

---

FIGURE 3.7 **Conceptual Features of Postmodernism**

open classroom where small groups of students are simultaneously studying different aspects of the course of subject matter, and others are engaged in individual tutorials with the teacher or other knowledgeable persons" (p. 21). The nature of such tutorials is decidedly political, which is where similarities with the romantic naturalism ends.

Because postmodernism features a cultural criticism of the school, it is difficult to completely understand its standing in the curriculum. Postmodernism operates in the school much in the way that we might expect romantic naturalism to operate, with one important difference. The postmodern position has an ideological prod that pushes the student in the direction of confronting the dominant ideology and ultimately understanding the oppression inherent in dominant thinking. But the main problem with the postmodern position from the standpoint of the curriculum is that it is decidedly non-normative in orientation, while the public school curriculum is, at its very core, a normative project.

THE PRACTICAL AND THE ECLECTIC

Attentive readers might have by now concluded that when it comes to curriculum design, only a limited range of philosophical dispositions seem viable. (Here I am referring to the development of the public school curriculum, and not to any private school initiative or nonschool enterprise.) The philosophical views discussed in the conservative tradition and the Deweyan variant of progressivism stand the best chance of giving their whole spirit to the public school curriculum. This is not because they are intrinsically superior, but because they have something to offer to the normative agenda of the school and take seriously the three factors discussed. But it does not mean that all other philosophical views are lost and forgotten.

In fact we can get a bit carried away with categorizing philosophical possibilities in the curriculum. Some expression of a value system will always prevail but will rarely be identifiable as any one philosophical view. Moreover, the exercise of different philosophical tendencies will likely occur at the different levels of the curriculum (macrocurricular and microcurricular) and affect different elements within these levels. A teacher's philosophy, for instance, will speak to instructional and pedagogical judgments, while the philosophy affecting the macrocurriculum will speak most directly to the framing of key purposes in the school. As a result, the possibilities for an eclectic expression of philosophical dispositions in the curriculum are numerous. Curriculum developers should understand that the most effective strategies in the curriculum are not drawn from philosophical pledges but from an effort to confront purposes in a way that will ensure their attainment.

As a result, we might find that in the development of the general education coursework for a high school, a more experimentalist position might be taken, one that highlights the importance of citizenship education concerns, heterogeneously mixed classrooms, and interdisciplinary course content, all framed around common socio-personal focal points. But in the specialized phase of the curriculum, especially in the design of the coursework dedicated to enrichment and advanced-placement work, we might find that an essentialist position is best at highlighting the importance of discipline-centered learning experiences. Or we might design some blending of each philosophical perspective for both general education and specialized education purposes. Design depends on what is revealed to work best, as determined by ongoing evaluations. In the elementary school, we might find a third-grade teacher who is child-centered (let's say a teacher who even borders on romantic-naturalism) and predisposed to using a constructivist instructional approach. And although such a teacher will be required to fulfill the normative purposes of the school, we might find that much of her classroom embraces exploratory learning possibilities and self-initiated learning experiences at a level of intensity that might not exist in another classroom. At the level of remediation, competency-based instruction that specifically targets particular skills needing correction and extra support might prove to be most useful. This is all another way of saying that if the school curriculum and its teachers are making judgments in the interests of what works best, some eclectic form of philosophical expression should be expected.

The devining rod for philosophy in the curriculum is really at the level of forging the mission and the purposes of the school curriculum. The formulation of a school (or classroom) philosophy is not made to assure the public that the school is moved by high-minded purposes, but is a serious commitment to a theory of conduct. The statement of philosophy for a school, typically required for accreditation procedures, often makes reference to objectives in the public mandate, such as fostering democratic values, assuring equal opportunities to learn, nurturing an attitude for life-long learning, and so forth. Such statements of philosophy are only meaningful if they are also commitments to practice. A philosophy, in this way, is a kind of resolution on the part of the school and its staff to not only reflect its expressed ideals in its classroom but to also be judged against them.

If the expression of school-wide purposes takes on, say, a perennialist tint, such as immersion in the Great Books, the curriculum obviously has slightly less room for the kind of eclecticism discussed above, although it would certainly still exist at the microcurricular level. If school-wide purposes make no mention of democratic skills and values, or emphasize the need for free activity in the curriculum (likely to be only found in a private school), then again we could appreciate the space that might open up for some philosophies. But we should also remember that the framing of the curriculum is a collaborative and deliberative process, involving various key people, and hence very much influenced by the many perspectives represented. So, with this in mind, we move next into discussing the issues involved in helping to define the school's purposes. We take our first big step away from theory and toward practice.

SUMMARY

Philosophy has an undeniably profound place in the classroom and school. It is the source of considerable variation in teaching style one sees across classrooms and schools. This is not to say, however, that all philosophies necessarily have equal standing in the school. Fascist or authoritarian views, for instance, are obviously not reconcilable with the schools of a democracy. And where a philosophy wants to make a stand in a classroom, it must have some perspective on the three fundamental factors (the learner, the society, and subject matter) in the educative process. In this way, a philosophy acts as a kind of screen through which ideas are filtered.

Three philosophical traditions characterize discussion of the purpose and practice of the schooling. Conservative views are deeply subject-centered, still associated with the psychology of mental discipline and very much wedded to the idea of transmitting culture through the knowledge embodied in the traditional academic subjects and the Great Books. Progressive experimentalist views are less mentalistic than the conservative views and are more attached to teaching the very skills, competencies, and attitudes needed to conduct an intelligent life in a democratic society. Essential to this process is the involvement of the scientific method applied to social thinking. The romantic variant of the progressive education movement is child-centered and allegiant to the naturalist views of Rousseau. And the social efficiency tradition, although furnishing progressive credentials in support of activity and engagement to life conditions in the curriculum, steps into antiprogressive territory as well by shedding a democratic social theory and putting its stock in life adjustment and using highly specific learning objectives as the main building blocks of the curriculum. Finally, the radical tradition offers a social reconstructionist view that embraces a politicized curriculum as the best way to rid the nation of capitalist oppression, and it takes a postmodern position that seeks inner understandings through the dislocation and deconstruction of dominant views.

DISCUSSION QUESTIONS AND SUGGESTED ACTIVITIES

1. Observe teachers and make some determinations about the philosophical prejudices that might underpin their teaching. Interview them about why they do what they do.

2. Of all the seven orientations discussed in this chapter, with which might your own views align most closely? Is there a way to shape a kind of eclectic approach to philosophy, taking the best of each tradition?

3. Examine one phase of the school curriculum (e.g., multicultural education, the reading program, the math program) and analyze the philosophical tradition behind it.

4. Get a copy of a school's mission statement and analyze it in terms of the seven orientations described in the chapter.

5. What do perennialists mean when they declare the need for youth to be engaged in the permanent studies?

6. Conservatives share a commitment to the development of a common culture with experimentalists. Explain the connection and the vital difference between the two.

7. Ralph Tyler referred to philosophy as a screen through which ideas are filtered. Try another metaphor to explain the role of philosophy in teaching. In what way is philosophy like an engine, a foundation, a compass, or a recipe? How adequate are these metaphors?

8. Explain the term *experimentalism* and its association with the work of John Dewey.

9. What is the reconstruction of experience and how is it vital to the work of John Dewey?

10. Rousseau used this aphorism to advise a student: "God makes all things good; man meddles with them and they become evil." Explain how this statement plays into a romantic naturalist view of the world.

11. In 1933, George Counts helped to author a report titled *A Call to the Teachers of the Nation*. The report maintained that "teachers will have to emancipate themselves from the dominance of the business interests of the nation, cease cultivating the manners and association of bankers and promotion agents, repudiate utterly the ideal of material success as the goal of education, abandon the smug middle-class tradition on which they have been nourished in the past, acquire a realistic understanding of the forces that actually rule the world, and formulate a fundamental program of thought and action that will deal honestly and intelligently with the problems of industrial civilization" (p. 20). Do you believe that such matters should be part of a teacher's responsibility? Why or why not?

12. Observe a classroom with an eye toward looking for evidence that supports or contradicts the social reconstructionist's view that public education serves capitalist interests.

13. In what ways does postmodernism lead to child-centeredness?

14. What are the basic similarities between postmodernism and social reconstructionism?

15. Examine the literature used to teach English in middle or secondary school (language arts in elementary school) as it is used in a classroom with which you are familiar. Conduct a postmodern analysis, looking for the dominant ideology used to color the worldviews of children, especially children from minority or subordinate groups.

NOTES

Adler, M. (1988). *Reforming education: The opening of the American mind.* New York: Macmillan Publishing Co.

Adler, M. (1984). *The paideia program: An educational syllabus.* New York: Macmillan Publishing Co.

Aronowitz, S. & Giroux, H. (1991). *Postmodern education: Politics, culture and social criticism.* Minneapolis: University of Minnesota.

Bagley, W. (1907). *Classroom management.* New York: Macmillan Publishing Co.

Bennett, W.J. (1993). *Book of virtues: A treasury of great moral stories.* New York: Simon & Schuster.

Bennett, W.J. (1986). *First lessons: A report on elementary education in America.* Washington, DC: United States Department of Education.

Bode, B.H. (1938). *Progressive education at the crossroads.* New York: Newson and Co.

Counts, G.S. (1922). *The selective character of American secondary education.* Chicago: University of Chicago Press.

Counts, G.S. (1932). *Dare the schools build a new social order?* New York: The John Day Co.

Dewey, J. (1916). *Democracy and education.* New York: Free Press.

Dewey, J. (1938). *Experience and education.* New York: Macmillan.

Finn, C. & Ravitch, D. (1987). *What do our 17-year-olds know?* New York: Harper & Row.

Hirsch, E.D. (1987). *Cultural literacy: What every American needs to know.* Boston: Houghton Mifflin.

Hook, S. (1973). John Dewey and his betrayers. In C. Troost (Ed.), *Radical school reform: Critique and alternatives.* Boston: Little, Brown and Company.

Hutchins, R.M. (1972). The great anti-school campaign. In R. Hutchins & M. Adler (Eds.), *The great ideas today.* Chicago: Encyclopaedia Britannica.

Hutchins, R.M. (1936). *The higher learning in America.* New Haven: Yale University Press.

Jackson, P.W. (1975). Notes on the aging of Franklin Bobbitt. *Elementary School Journal, 75,* 118–133.

McLaren P. (1989). *Life in schools: An introduction to critical pedagogy in the foundations of education.* New York: Longman.

McCraken, S. (1973). Quackery in the classroom. In C. Troost (Ed.), *Radical school reform: Critique and alternatives.* Boston: Little, Brown and Company.

Tyler, R.W. (1949). *Basic principles of curriculum and instruction.* Chicago: University of Chicago Press.

Van Doren, M. (1943). *Liberal education.* New York: Henry Holt and Co.

Wink, J. (2000). *Critical pedagogy: Notes from the real world.* New York: Longman.

CHAPTER FOUR

DEFINING PURPOSES

An aim denotes the result of any natural process brought to consciousness and made a factor in determining present observation and choice of ways of acting. It signifies that an activity has become intelligent
—John Dewey

To understand the curriculum, one must examine its intentions. The school curriculum exists by some formulation of intention or by some vision of an ideal to be accomplished. If we say the curriculum is deliberately conceived, we mean that it is conceived in the expectation of fulfilling a particular mandate or purpose. The curriculum, in this sense, is always purposeful, always full of a sense of what is desirable in the experience of school children.

Because so many causes and so many different aims and objectives are addressed by the curriculum, the task of organizing purposes becomes among the more significant responsibilities of the curriculum worker. Having high prospects in the curriculum is a relatively simple matter, but articulating these prospects in a way that captures the whole of the school experience and ensures the delivery of experiences attendant to these prospects is a complicated and demanding process. To think about what one wants to accomplish is a slightly more comfortable exercise than thinking about how exactly to accomplish it. It is the difference between having an idea and seeing an idea to its realization. The curriculum worker, of course, does not have the luxury of simply having ideas. The very nature of curriculum work is implementational and is relevant only as it is engaged with the realities of the educational situation. Our job as curriculum developers is to define purposes and mark out the school experience in a way that translates to the teacher and to the overall development of intelligent instructional and evaluative strategies.

The need to define and organize purposes in the curriculum inevitably brings us to the undertaking of developing aims, goals, and objectives. If you have ever had any experience teaching children, you have probably come face to face with this kind of work, and the experience, I bet, was not always positive. I recall, from my own time in the classroom, being required to design lesson objectives that followed a particular formula, which included being told that objectives must start with the statement "the student will." The rationale was to keep the focus on student performance by designing objectives that detailed what the students should be able to demonstrate when they achieved the objective. I also recall being advised that only highly detailed objectives, which were measurable or which exhibited a behavioral characteristic, were valid. And then, when putting all the proper formulaic pieces together, I found myself in good company with other teachers, as we were all confused over how to distinguish between objectives that referred to learning outcomes (effects) and those that referred to learning processes (means). And in the end, we all understood that the full panoply of content, skills, and values taught in our school could not be properly represented in the writing of objectives. It all became quite confusing, and at times, frustrating.

This chapter explores the procedures involved in defining the purposes of the school. We start with the framing of an overarching statement of purpose or mission in the school. This statement of mission will allow us to better understand how to handle later formulations of aims, goals, and objectives. It will also help us to think of ways to organize key skills and content in the curriculum.

DEVELOPING A SCHOOL MISSION

Although every school with which I have been associated possessed a public (and published) mission statement, they did not all abide by a sense of mission. And contrary to what one might intuitively think, the absence of mission in the school was not always attributable to an operational or implementational failure. Sometimes the failure was on the other side of the problem; that is, the mission statement itself was inadequately constructed and fell short of conveying any real impression of mission or purpose.

Why does this sometimes happen? One problem is that the formation of school mission statements tends to get entangled with so many other agendas that the actual identity of the mission gets lost. For instance, schools commonly use mission statements as an excuse to offer platitudes about their high-minded nature, at times using glowing language about the love their teachers have for children or even the dedication their teachers exhibit toward their chosen profession. On occasion, a school's declared mission is gratuitous, assuring the public of their commitment to the obvious. One could hardly encounter a mission statement these days without finding some reference to securing the safety of the school or some observation about believing in the potential of all students. No one I know supports unsafe schools or would tolerate teachers who did not show some commitment to all their students. We might understand why a school might choose to emphasize these traits, but we should also understand that such a mission statement does not help with the cause of projecting the school's sense of purpose and vision.

Here is a mission statement that might sound familiar to many of you. It is fictional, but it is not unlike what you might find written at your local school:

> Central Elementary School provides an environment where all children can learn the skills needed to become caring and productive individuals. We believe in a nurturing environment that promotes life-long learning and that enables each child to become a positive member of a global society. The staff of Central School is committed to the self-worth and full development of each child.

I can see about five important considerations emerging from the statement: (1) the school is committed to teaching everyone; (2) it values caring and productive individuals; (3) it wants its education to be sustainable throughout life; (4) it believes that some educational connection has to be made to a global society; and (5) it is especially concerned about self-worth and something known as full development. Is this enough to truly give the school a sense of mission and purpose? I think not. First, the statement needs some clarification. What do *caring and productive individuals, global society,* and *full development* mean? The purposeful sense of endeavor in the school will be enhanced with clarification on these points. And this means digging a little more deeply into the contours of these terms. Second, the statement seems to be missing some pretty important ingredients. Did you notice, for instance, that the word democracy or citizenship never surfaced? What a school does not include in its mission statement says a lot about the mission statement.

The first thing we should look for in a mission statement is some exposition that helps to unify the structure of the entire school experience (Krug, 1950). What is it that all teachers, irrespective of grade level or subject area, are committed to accomplishing in the school? And what is it about the school that makes it unique and especially critical in the education of youth? The statement should be formed at a level of high generality, but phrased in a way that allows lay people and educators alike to understand what the school truly values in the education of its children. And although we do not want the mission statement to take on the length of a tome, we do want it to convincingly convey its mission, and that sometimes requires slightly more detail than is typically the case.

Not infrequently, school mission statements accent matters of process rather than purpose, highlighting the importance of particular methodologies or instructional approaches in the school. We should be reminded that such efforts only make sense in the mission statement if they point to the fulfillment of key purposes in the school. In other words, the school can say it values instructional approach x because it is viewed as especially effective at fulfilling purposes y and z. Charter schools, as well as other alternative schools, are likely to see themselves this way because they usually tout distinctiveness in both method and purpose, meaning that they not only aim at unique targets but also their methods of approach are unique. For instance, the mission statement for one charter school in Philadelphia starts by asserting that it is "an African-Centered, Science, Mathematics and Technology School." This likely means that the content of the curriculum will somehow be justified as African-centered, which would certainly give it some unique status. The statement continues by noting that the school will "provide an instructional program for high school students that focuses on high academic standards and character development" and that "it will use a standards-driven constructivist approach of teaching and learning." Thus, the mission of the school is embodied in not only its purposes but also its instructional approach. Presumably parents who enroll in this "choice" school understand the instructional mission and believe it to be best for their children. But a mission-based commitment to an instructional approach can be more complicated in a neighborhood school setting, where the expectation will be that teachers should make wholly independent instructional judgments. So, in most public school settings, the development of a mission statement should be less about process and more about purpose.

One way to begin the process of articulating a mission of purpose for the school is to think about categorical ways to shape or frame the school agenda. Historically speaking, four main categories have prevailed in the comprehensive mandate of the public school: personal-individual development, socio-civic development, academic-intellectual development, and vocational development. Some schools might value these equally, others might emphasize the academic over the vocational, and yet others might find some other combination of categories useful. When I say that these four main categories could be useful, I mean that they generally cover what schools typically aim to do (Goodlad, 1984). In considering personal-social development, for instance, to what extent will the school express its commitment to emotional and physical well-being issues, to creativity and aesthetic expression concerns, or to self-realization considerations? In regard to socio-civic development, will the mission statement make some direct reference to interpersonal understandings, to citizenship participation, to moral and ethical character, and to enculturation concerns? If the academic-intellectual development is a primary concern, does the mission statement relate to the mastery of certain intellectual skills and academic knowledge? And what of vocational development matters? Will it support only job training issues or will it also reach into important habits and attitudes? And certainly vocational education will be less of a concern in the mission statement of an elementary school than in that of a high school.

So, as a first matter, the development of a school mission statement should look to purpose and to the main categorical lines of the comprehensive agenda of the public school and try to see itself in terms that address goals related to personal-social, socio-civic, academic-intellectual, and vocational growth (Fig. 4.1). Let's put some detail into the endeavor.

Defining a sense of purpose in the realm of personal-social development might include the development of habits for independent learning, and the skills and attitudes needed to maintain good emotional, physical, and mental health. The statement might directly address the need for individuals to attain some degree of social belongingness and skills in interpersonal participation. It might also emphasize the need to develop individual responsibility, to honor individual uniquenesses and talents, and to generally serve the objectives of self-understanding and self-realization. These general commitments will naturally lead to more specific ones. A school where individual well-being is articulated in its mission statement will likely have to respond instructionally to matters such as influencing leisure time activities, helping youth to develop an honest and constructive self-image, and showing some regard for the spiritual and introspective needs of children. Can such things be ignored in the mission of a school? Perhaps, but the

FIGURE 4.1   **Elements of a Comprehensive School Mission**

argument for what is more important than personal-social development will have to be a compelling one.

The same is true for socio-civic development. We must think of the kinds of behavior, knowledge, skills, and values that are crucial to leading an informed and ethical life in a democracy. What school can ignore such matters in its mission? With a mission's commitment to socio-civic development in place, the school must then provide experiences that utilize civic virtues, such as social responsibility, cooperation, critical tolerance, and social equity. The school also might highlight the importance of interpersonal relations, outlining in specific terms what it views as the main roles and responsibilities of citizenship, addressing even political action skills, educating students in a heritage of common values and knowledge, or even offering some interaction with key moral and ethical concerns.

The development of academic and intellectual skills and knowledge is probably what schools best understand and most effectively reflect in their official undertakings. But even here the mission's language must be clear and carefully selected. Although most schools understand the normative agenda and properly reflect priorities to teach the fundamental skills of literacy, numeracy, and knowledge in the subject areas, they may not put the same emphasis on other intellectual skills. Will the mission statement, for instance, speak to problem-solving skills, higher-level thinking skills, inquiry skills, to the development of intellectual curiosity, and to an understanding of knowledge in its application contexts?

Vocation development concerns are of course most applicable to the high school, and to a lesser extent, the middle school. Because the school has such a full agenda, vocational interests are among the most likely to be ignored. Still, most schools can articulate vocational education purposes in a way that addresses the exploration of career options, focuses on life skills (related perhaps to auto and home ownership), and encourages positive attitudes toward work as well as pride in one's own workmanship. All of these purposes essentially take vocational education out of its traditional job-training capacity.

So, what makes a good mission statement? Simply put, we look for a powerful statement of mission or purpose. Mission statements should be about articulating missions and avoid lapsing into homilies or gratuitous public expressions. Some schools' missions might also describe the means by which they will attain key purposes. In most cases, these will be special-interest schools (private, charter, magnet, and the like), whose identity is wrapped up in both purpose and process. Of course, to the extent that the process reflects unique purposes, it becomes a necessary condition of the mission statement. Most American public schools embrace a comprehensive mandate that can be categorized along four important lines: socio-personal development, socio-civic development, academic-intellectual development, and vocational development. These four categories could prove to be helpful in assisting the school community frame its mission in a way that reflects the school's all-inclusive aspirations.

THE NATURE OF AIMS, GOALS, AND OBJECTIVES

We turn to John Dewey to initiate the argument for the vital place that educational aims have in the conduct of the school. Because an aim, as Dewey put it, "implies an ordered or orderly activity," it is especially well suited for the curriculum developer (Dewey, 1916, p. 102). But it is not the fact that the presence of aims creates an ordered environment that makes them so attractive or important; it is that they bring forth an ordered environment that school professionals can use to realize critical educational outcomes. Thus, educational aims become regulating conditions in the school that give the school meaning and that instruct everyone involved that their conduct should be at one with the school's intentions. But, as we will see, the approach one takes toward the construction of aims must not overstep certain boundaries and should keep other key principles in mind.

The aims, goals, and objectives used in the curriculum are really all of a piece, components that are rationalized and implemented at different levels of the curriculum. Zais (1975) uses the analogy of a target to characterize the relationship. An aim represents a target set far in the field. Educators might be able to see the distant target but because its particulars are not distinct, it is difficult to strike it directly. Here we are talking about the very kind of statements that would likely make their way into the articulation of a school's mission statement. If we speak of broad socio-civic or broad intellectual aims, for instance, we understand that such aims are, by their sweeping nature, next to impossible to strike directly. So, the natural reaction is to try to find a way to bring the target in, to make it more distinguishable to the eye in order to inspire some judgment on the instrumentation one might use to hit it. The movement in the direction of specificity is a movement in the direction of articulating goals and objectives as well as in the direction of defining purposes closer to the living experience of the teacher and the student. Sometimes, educators might want to bring the target in all the way, setting it close so that, tactically speaking, the target cannot be missed. Such targets are plainly visible and knowable—sitting ducks, as it were, for educators seeking their attainment—and are analogous to what we might traditionally view as instructional objectives in the curriculum. Objectives obviously become key to the work of classroom teachers, who use them to frame instructional events, but their degree of specificity in the microcurriculum (the classroom) is determined by teacher judgment. The macrocurricular goals affecting these judgments (which are intermediate to aims and objectives) are deliberately placed far enough in the field to allow for varied and less automated responses.

The target metaphor demonstrates some important differences between aims, goals, and objectives. Generally speaking, an aim is orienting or perspectival—it marks out a general commitment or purpose for the whole school, but is insufficient in guiding decisions at the microcurricular level. Thus, we will find aims taking their residence in the macrocurriculum. Objectives (and even goals), on the other hand, have a more tactical role. They are much more specific in outlining what should be done, but they still have their origin in a statement of aims. Objectives draw their sense of the particular from the general. A school, for example, might support the aim of developing critical-thinking skills, but each classroom within the school might go about contributing to this aim in a different way, accounting for learner and subject-matter differences. The development of objectives is useful in drawing out this more specific strategy. The distinction between goals and objectives can sometimes be blurred because the level of specificity required to conduct the classroom is ultimately in the teacher's hands. Curriculum developers abide by certain rules that help keep the formation of goals broad enough to still give teachers plenty of room for these situational judgments.

But the target metaphor is an incomplete one. Closer targets are not always better ones by virtue of being easier to hit. In fact, in the macrocurriculum, we deliberately set targets at a calculated distance. Furthermore, finding a balance between an aim (a target off in the distance) and multiple goals and objectives (closer targets) can be tricky. The metaphor is further flawed in that it implies that once aims or goals are struck, the work is complete, when in fact, in the context of a curriculum, all goals and aims lie on a continuum that subtly shifts over time and in different contexts.

Because Dewey (1916) understood that the formation of aims has a ripple effect in the curriculum, he outlined what he called "the criteria for good aims." He thought that three important factors had to be weighed.

First, the formation of aims had to rise up from the educational situation, "based on a consideration of what was already going on; upon the resources and difficulties of the situation" (Dewey, 1916, p. 104). In other words, to effectively set broad purposes in the school requires knowing the school, its resources and capacities, as well as what might be especially valued in the school community and needed in the light of evaluative data. The formation of aims or purposes is always affected by social and political realities as well as by resource limitations and various nuances in the nature of the school community. External normative aims given by state directive can be problematic in this sense, especially if they result in rendering the work of teachers, to use Dewey's characterization, "slavish or mechanical." Another threat is the present-day inclination among curriculum theorists to politicize aims and to assume a line of best fit between their ideology and the conduct of the school. Directives that arise from the states' departments of education or from "theory" violate one criterion of Dewey's good aims if they are imposed without due consideration of the local educational situation, and if they carry with them a rigid instructional will. Curriculum developers leave the instructional will of the school to the teacher while still influencing it through the formation of broader purposes or aims.

The second criterion of good aims refers to the tentative and flexible character of aims. To Dewey, good aims are elastic enough to allow for some range of interpretation as well as some flexibility in shifting course, or making other modifications as circumstance dictates. Aims help form a tentative plan and give the teacher a vision of the whole school experience, but they must be amenable to adjustments as conditions develop.

The third and final criterion of good aims is a variation of the second and represents a kind of paradox. I have been saying from the beginning of this book that curriculum development is a delimiting exercise and that the defining of purposes is one of the procedural ways we can begin to refine, focus, and simplify the school experience. But Dewey reminds us that the third criterion of good aims demands that aims produce a freeing or releasing of activities. This should not be viewed as a contradiction. The fine line that curriculum developers walk is between giving direction and allowing for the exercise of professional judgment. A good aim does not close down a teacher's options but opens them up in a focused and directive way.

Ralph Tyler (1949) must have read John Dewey because when he offered his own advice on the development of objectives in the curriculum in *Basic Principles of Curriculum and Instruction,* he cautioned against some of the very same concerns raised by Dewey. He wanted to keep objectives written at a high level of generality, one we might associate with a goal, and he wanted to keep decisions close to the hands of those who knew the school the best. The issue of specificity emerges then as a key principle in Tyler's work. He essentially rejected specificity in the development of objectives largely using the same argument that Dewey used to appeal for flexibility and a freeing of activity in the development of aims. At the same time, Tyler (1949) understood that there is tension here because objectives were, by their nature, supposed to be stated in a way that left little confusion about the kind of behavior and content to be integrated into the learning experience.

Tyler (1949) spoke in straightforward terms about objectives in the curriculum. For instance, he directly criticized the idea of defining the actual activity the teacher needed to accomplish, such as "the teacher will demonstrate the nature of inductive proof, or introduce four part harmony" (p. 44). These certainly were activities that might be worthy of a teacher's attention, but they were not statements of educational ends. They possessed no sense of behavior or skill that the teacher was to develop in the student; they were just descriptions of activities. Tyler also criticized the use of objectives that focused only on content and that often resulted in a simple listing of topics to be followed, as well as the use of objectives that referred only to key behaviors and skills without any reference to content. Not surprisingly, Tyler asserted that the best objectives were ones that included a content component and a behavioral or skill component. "The most useful form for stating objectives is to express them with terms which identify both the kind of behavior to be developed in the student and the content or area of life in which this behavior is to operate" (p. 46). The two-dimensionality of Tyler's objectives ensures that both behavioral and content concerns are integrated in the statement of purposes. As Taba (1962) noted, "this double concept of scope should go a long way toward eliminating the bugaboo of coverage (of content) as the sole index of achievement and growth" (p. 200).

TWO-DIMENSIONALITY IN THE
FORMATION OF OBJECTIVES

We will be working with Tyler's proposition that the formation of objectives in the curriculum (the purposes closest to the teacher) are most useful when they specify the kind of behavior or skill expected and the content to which it applies. So, if we say we want to encourage a set of communication skills (such as writing or debating persuasively), we should take some notice of what it is we are writing or debating about. This puts the teacher in the spot of simultaneously supporting content mastery and the development of a variety of behaviors, skills, values, and attitudes. This method not only makes certain that content is integrated in learning experiences (one feature of the three factors in the educative process) but it also gives approval to the broadening of experience, as it extends into behaviors and skills and the like.

Dimension One: Pervasive Behaviors, Skills, and Values

Let's start with explaining the behavioral side of the two-dimensional process by thinking about the general behaviors, skills, and values we might support across most, if not all, subject areas in the curriculum. We should first look at the comprehensive agenda of the school, as it might be expressed in the school's mission statement. The curriculum developer might seek to understand the kinds of general behaviors and skills indicative of personal, academic, intellectual, and sociocivic growth. Such behaviors and skills are *pervasive* in the curriculum; they have no particularized place in any one realm of inquiry or subject matter. And although some skills are likely to be more applicable to some classroom setting than others, taken together, they give the curriculum some unity of purpose and focus.

The focus on the general is deliberate. The intention is to give teachers direction without compromising their instructional authority. The purposes of the school curriculum are to act as a guide to teachers without coming at the cost of individual ways of conducting instruction.

But what might these skills and behaviors be, and once we have identified them, how might we organize them? If we think about the kinds of skills and behaviors that should pervade or infuse virtually every phase of the curriculum—we could begin to make our list. It might include thinking, communication, inquiry, and study skills. The list probably should include some reference to civic virtues and responsibilities as well as common moral and ethical values. Other curriculum workers might organize their list differently, but I have found that these areas cover good ground. And remember that, at this point, we are only discussing the behavioral side (which includes skills and values) of the formation of an objective, and that we are only thinking of behaviors that are applicable to many subject areas, although with varied degrees of involvement.

Thinking.   Thinking is a pervasive skill. But to simply say that thinking skills must be integrated into the whole of the school experience does not help much. The question inevitably becomes what types of thinking skills are we planning to integrate into the curriculum and how will we design them so that the entire school comprehends their importance? And because the question of how to organize the attendant skills and behaviors of thinking in the curriculum is a philosophical one, there should be considerable discussion and debate in the school community.

Educators often make reference to all sorts of thinking skills: creative, critical, reflective, introspective, metacognitive, logical, mathematical (or quantitative), scientific, or even artistic thinking. So, which set of thinking skills gets included? The answer is all or some combination, depending on which skills the school wants to identify as pervasive skills in the curriculum. If mathematical or scientific thinking skills, which already have some residency in a particular discipline, are viewed as important enough to integrate into all the features of the school, the curriculum developer could help to design the curriculum accordingly. Or the curriculum worker might just use a different approach altogether by framing thinking skills and behaviors from the standpoint of problem solving, as a construct that contains the behavioral elements of decision making. When approached from this perspective, the organization of thinking skills will emphasize purposes different from other schemes of thinking.

Among the more popular ways to organize thinking skills in the curriculum is to reflect on the upper cognitive levels of Bloom's taxonomy, a well-known hierarchical arrangement of thinking skills. The most recently revised upper levels of the taxonomy are organized as analysis, evaluation, and creation (Anderson and Krathwohl, 2001).

Analysis "involves breaking material into its constituent parts and determining how the parts are related to one another and to an overall structure" (p. 79) and could include the ability to

- Distinguish fact from opinion (reality and fantasy)
- Connect conclusions with supporting statements
- Distinguish between relevant and extraneous material
- Compare and contrast
- Recognize patterns (cause-and-effect pattern)
- Classify data

- Identify assumptions
- Understand main ideas
- Find sequences.

Evaluation "is defined as making judgments based on criteria and standards" (p. 83) and could include the ability to

- Check for inconsistencies and fallacies
- Evaluate facts, disadvantages, shortcomings, strengths, and achievement
- Create new ideas
- Offer independent judgment, including justifiable opinions and creative responses
- Critique.

Creation "involves putting elements together to form a coherent or functional whole" (p. 84) and could include the ability to

- Draw conclusions, inferring inductively and deductively
- Summarize
- Construct an original product (a solution to a problem)
- Apply knowledge to life situation
- Develop generalizations.

If the three upper levels of Bloom's taxonomy had a front-and-center place in the formation of objectives, the types of thinking skills to be used in the school would be clear. Obviously, those thinking skills would presume formal operations and would be best placed in a middle school or high school setting. And when used in the classroom, they will take on a more specific interpretation. Such upper-cognitive concerns could be systematically integrated into the curriculum to support the school's goal of teaching thinking skills. But the school might not be satisfied with only these thinking skills. It might want to support more open-ended and creative thinking and thus design a list of skills that might approximate the following (Iowa Department of Education, 1989):

> *Analogical thinking,* which is the use of figurative language to express ideas in innovative and analytically penetrating ways, and could include the ability to use metaphors, similes, personification, and other literary forms to gain a clearer understanding of abstract or complex ideas.
>
> *Hypothesizing,* which is the development of a testable explanation for a given problem, and could include the ability to make generalizations about observed data, to inquire into and understand existing data pertaining to the given problem, and to properly connect problem solutions.

Imagining, which moves beyond what is factual and logical and into the realm of informed speculation and the production of novel expressions of insight, and could include the ability to make informed predictions, to speculate about possibilities, and to offer new visualization of insight.

Elaborating, which represents a contribution to the improvement of an idea. This might mean seeing an idea in a unique context or refining it in some way and could include skills pertaining to expanding on existing ideas, modifying them, extending to new contexts, or shifting them in an alternate direction.

This list obviously sends a different charge through the curriculum than the list based on Bloom's taxonomy. But they are not, in fact, mutually exclusive. The skills inherent to analogical thinking, hypothesizing, imagining, and elaborating are all, more or less, within the creation level of Bloom's taxonomy. But to put the emphasis on the categorical elements of creativity thinking makes the case that much stronger for its place in the curriculum. The point is that the curriculum worker has quite a bit of room here to structure general behaviors and skills in a way that ensures the applicability of a certain range of thinking skills in the school experience.

An altogether different approach to thinking might be to stress the act of problem solving and to identify those behaviors that utilize it. A list of such behaviors might look something like the following (Dressel and Mayhew, 1954):

Recognizing the existence of a problem, which could include the ability to recognize conflicts and issues in a situation.

Defining a problem, which could include the ability to identify the nature of a problem, to properly phrase it, to break it down into workable parts, and to eliminate any extraneous elements.

Selecting information pertinent to the solution to a problem, which could include the ability to recognize assumptions bearing on a problem, to distinguish between reliable and unreliable sources, to recognize relevant information, and to select information from personal experience.

Making relevant hypotheses, which could include the ability to check the consistency of a hypothesis with existing data sources.

Drawing valid conclusions from assumptions, hypotheses, and other pertinent information, which could include the ability to distinguish a necessary inference from a probable one, and to detect logical inconsistencies in an argument.

Judging the validity of the process leading to the conclusion, which could include the ability to recognize the condition necessary to verify a conclusion and to judge the adequacy of a conclusion to a problem.

This list dismantles the act of thinking into key components teachers can, in the end, systematically integrate into their lessons and instructional events. Adjustments, of course, need to be made according to age and grade levels.

In the end, the pattern of thinking skills that will hold some centralizing influence in the curriculum will be as comprehensive as possible and include some display of critical, creative, and problem-solving skills. The key principle in designing this pattern is to make the behavioral characteristics of the general skill clear enough to give the teacher some direction on how to proceed.

Communicating.   Communication skills are also pervasive in the curriculum. They include what is traditionally viewed as literacy (learning to read) but they also get into other behaviors, including writing, speaking, debating, visual communication, and artistic expression. Unlike the skills of thinking, those involved in communications are sometimes taught separately. Schools employ teachers who teach reading, writing, speech, and debate.

Reading is a special case. It gets a lot of direct attention in the earlier grades because it is a basis for all learning. Good reading skills are fundamental to virtually every learning experience in the school. Their educational impact is especially profound because once children learn to read, they begin to explore ideas independently and even, at some level, begin to educate themselves. Reading absolutely has some independent status in the elementary school. In some ways, the considerable body of skills that contribute to phonemic awareness, auditory processing, grammatical structure, and general comprehension could be viewed as the content of a reading program. (We could also make a similar case for writing.) Furthermore, children cannot read reading, as it were—they have to read something. Hence, the content of the reading can address another subject.

Reading, however, is also pervasive in the curriculum. It is not the exclusive domain of reading teachers. And although reading teachers will target certain skills at a level of specificity and attention that we could not expect from the science or math teachers, we should remember that some reading skills apply to all content areas.

It goes without saying that other communication skills (writing, speaking, and other expressive skills) also apply across the curriculum. Thus, the curriculum designer has some obligation to reflect a range of communication skills throughout the curriculum. I organized a range of communication skills along four lines: reading, writing, speaking, and expressive skills. These are skills that have a wide-ranging or pervasive applicability in the curriculum. So, when we look to reading, we ask what we might expect not just from reading teachers but from all other teachers in the school. This means that reading, as a pervasive skill, will likely touch on factors such as reading critically and efficiently. Similarly, writing (as a pervasive skill) will be less focused on developmental concerns about writing (identifying audiences, prewriting, editing, and revision), which we mostly leave to the English or language arts experience, and more on stylistic concerns (the use of different forms and different genres of writing) or perhaps concerns related to the application of technical vocabulary and usage. Speaking and listening skills go directly to presentation and oration skills, as well as skills in debate and argumentation. Finally, expressive skills point to abilities such as the effective use of visual and data-driven displays as well as the use of other nonverbal forms of communication. Our skills could be organized in the following way:

Pervasive reading skills, which could include the ability to

- Use skimming skills and other reading efficiency strategies
- Recognize author style
- Critically question the narrative (to identify the bias and the emotive in the narrative)
- Read with discrimination for informational or research purposes
- Read for recreational or enjoyment purposes
- Increase and develop vocabulary.

Pervasive writing skills, which could include the ability to

- Write clearly and persuasively
- Understand different genres of writing (poetry, narrative, informational)
- Use correct grammar and conventional spelling
- Use different forms of writing (editorials, metaphorical, legalistic, expository, humorous).

Pervasive speaking and listening skills, which could include the ability to

- Use skills in oral presentation
- Use skills in debate and argumentation
- Ask clarifying questions and take good notes
- Listen reflectively and critically
- Use technological tools that could assist with presentations.

Pervasive expressive skills, which could include the ability to

- Use skills in the presentation of charts, graphs, tables, and other nonverbal tools of communication
- Use a variety of expressive forms, including musical, visual, theatrical, dance, mathematical expressions
- Use technological resources, including word processing technologies, presentation technologies, data representation technologies, drawing tools, video streams, and digital cameras
- Communicate with diverse audiences, in a variety of ways for a variety of purposes.

Although these skills are viewed as pervasive in the curriculum, all teachers will not necessarily engage them. The image of a mathematics teacher actively involved in teaching math in a way that results in some instructional focus on grammar and conventional spelling concerns might be too much for some of us. The fact is that we cannot fully understand the place that each of these pervasive skills takes in the curriculum until we discuss the issue of horizontal articulation, which will be covered in the next chapter. For now, however, we are looking for general behaviors and skills that might find their way into multiple classroom settings, understanding that the fit may not be suitable in all settings. And in some cases, the effort to reach out to communications skills in a specialty area (such as art, music, or dance) might result in specially designed courses or units that might involve a team teaching or collaborative teaching arrangement. The purpose is not for all teachers to become reading and writing teachers, but for all teachers to properly reflect pervasive communication skills that are appropriately and suitably matched with the nature of the subject matter and the instructional style of the classroom teacher. And because the curriculum worker must be cognizant of the nature of the learner, each of the aforementioned communication skills would need to be adjusted to the developmental and maturity level of the child.

Inquiring and Studying.   The ability to find and understand credible knowledge that contributes to one's understanding of the world, including one's ability to solve a problem or to use knowledge in a way that informs enlightened behavior, is an important characteristic of being educated in a democracy. The curriculum should find a way to emphasize inquiry-based skills as well as to provide insight on how to study and organize one's academic or intellectual life. In this sense, inquiry and study skills could be constructed as pervasive skills. Much of what we might offer as inquiry skills overlap conceptually with certain thinking skills, but the overall flavor of inquiry is different enough to justify its own spot in the curriculum. Where such skills are taken seriously, the possibilities for more problem-focused and inquiry-based instructional activities likely increase, as do the possibilities for higher-level thinking engagements in the classroom. Here is one organizational scheme:

Inquiry skills, which could include the ability to

- Collect facts and data from multiple sources
- Understand the difference between primary and secondary source material
- Select dependable sources of data
- Discriminate between important and unimportant facts
- Read graphs, charts, tables, and maps
- Employ all of the reference tools available in a library
- Use technological methods of research, including Internet tools, as well as other electronic resources
- Document sources.

Studying skills, which could include the ability to

- Use an effective note-taking method
- Outline and summarize
- Plan, organize, and properly manage one's time
- Use good studying methods.

There are no surprises here. These objectives apply, one way or another, to all knowledge domains, including science, mathematics, history, social studies, and language arts. Some of the skills are quite detailed and precise, specificity, such as the reference to discriminating between important and unimportant facts, while others, such as the reference to using library references skills, might call for further specificity.

Interpersonal Engagements.   Although schools often give lip service to socio-civic behaviors and skills in the school, they rarely take them seriously enough to integrate them into the whole of the curriculum. Interpersonal engagements refer to the kinds of pervasive behaviors that can manifest in any classroom setting and that are important enough to be part of the teacher's instructional and pedagogical consciousness. These are the kinds of behaviors that contribute to our prospects for a civil and democratic society. They are not geared at citizenship per se because they are designed to infuse the macrocurriculum. So, the focus is on cooperation (and other group dynamics), character and ethics, and democratic values.

Interpersonal engagements refer to the behaviors, values, and attitudes that are central to a civil society, and which could include the ability to

- Form productive and satisfying relations with others based on respect, trust, cooperation, consideration, and caring
- Balance compromise with steadfastness
- Judge people by their character and behavior
- Use democratic values and practices in group activities
- Communicate effectively in groups and fulfill group goals
- Develop an understanding and appreciation of cultures different from one's own
- Work cooperatively with others and seek multiple perspectives
- Work in the interest of school and community problems.

These interpersonal skills could be integrated into instructional decisions and into the general social atmosphere of the school and classroom. If these interpersonal engagements had a primary place in the development of the micro-curriculum, the school experience would likely feature more cooperative engagements, more efforts to encourage conversation, and more opportunities to deal with diversity concerns (as they relate to common values and common out-looks), than would otherwise be the case. The point is that if these interpersonal behaviors are important to the school, they must be reflected in the school's key purposes and taken seriously as pervasive skills in the curriculum.

Personal Development.   The curriculum, of course, also has some responsibility to attend to the skills of personal or individual development. An enlightened so-ciety depends on informed individuals who have a constructive outlook on life. Individual well-being concerns speak to variables such as emotional stability, cop-ing with change, habits of individual responsibility, the constructive use of leisure time, and maintaining an honest and healthy self-image. The possibilities for or-ganizing the key skills of personal development are many. Goodlad (1984) high-lighted the skills using three categories: emotional and physical well-being, creative and aesthetic expression, and self-realization.

Under *emotional well-being,* we could include skills, such as the ability to

- Engage in constructive self-criticism
- Learn to make effective use of one's leisure time
- Expand on one's affective sensitivities (one's sense of caring, compassion, appreciation, and gratitude) and develop the adjustment skills one needs to deal with change.

Under *aesthetic expression,* we might point to skills such as the ability to

- Be flexible and to consider different viewpoints
- Experience, evaluate, and enjoy different forms of aesthetic expression. (These could also be listed as communicative skills.)

Finally, under *self-realization,* we might emphasize skills such as the ability to

- Develop a balanced philosophy of life
- Develop the self-confidence for knowing and confronting oneself
- Assess and live with one's limitations and strengths
- Develop a willingness to accept responsibility for one's own decisions.

It is clear that such personal development skills dovetail nicely with the con-tent of the language arts. Without question, high school English teachers and lan-guage arts teachers in the middle and elementary schools will have a much more prominent role in dealing with personal development concerns. But these are also skills that can be dealt with in other settings and are almost always at work in the latent curriculum of all classrooms. Where these skills might extend and how they might be represented will be partly the consequence of the curriculum devel-oper's design.

Dimension Two: Specific Content

We now turn to the issue of content as it relates to the formation of objectives. The presupposition we will be working with here is that all educational experiences must possess content; that is, they must endeavor to offer some interaction with a body of knowledge (expressed as facts, principles, definitions, skills, and ideas) that is organized in some representational or categorical form. Learning how to do science means not only to be acquainted with specific scientific skills but also with the considerable accumulation of wisdom embodied in the various subdisciplines or knowledge areas of science. To think, communicate, or inquire means to think, communicate, or inquire about something. Even skill-based content areas such as reading and mathematics can be seen as interacting with other forms of content. In the case of reading, there might be an interplay with literature choices and in the case of mathematics, a select set of quantitative skills could be used in relation to inquiries in science or social studies. As Taba (1962) noted, "if the behavior denotes knowing or remembering, the statement of objectives should also indicate what is to be known or remembered. If the statement specifies an attitude, then it should also state what the attitude is about" (p. 200).

As previously discussed content categories of the curriculum require us once again to consider the balance between specificity and generality. Tyler's advice is no different on the content side of the objectives than it is on the behavioral side. He makes it clear that we should favor generality, doing enough to lay out the content in categorical terms in order to give definite meaning to the function of subject matter in the curriculum. So how do we do this?

Four Levels of Content. Taba offers a design approach that organizes content along four levels. The first level is what she refers to as specific facts and processes. Although educators can get carried away with a concern for facts, so much so that education can begin to become more fact-driven than idea-driven, the reality is that some basic facts are investments in higher level engagements. They are, as Taba (1962) phrased it, the raw material for the development of ideas and the main building blocks for the construction of generalizations and insights (pp. 175–176). Some facts are, of course, trivial. The curriculum developer should guard against the prospect of allowing the content of the curriculum to collapse into content triviality (e.g., Abraham Lincoln's hat size). Under no circumstances should the mastery of facts become the exclusive concern of educators, but the role that facts play in shaping concepts, ideas, generalizations, and even good criticism, cannot be ignored. So, we can say that one level of concern about content is the acquisition of some specific facts and processes. The kinds of facts that Taba had in mind could be stated at a relatively general level, such as knowing the branches of government, characteristics of the digestive system, specific rules of grammatical usage, or specific computational processes.

But the best form of protection against content minutiae is to be sure that the facts we are seeking to integrate into the learning experience are tied to important ideas. Thus, Taba's second level refers to the organization of basic ideas. At this level, knowledge is organized by general ideas that explain key principles and key phenomena. Facts inherent in ideas are not always obvious and the ideas themselves could be described in any number of ways. In science, for instance, some basic ideas related to the teaching of matter and energy in the upper-elementary-school grades might be that the sun is the chief source of energy for the earth, that chemical changes are constantly occurring in nature (photosynthesis, corrosion), that atomic energy has multiple uses, and that matter is composed of molecules which can be broken down into atoms (Beauchamp, 1975, pp. 160–161). In elementary school science, an instructional unit in life science for the earliest grades might include knowing the difference between living and nonliving things, understanding organisms according to selective characteristics, knowing the basic needs of organisms, and understanding the interrelatedness of living systems. These basic ideas explain multiple phenomena and cover a wide swath of territory through which a river of facts might flow. The identification of basic ideas is clearly linked to the acquisition of facts.

Taba's (1962) third level of content organization is composed of concepts, which she describes as "complex systems of highly abstract ideas which can be built only by successive experiences in a variety of contexts" (p. 178). In elementary school mathematics, the main concepts of the curriculum might be described as sets, numbers, operations, functions and graphs, measurement, geometry, statistics and probability, primitive number theory, and relations (Michaelis and others, 1975, p. 266; see Table 4.1). Concepts related to science might be organized around cross-grade referents, such as living things, earth and space, and matter and energy; in the study of societies, they might be represented as big ideas, such as roles, interaction, interdependence, and social control (Michaelis and others, 1975, p. 330). These concepts are recurrent in the curriculum, surfacing in different ways at different grade levels. In fact, concepts are often used to establish the vertical articulation of the content in the curriculum, which is how content can be threaded through grade levels, an especially critical concern in the elementary school. The concept of *living things*, for instance, might have a cyclical place between grade levels, resulting in a different listing of ideas and attendant facts for each grade. But it also stands as a unifying concept within the science curriculum (see Table 4.2, pp. 108–110).

Finally, Taba pointed to the existence of discipline-centered thought patterns and methods of inquiry that could be represented as content. In other words, what are the ways of thinking particular to a discipline that could be included in the content side of the curriculum objective? We could say that there is a scientific way of thinking, a mathematical way of thinking, and ways of thinking historically, politically, sociologically, psychologically, and even musically. Language arts could offer ways to think through the use of different literary instruments, so that we could think as a poet, a humorist, or an editorial writer. The question is, can such modes of thinking be identified in a way that allows for their integration into the curriculum?

TABLE 4.1   Concepts Underpinning the Content of Mathematics Education in the Elementary School

CONCEPTS	BASIC IDEAS
Sets	Collection, elements, one-to-one correspondence, pairing, matching or equivalent, equal, serial ordering, proper, improper, finite, infinite, empty or null, subset, operation, intersection, union, disjoint, complement, Cartesian product
Numbers	Property of set, cardinality, ordinality, counting, betweenness, natural, zero, whole, integers, rational, irrational, real, positive, negative, prime, composite, factors, multiples, numeration, patterns, density, equality, inequalities, ordered pairs, equivalent class
Operations	Addition, multiplication, subtraction, division, basic facts, inverses, sentences, interactions, algorithms, role of computating, flexibility, compensation, identity, commutation, association, distribution, closure, binary and unary, nondecimal bases
Functions and Graphs	Ordered pairs, functional relationship, continuous variables, graphs in one, two, and three dimensions, coordinates, axis, slope, inter-cepts, interpolation, extrapolation, interpretation, linear, quadratic, exponential
Measurement	Comparison, units, dimensions, arbitrary and standard units, likeness, number, scale, calibration, precision, accuracy, error, relative error, absolute error, approximate numbers, significant digits, metric system, conversions
Geometry	Classification, point, line, segment, plane, region, three-dimensional space, ray, arc, end point, vertex, intersection, union, polygon, parallel, perpendicular, bi-section, similarity, congruence, metric, nonmetric
Statistics and Probability	Prediction, probability, chance, distribution, average, mean, median, mode, variance, standard deviation, correlation, graphing, models, sampling
Primitive Number Theory	Factors, multiples, primes, composites, least common multiple, greatest common factor, tests for divisibility, relations

Source: Adapted from J.U. Michaelis, R.H. Grossman, & L.F. Scott. (1975). *New designs for elementary education curriculum and instruction.* New York: McGraw-Hill.

TABLE 4.2   **Vertical Articulation through Concepts**

CONCEPT	GRADE 2 BASIC IDEAS	GRADE 3 BASIC IDEAS	GRADE 4 BASIC IDEAS
Living Things	All living things are either plants or animals. Most plants stay in one place; most animals move around. Each kind of animal has characteristics that make it different from other kinds of animals.	Green plants need air, light, and water in order to manufacture food. All food comes from green plants directly or indirectly. Living things and their products are used for food.	Some insects change from one form to another as they grow to maturity. Some insects are useful to man; some are harmful. Spiders differ from insects.
	Each part of a plant has its own work to do. Each part of a seed helps in the growing of a new plant. A seed grows a plant like the plant from which the seed comes. The flowers and leaves of plants have many colors and shapes. Some animals are raised by people and are tame. Domestic animals eat plants and other animals. Some domestic animals are hatched from eggs. Some domestic animals are born. Domestic animals give us food and other products.	Some birds remain in this area the year around. Some birds are migratory. Living things go through different stages of growth. Animals have different ways of moving, eating, and protecting themselves. Some animals can breathe under water; others cannot. Some animals today are different from those of long ago.	Some plants reproduce from roots; some from stems; and some from leaves. Environment affects the growth of plant life. Plants are useful to other living things by providing shelter, food, clothing, furniture, heat, paper, and beauty. Plants and animals are especially fitted for the environment in which they live. Some animals tend to live together in groups and/or packs. Some animals destroy or damage food crops. Some animals are useful to man and are protected. Some plants are useful; some are harmful.
Earth and Space Beyond	The sun gives off heat and light. The sun is the nearest star to the earth, but it and all other stars (suns) are very far away. The sun seems to rise in the east and set in the west.	The earth is made up of land, water, and air. Soil is always being made. Earth's different surfaces affect weather. Air contains water vapor and dust.	Stars look small because they are so far away. The sun is one of billions of stars. Stars are moving through space. The sun is many times the size of the moon.

TABLE 4.2 Continued

CONCEPT	GRADE 2 BASIC IDEAS	GRADE 3 BASIC IDEAS	GRADE 4 BASIC IDEAS
Earth and Space Beyond (*cont.*)	The sun causes the seasons. The earth is a round ball of matter. The earth has no light of its own. The moon reflects sunlight to the earth. Groups of stars form constellations.	Air expands when heated; contracts when cooled. Air has weight and occupies space. The weight of air presses down and up and on and within all things. Water has many uses. There is more water than land on the surface of the earth. Water can be a solid, a liquid, or a gas. The amount of water vapor and the temperature of the air affects our weather.	All planets receive heat and light from the sun. Comets and meteors are star particles. Earth turns once in its axis each day causing daytime and nighttime. Earth's revolution around the sun causes years. Seasons are caused by the tilt of the earth on its axis and the revolution of the earth around the sun. Earth's mass exerts pull. Moon's gravitational pull causes tides. The moon cannot support life. The moon circles the earth once a month.
Behavior of Matter and Energy	Everything (matter) takes up space (volume) and has weight. Sometimes objects of the same size have different weights. Sometimes objects that weigh the same take up different amounts of space. Materials can be recognized by the ways that they act when we work with them. Magnets have unlike poles and a zone around them in which they can push and pull. Magnets can make other magnets.	All matter is found either as elements, compounds, or mixtures of them. Electricity flows only when it has a complete path called a circuit. A switch is used to start or stop the flow of current. Heat and light are produced by electricity. Electric current can make magnets. These are called electromagnets. A simple machine is one which performs works advantageously. Complex machines are combinations of the simple machines.	Matter consists of particles which are in motion (molecules). Molecules attract each other; the farther apart they are the less the attraction. Sound is caused by the vibration of objects. Sound waves can be directed and reflected. Pitch refers to the highness or lowness of a sound and is determined by the number of times an object moves back and forth per second. Intensity of sound refers to its loudness or softness and is

(continued)

TABLE 4.2   Continued

CONCEPT	GRADE 2 BASIC IDEAS	GRADE 3 BASIC IDEAS	GRADE 4 BASIC IDEAS
Behavior of Matter and Energy (*cont.*)	Some things can be made into magnets, other things cannot be made into magnets. We can make one kind of electricity if we rub certain things together. One kind of electricity is called static electricity; it can pull some things; it can push other things.	Friction causes wear (machine wear, soil erosion, etc.). Friction is useful in starting and stopping moving objects. Lubrication reduces friction.	determined by the amount of energy used to make the sound. A force is a push or pull. Some forces are used to set certain machines in motion. Work is applied force acting through distance. Energy is the ability to do work.
	Some materials, usually metals, produce either positive or negative electrical charges when they are placed in a certain liquid.		
	The kind of electricity we use in our homes is called current electricity. This is the kind of electricity that keeps moving through wires. Current electricity can make heat and light. Temperature can be measured. We can make some things hot by rubbing them. Simple machines make work easier.		

Source: Adapted from G.A. Beauchamp. (1975). *Curriculum theory* (3rd ed.). Wilmette, IL: Kagg Press. Reprinted with permission.

Dresell and Edwards (1954) listed a set of assumptions and principles inherent to science that could be interpreted as a thought pattern or mode of thinking particular to scientists. As Table 4.3 (pp. 112–113) illustrates, the list includes principles such as objectivity, consistency, tentativeness, causality, dynamism, and so forth. Because these are principles that are integral to all of the subject matter iterations of the science curriculum, the curriculum developer could fold them into the content side of the curriculum objective, using the argument that such principles are particular to the study of science and should be part and parcel of science education. However, if the school wanted to use such principles in a manner that pervades all of the content areas of the curriculum, as might be the case in a science-themed magnet school, those principles could then be shifted to the behavioral side of the stated objective so that scientific thinking is infused across the curriculum.

The same is true of mathematical thinking, which one might see in relation to data management, data representation, and probability—something that could be valued either in mathematics classes or in another content setting as well. Skills might include the ability to collect, organize and analyze data; to use tally charts, frequency tables, and stem-and-leaf plots; to understand mean, median, and mode as ways to represent central tendencies; to manipulate and present data using spreadsheets; to use bar and line graphs, pie charts, pictographs, and histographs; and to construct various graphic representations of data using simple statistical methods and computer programs. This could be a critical aspect of a mathematics course (and hence framed as mathematics content) or it could be used more widely in the curriculum (and hence framed as a pervading skill across the curriculum).

So, in thinking about the content of the curriculum, we have four levels of concern. The acquisition of facts as they are tied to the construction and understanding of basic ideas and principles represent two synergetic levels. Facts are important to the extent that they inform key ideas in the content. Imagine trying to understand the idea of "government by the consent of the governed" without understanding the branches of government (and their attendant functions) that are used to actualize such an idea. The third level of content focuses on big ideas or big concepts that take their purpose largely as organizing elements in the curriculum.

We use concepts as organizing tools that give coherence to the content across grade levels of the curriculum. These are often unifying concepts. The National Science Foundation uses the following concepts to unify the content standards they designed for grades 5–8: systems order and organization; evidence, modes, and explanation; change, constancy, and measurement; evolution and equilibrium; form and function. Finally, the remaining organizational level of content refers to particular modes of thinking embedded in a content area. Such thinking processes could be limited strictly to their discipline moorings in the curriculum

TABLE 4.3   **Basic Assumptions of a Scientist**

PRINCIPLE OF	ASSUMPTION
Objectivity	A scientist cultivates the ability to examine facts and suspend judgment with regard to his observations, conclusions, and activities.
Consistency	A scientist assumes that the behavior of the universe is not capricious, but is describable in terms of consistent laws, such that when two sets of conditions are the same, the same consequences may be expected.
Tentativeness	A scientist does not regard his generalizations as final, but is willing to modify them if they are contradicted by new evidence.
Causality	A scientist believes that every phenomenon results from a discoverable cause.
Uniformity	A scientist believes that the forces which are now operating in the world are those which have always operated, and that the world and the universe which we see are the result of their continuous operation.
Simplicity	A scientist prefers simple and widely applicable explanations of phenomena. He attempts to reduce his view of the world to as simple terms as possible.
Materiality	A scientist prefers material and mechanical explanations of phenomena, rather than those which depend on nonmaterial and supernatural forces.
Dynamism	A scientist expects nature to be dynamic rather than static, and to show variation and change.
Relativeness	A scientist thinks of the world, and of things in it, as sets of relationships rather than as absolutes.
Intergradation	A scientist thinks in terms of continua; he distrusts sharp boundary lines, and expects to find related classes of natural phenomena grading imperceptibly into one another.
Practicality	A scientist expects that in any situation involving competition among units of varying potentialities, those which work best under existing circumstances will tend to survive and perpetuate themselves.
Continuous Discovery	A scientist hopes that it will be possible to go on learning more and more about the material world and the material universe of which it is a part, until eventually all may be understood.

TABLE 4.3 Continued

PRINCIPLE OF	ASSUMPTION
Complementarity	A scientist attempts to incorporate all phenomena into a single, consistent, natural scheme, but he recognizes that contradictory generalizations may be necessary to describe aspects of certain things as they appear to us.
Social Limitation	The social framework within which a scientist operates may determine and limit the kinds of problems on which he works, and the data which he collects, and may also influence his conclusions.

Source: Adapted from P.L. Dressel & L.B. Mayhew. (1954). *General education: Explorations in evaluation.* Washington, DC: American Council on Education.

or they could be designed in a way that gives them wide applicability across different content areas of the curriculum.

Content Standards. Are current efforts to identify content standards for the curriculum helpful in our quest to ensure the proper place of content in the school experience? The answer is that it depends. Taba's ideas on content organization might show us how standards might prove to be either an advantage or a hindrance. We should ask, for instance, whether content standards help to identify key ideas and facts to be used in the learning experience and whether they yield concepts that provide some center of gravity for the content across the grade levels. We should also ask whether certain modes of thinking particular to disciplines are promoted via standards. And we would be remiss if we did not question whether standards produced side effects that are less than good for the curriculum.

Without question, content standards are meant to set a direction for curriculum content. Some standards advocates want them set at a national level, while others, understanding the decentralized nature of the public school system, would prefer to see them set at the state level. And interestingly, some states, such as Iowa, mandate standards but see their development as an exclusively local concern. Most of the arguments in support of standards speak to public accountability. Advocates of standards assert that the skills and knowledge that reside in the normative agenda of the school (common knowledge in math, science, and literature as well as the common skills of reading, numeracy, and writing) should be identified, codified, integrated in the curricula of all schools. Such skills and knowledge, they argue, should be tested and the results made public. Such desire for accountability is motivated by anxiety over the national implications of low achievement in the normative agenda, as well as over equity concerns and the possibility that certain school districts, absent the strong arm of standards, will deny certain children the opportunity to learn key knowledge and skills (Ravitch, 1995).

Our concern here is about whether content standards can fulfill the obligation to frame curriculum content. We should understand that most content standards are rarely only content standards. Often they are accompanied by what are known as performance and proficiency standards. Content standards are simple enough, outlining what should be taught. But when accompanied by performance and proficiency standards, content standards take on a different life in the curriculum. Performance standards describe how students will show that they achieved the content standards, and proficiency standards provide criteria with which to measure the degree of performance progress. It is important to note that content standards, when tied to performance and proficiency standards, begin to do more than simply outline curriculum content. They actually begin to get tied into ways of testing. This raises the possibility that the content standard could become less important than the proficiency standard, causing the teacher to look first to the test rather than to the content. The ultimate effect is that the potential for more varied and responsive instruction is weakened.

Can the curriculum worker at least use content standards to organize the content of the curriculum? In most cases, content standards adequately cover the general facts, ideas, concepts, and thinking modes of various subject areas. But to organize content with more specificity, some states use a style of standard-setting known as benchmarks. The content standards reflect basic ideas, while benchmarks, which accompany the standards, articulate what the student should be able to know and do. This could prove to be quite helpful for teachers as they develop instructional objectives, but because the benchmarks tend to target specific elements, they take some flexibility out of the process of defining purposes. Benchmarks also can be easily converted into test items that could, in the end, set the conditions for a test-driven curriculum.

A select section of the National History Standards (National Center for History in the Schools, 1996; shown in Table 4.4) demonstrates the utility of setting content standards. The standards are aligned with some of the content levels discussed by Taba. One overarching concept for the history curriculum in grades 5–12 is "Revolution and the New Nation (1754–1820s)," which focuses on the causes of the American Revolution, the reasons for the American victory, the impact of the revolution, and the institutions created at the time that provided some foundation for the new American nation. The concept helps to orchestrate the content of the history curriculum, much in the style of a fugue, as each grade level embraces some variation on a common conceptual theme. The actual content standards themselves reside within these common concepts and are largely stated as basic ideas. Thus, a standard such as "students [will] understand the causes of the American Revolution, the principles articulated in the Declaration of Independence, and the factors affecting the course of the war and

TABLE 4.4   Content Standards and Content Levels

CONCEPTS USED FOR VERTICAL ARTICULATION IN THE U.S. HISTORY
STANDARDS FOR GRADES 5–12

Revolution and the New Nation

BASIC IDEAS USED TO CONSTRUCT CONTENT STANDARDS

- The student understands:
  - The causes of the American Revolution.
  - The principles articulated in the Declaration of Independence.
  - The factors affecting the course of the war and contributing to the American victory.

FACTS AND INFORMATION EMBODIED IN A DESCRIPTION OF
THE BENCHMARK

- The student is able to:
  - Explain the consequences of the Seven Years War and the overhaul of English imperial policy following the Treaty of Paris in 1763.
  - Reconstruct the chronology of the critical events leading to the outbreak of armed conflict between the American colonies and England.
  - Explain the major ideas expressed in the Declaration of Independence and their intellectual origins.
  - Explain how key principles in the Declaration of Independence grew in importance to become unifying ideas of American democracy.
  - Appraise George Washington's military and political leadership in conducting the Revolutionary War.
  - Compare and explain the different roles and perspectives in the war of men and women, including white settlers, free and and enslaved African Americans, and Native Americans.

the eventual American victory" is really a commitment to teaching basic ideas, within which many different content possibilities can be found. The history benchmarks, however, specify the point of direction, stipulating that students (again, grades 5–12) should be able to "explain the consequences of the Seven Years War and the overhaul of English policy following the treaty of Paris in 1763, explain how the key principles in the Declaration of Independence grew in importance to become unifying ideas of American democracy, and appraise George

Washington's military and political leadership in conducting the Revolutionary War." Because these benchmarks discuss knowledge of the Seven Years War, the Treaty of Paris, the principles of the Declaration of Independence, and details related to Washington's political and military leadership, we might then organize our content thusly: "students will know and understand the Seven Years War, the Treaty of Paris, the principles of the Declaration of Independence, and details related to Washington's political and military leadership." Such standards could articulate an even more refined factual mandate. So, when it comes to content standards, there is some play in the level of factual specificity that gets articulated.

As indicated earlier, content standards could also make some reference to specific modes of thinking. When that happens, our standards and benchmarks target process more than content. Content standards for the science curriculum, for instance, often sound more like process standards, as is the case with some of the National Science Education Standards (National Committee on Science Education Standards and Assessment, 1996), which underscore understanding the processes of scientific investigation and the actual design, conduct, and evaluation of such investigations. The content standard, in this case, is targeted at abilities and understanding tied to scientific inquiry. We will not find references to facts or information but references instead to matters of process, such as (in grades 9–12), "identifying questions and concepts that guide scientific investigations; designing and conducting scientific investigations; formulating and revising scientific explanations and models using logic and evidence; recognizing and analyzing alternative explanations and models, and communicating and defending a scientific argument." Similarly, the National History Standards make it a point to identify "historical thinking standards," which include chronological thinking, skills in historical comprehension, interpretation, and analysis, as well as historical decision making. The benchmarks for chronological thinking, for grades 5–12, include items such as "distinguishing between past, present, and future time, identifying the temporal structure of historical narrative, establishing temporal order in historical narrative, measuring and calculating time, interpreting data presented in time lines, reconstructing patterns of historical succession and comparing models of periodization." As these examples make clear, content can be constructed as a mode of thinking inherent to a discipline or to a particular form of inquiry or study.

In some cases, an entire discipline of study could be interpreted as a skill-based one. Thus, the content of the subject does not boil down, in the end, to the acquisition of facts and information, but to the application of certain skills. This is especially the case for reading and other language arts subjects; thus, reading and writing, pervasive skills that cut across the curriculum, can be designed in a way that is especially suitable for the specialized reading or specialized writing teacher. The New Jersey Core Curriculum Standards for Language Arts (New Jersey Department of Education, 1998) show that the "content" of the language arts can be largely skill based. Some of the basic reading curriculum concepts include phonological awareness, decoding and word recognition, fluency, reading strategies, vocabulary development, and comprehension skills. These concepts yield different reading standards for different grade levels. As Table 4.5 (pp. 118–120) demonstrates, the content for the language arts in grades 7 and 8, as it relates to reading, is decidedly skill based and designed for the specialized language arts teachers, as it relates to writing.

Bringing the Two Dimensions Together

To recall Tyler's earlier advice, the most useful form of objective identifies the behavior to be developed, which is articulated by the curriculum as a pervasive skill, and the content area in which this behavior takes place. These two dimensions eventually have to be synthesized into working objectives for the teacher.

So, to encourage the development of thinking or communication skills, educators have to simultaneously think about the content that will accompany such an undertaking. Tyler (1949) recommends a graphic representation that sets off the two dimensions in a way that allows teachers to begin to consider both in the construction of their microcurricular objectives. Thus, if the high school curriculum dedicates a course to the study of government, the course also will be expected to take on some of the pervasive behavioral skills discussed earlier. Let's say it chooses a uniquely patterned set of seven key skills areas: thinking, writing, listening and speaking, expression, inquiry, study, and interpersonal relations. This choice would result from a macrocurricular discussion that ensures a balanced and well-distributed treatment of key behavioral skills across the whole school curriculum. But we are only halfway there, as the course must also reflect some position on the content aspect of the objective. Here the course designer could use the district's content standards or some other form of content organization that follows the four levels discussed by Taba. The course might start with the structure and purpose of government and deal with topics: the essential characteristics of various systems of government from both historical and contemporary perspective; the distribution of powers in government; the organization and function of local, state, and national government; the responsibilities of the national government for domestic and foreign policy; and the financing of government through taxation. Now both dimensions of the objective are clarified for the teacher.

The intersections in the chart essentially represent instructional opportunities to teach x content in relation to x behavior. It also acts as a kind of accountability instrument by visually demonstrating what content and what behavior was covered in the course of the school experience. Discussion returns to the two-dimensional chart in Chapter 6 (see Fig. 6.1, p. 161), which addresses instructional judgments.

Finally, it should be made clear that the two-dimensional chart cannot capture the entirety of the curriculum. The chart structures the school experience and helps to keep activity on track and accountable to macro purposes, but

TABLE 4.5   Skill-Based Content Standards in the Language Arts Curriculum

<table>
<tr><th colspan="5" align="center">GRADES 7–8</th></tr>
<tr><th></th><th colspan="2">READING</th><th colspan="2">WRITING</th></tr>
<tr>
<td>Concepts
About
Print/Text</td>
<td colspan="2">1. Identify and use common textual and graphic features and organizational structures to comprehend information. These include: textual features (e.g., paragraphs, topic sentence, index, table of contents); graphic features (e.g., charts, maps, diagrams); and organizational structure; (e.g., logical order, comparison/ contrast, cause/effect).</td>
<td>Writing as a Process (pre- writing, draft- ing, revising, editing, post- writing)</td>
<td>1. Engage in the full writing process (from prewriting through post- writing) by writing daily and for sustained amounts of time.
2. Revise drafts by revealing for meaning, narrowing focus, elabo- rating, deleting, reorganizing, cre- ating sentence variety as needed, maintaining consistency of voice, and reworking introductions, transitions, conclusions, and awk- ward passages.
3. Review and edit work for spelling, usage, clarity, organiza- tion, and fluency.
4. Demonstrate understanding of a scoring rubric to improve and evaluate writing.
5. Compose, revise, edit, and pub- lish writing using appropriate word processing software.</td>
</tr>
<tr>
<td>Decoding
and Word
Recognition</td>
<td colspan="2">1. Distinguish among the spellings of homophones (e.g., cite, site, and sight).
2. Apply spelling rules that aid in correct spelling.
3. Continue to use structural analysis and context analysis to decode new words.</td>
<td>Writing as a Product (prewriting in a formal product or publication)</td>
<td>1. Extend knowledge of specific characteristics, structures, and appropriate voice and tone of se- lected genres and use this knowl- edge in creating written work, considering the purpose, audi- ence, and context of the writing.
2. Write pieces that contain narra- tive elements, such as short sto- ries, biography, autobiography, or memoir.
3. Write reports and subject- appropriate nonfiction pieces across the curriculum based on research and including citations, quotations, and a bibli- ography or works cited page.
4. Write a range of essays, including persuasive, descriptive, personal, or issue-based.</td>
</tr>
</table>

TABLE 4.5   Continued

	GRADES 7–8		
	READING		**WRITING**
Fluency	1. Read aloud in selected texts reflecting understanding of the text and engaging the listener. 2. Read increasingly difficult texts silently with comprehension and fluency. 3. Apply self-correcting strategies automatically to decode and gain meaning from print both orally and silently.	Mechanics, Spelling, and Handwriting	1. Use Standard English conventions in all writing (sentence structure, grammar and usage, punctuation, capitalization, spelling). 2. Use a variety of sentence types correctly, including combinations of independent and dependent clauses, prepositional and adverbial phrases, and varied sentence openings to develop a lively and effective personal style. 3. Understand and use parallelism, including similar grammatical forms, to present items in a series or to organize ideas for emphasis. 4. Experiment in using subordination, coordination, apposition, and other devices to indicate relationships between ideas. 5. Use transition words to reinforce a logical progression of ideas.
Reading Strategies (before, during, and after reading)	1. Monitor reading for understanding by automatically setting a purpose for reading, asking essential questions, and relating new learning to background experiences. 2. Use increasingly complex text guides, maps, charts, and graphs to assist with reading comprehension.	Writing Forms, Audiences, and Purposes (exploring a variety of forms)	1. Gather, select, and organize the most effective information appropriate to a topic, task, and audience. 2. Apply knowledge and strategies for composing pieces in a variety of genres (narrative, expository, persuasive, poetic, and everyday/workplace or technical writing, etc.). 3. Write responses to literature and develop insights into interpretations by connecting to personal experiences and referring to textual information. 4. Write personal narratives, short stories, memoirs, poetry, and

(continued)

TABLE 4.5   Continued

GRADES 7–8			
READING		**WRITING**	
			persuasive and expository text that relate clear, coherent events or situations through the use of specific details.
			5. Use narrative and descriptive writing techniques (e.g., dialogue, sensory words and phrases, background information, thoughts and feelings of characters, and comparison and contrast of characters).
Vocabulary and Concept Development	1. Develop an extended vocabulary through both listening and reading independently. 2. Clarify word meanings through the use of a word's definition, example, restatement, or contrast. 3. Clarify pronunciations, meanings, alternate word choice, parts of speech, and etymology of words using the dictionary, thesaurus, glossary, and technology resources. 4. Expand reading vocabulary by identifying and correctly using idioms and words with literal and figurative meanings in their speaking and writing experiences.	Writing Forms, Audiences, and Purposes (exploring a variety of forms)	1. Gather, select, and organize the most effective information appropriate to a topic, task, and audience. 2. Apply knowledge and strategies for composing pieces in a variety of genres (narrative, expository, persuasive, poetic, and everyday/workplace or technical writing, etc.). 3. Write responses to literature and develop insights into interpretations by connecting to personal experiences and referring to textual information. 4. Write personal narratives, short stories, memoirs, poetry, and persuasive and expository text that relate clear, coherent events or situations through the use of specific details. 5. Use narrative and descriptive writing techniques (e.g., dialogue, sensory words and phrases, background information, thoughts and feelings of characters, and comparison and contrast of characters).

anyone who has ever been in the class will know that much of what an educator does is not always rationalized by objectives. Sometimes emergent things happen in the classroom that stem from an interest in exploration, having fun, or otherwise responding to a situation or problem that was not anticipated in the moving objectives of the curriculum. Eisner calls such emergent activities *expressive outcomes*. We cannot rely on expressive outcomes in the curriculum; they are too idiosyncratic. But we should honor them as important factors—born of teacher intelligence and creativity—in a child's education. Chapter 6 addresses this topic.

SUMMARY

When we define the main purposes of the school, we create the main engine for the curriculum. Curriculum developers are wise to begin this process by thinking widely about the comprehensive agenda of public education and relating it to the priorities of the local school. Articulating the school's mission statement puts the whole process into motion. If citizenship for instance, truly means something in the school, it should be boldly declared in the mission statement, giving the school the impetus needed to define the appropriate aims, goals, and objectives in the curriculum. The school cannot conduct itself consciously or deliberately without using some matrix to do this. These three iterations of purpose are used to channel teacher judgment and to refine the conceptual lines within which objectives can be flexible, open to modification, and helpful in focusing the application of teacher artistry. The best matrix of objectives is general in its outlook and is inclusive of both behavioral and content ingredients.

The translation of purposes into working objectives for teachers is most easily accomplished by considering a two-dimensional approach that insists on blending pervasive skills with specific content areas. Pervasive skills are those behaviors, skills, and values that pervade all features of the curriculum (thinking, communicating, inquiring, listening, studying, and so forth). Content standards can be used to organize the subject-matter side of the objective, but we must be wary of the connection content standards often have to standardized tests—one that can result in stripping the gears of purpose in the curriculum (while replacing them with a mandate to raise test scores). Ideally, an organizational scheme of the content in some way integrates Taba's four levels of content, which include the treatment of facts as investments in ideas that are themselves organized within larger concepts and the distillation of distinctive or discipline-bound modes of thinking or modes of inquiry. So, the defining of purpose in the school ultimately boils down to producing some sketch of the behaviors, skills, values, and content desired in the school and setting the conditions for these factors to be instructionally managed in some coherent and consistent manner. This latter concern is the topic of the next chapter.

DISCUSSION QUESTIONS AND SUGGESTED ACTIVITIES

1. Select a mission statement from a school or school district and evaluate how effectively it conveys its mission. What in the statement, if anything, clearly speaks to purposes that could unify the school? How satisfied are you with the actual statement of purpose as it might relate to the comprehensive agenda of the school? What might be missing in the mission and what in it might strike you as unnecessary or gratuitous?

2. Consider the metaphor that likens the framing of aims, goals, and objectives to setting targets. Where are the flaws in the metaphor? Can you think of a better one?

3. If the design of the school is, as indicated in Chapter One, to simplify the school experience, how can we then reconcile Dewey's point that one of the key factors in the design of school objectives is to free or release activities?

4. What is the essential message sent to the curriculum developer in Dewey's "criteria for good aims"?

5. Why does Tyler advise that the design of curriculum objectives should err on the side of generality rather than specificity? And how does this relate to the need to state clear and useful objectives?

6. How might you design the pervasive skills of thinking in the curriculum for a fourth grade classroom? Will you try to include Bloom's taxonomy, some expression of creative thinking skills or even use thinking skills that describe a decision-making process?

7. What might it mean to teachers whose content obligations in algebra require them to cover a set of pervasive inquiry skills?

8. Examine the mission statement of a charter or an alternative school. Separate the purposes that relate to outcomes from those that relate to process or method. To what extent does this mission accord with the three factors in the educational process?

9. Study a collection of objectives used in a school curriculum. How would you judge the adequacy of these objectives and how might you find a way to improve them?

10. Examine a set of content standards developed by a state or a professional teacher's organization. To what extent does it reflect Taba's four levels of content?

11. How can content standards help with and/or hinder the task of developing useful curriculum objectives?

12. Explain how reading can be organized as both a pervasive skill and as content in the design of objectives.

13. How does the organization of content factor into the vertical articulation of the school curriculum?

14. What are the main arguments offered in support of and against national content standards?

15. What are expressive outcomes and why are they important for a curriculum developer to understand?

NOTES

Anderson, L.W. & Krathwohl, D.R. (2001). *A taxonomy for learning and assessing: A revision of Bloom's taxonomy of educational objectives.* New York: Longman.

Beauchamp, G.A. (1975). *Curriculum theory* (3rd ed.). Wilmette, IL: Kagg Press.

Dewey, J. (1916). *Democracy and education.* New York: Macmillan Co.

Dressel, P.L. & Mayhew, L.B., (1954). *General education: Explorations in evaluation.* Washington, DC: American Council on Education.

Goodlad, J. (1984). *A place called school.* New York: McGraw-Hill.

Iowa Department of Education. (1989). *A guide to developing higher order thinking across the curriculum.* Des Moines, State Department of Education.

Krug, E. (1950). *Curriculum planning.* New York: Harper and Brothers.

Michaelis, J.U., Grossman, R.H. & Scott, L.F. (1975). *New designs for elementary education curriculum and instruction.* New York: McGraw-Hill.

National Center for History in the Schools. (1996). *National history standards.* Washington, DC: Department of Education.

National Committee on Science Education Standards and Assessment. (1996). *National science education standards.* Washington, DC: National Academy Press.

New Jersey Department of Education. (1998). *New Jersey language arts curriculum framework.* Trenton, NJ: New Jersey Department of Education.

Ravitch, D. (1995). *National standards in American education.* Washington, DC: The Brookings Institution.

Taba, H. (1962). *Curriculum development: Theory and practice.* New York: Harcourt, Brace and Jovanovich.

Tyler, R. (1949). *Basic principles of curriculum and instruction.* Chicago: University of Chicago Press.

Zais, R.S. (1976). *Curriculum: Principles and foundations.* New York: Crowell.

CHAPTER FIVE

ORGANIZING THE MACROCURRICULUM

The environment is whatever conditions interact with personal needs, desires, purposes, and capacities to create the experience that is had. Even when a person builds a castle in the air, he is interacting with the objects that he constructs in his fancy

—John Dewey

Although the missions of public schools vary according to local prerogatives, the public school is usually organized along two key mandates. The first mandate is related to what we call general education, which represents a commitment to common educational experiences and the learning of common skills, knowledge, and values. This is what we typically associate with the normative agenda— the obligatory common learnings for all youth. Obviously, the teaching of literacy and numeracy skills applies here, as does the teaching of various other requisite skills, such as critical thinking, a range of communication skills, and general inquiry or research skills. The common core also embraces common ethical values as well as an exposure to common knowledge. And although such a process is committed to amalgamating the student population along a core foundation of skills, knowledge, and values, it does not mean that diversity issues are ignored. The common experience, in fact, should also represent an enlarging experience, where school children look toward a new horizon of ideas and gain encounters with peers who bring different views of the world with them to school.

The second key mandate has to do with encouraging individual development. The school must, through instruction, address a wide range of individual interests, talents, and needs. So, in the curriculum design, some of its organizational structure must provide for specific experiences directly responsive to individual interests, career goals, aptitudes, and special needs. Because the coursework justified under this mandate aims to specialize the educational experience of the individual, we refer to it as *specialized education.*

The dual mandate in the macrocurriculum (general education and specialized education) is useful in that every school with a mission likely has a sense of what it values in the common education of its charges as well as what it values in the more individualized side of the curriculum. I am going to use the ideas of general education and specialized education to demonstrate how they can be applied as overarching structures for the organization of school purposes in the macrocurriculum. And because the school curriculum also advances its causes outside of the classroom, I am also going to discuss the role that extra-classroom experiences can play in the organization of the macrocurriculum.

GENERAL EDUCATION AND SPECIALIZED EDUCATION

The design of both the general and specialized education phases of the curriculum is centered on the task of translating the overarching purposes of the school into some structure for coursework. At the high school and middle school levels, for instance, questions arise about what coursework will be required in general education, what percentage of the school program will be taken up with such requirements, and how essential subject matter and skills within and between courses will be organized. Complicating matters are issues related to curriculum tracking and other forms of curriculum differentiation. At the same time, the middle school and high school curricula might seek to offer experiences tailored to the individual, such as special advanced-placement courses, various elective courses, career-based or vocational studies, and extra-classroom experiences responsive to specific talents and interests. At the elementary school, similar questions appear. For instance, will the teaching of reading and mathematics, both of which fall under the purview of general education, be differentiated? Will general education be block-scheduled into the self-contained classroom or will some between-class ability grouping or subject compartmentalization prevail? And just how will the individualized phase of the curriculum be handled in the elementary school?

At the high school level, partial answers to these questions can be found in state directives that obligate the school to teach a certain body of knowledge. Most states retain course area requirements for high school graduation, stipulating exposure to a list of four or five core subject areas (commonly the language arts, social studies, mathematics, science, and physical education/health, Fig. 5.1). These are typically expressed as Carnegie unit requirements. One Carnegie unit represents a 120-hour instructional obligation to a subject area over the course of an

State	English	Math	Science	Social Studies	Health/PE
Alabama	4	4	4	4	1.5
Alaska	4	2	2	3	1
Arizona	4	2	2	2.5	0
Arkansas	4	3	3	3	1
California	3	2	2	3	2
Colorado	1	1	1	1	1
Connecticut	4	3	2	3	1
Delaware	4	3	3	3	1.5
Florida	4	3	3	2.5	1
Georgia	4	3	3	3	1
Hawaii	4	3	3	4	2
Idaho	4	2	2	2	1.5
Illinois	3	2	1	2	4.5
Indiana	4	4	4	3	1
Iowa	—	—	—	1.5	—
Kansas	4	2	2	3	1
Kentucky	4	3	2	2	1
Louisiana	4	3	3	3.5	2
Maine	4	2	2	2	1.5
Maryland	4	3	2	3	1
Massachusetts	—	—	—	1	4
Michigan	—	—	—	—	—
Minnesota	—	—	—	—	—
Mississippi	4	2	2	2	—
Missouri	4	3	2	3	1
Montana	4	2	2	2	1
Nebraska	—	—	—	—	—
Nevada	4	2	2	2	2.5
New Hampshire	4	2	2	2	1.25
New Jersey	4	3	2	3	4
New Mexico	4	3	2	3	1

FIGURE 5.1 **High School Graduation Requirements: Carnegie Units in Curricular Areas**

(continued)

State	English	Math	Science	Social Studies	Health/PE
New York	4	2	2	4	2.5
North Carolina	4	3	3	3	1
North Dakota	4	2	2	3	1
Ohio	3	2	1	2	1
Oklahoma	4	3	2	2	0
Oregon	3	2	2	3.5	2
Pennsylvania	4	3	3	3	1
Rhode Island	4	3	2	2	—
South Carolina	4	4	4	4	1
South Dakota	4	2	2	3	—
Tennessee	4	3	3	3	1
Texas	4	3	3	4	2
Utah	3	2	2	3	2
Vermont	4	0 to 5	0 to 5	3	1.5
Virginia	4	3	3	3	2
Washington	3	2	2	2.5	2
West Virginia	4	2	2	3	2
Wisconsin	4	2	2	3	2
Wyoming	4	2	2	3	—
District of Columbia	4	3	3	3	1.5

FIGURE 5.1   Continued

academic year. This usually means that a subject area will be taught regularly—say, 40 minutes per day—during a 35-week academic year. But because these requirements are listed as subject areas, they do not necessarily translate into common core experiences in high schools, although they can. Carnegie unit requirements can be fulfilled, for instance, through a menu of courses sorted by ability level.

General education in high schools is also very much influenced by the admissions requirements of universities, which typically set a higher standard than do the states. Public schools are often motivated to teach those skills that universities want to see in high school graduates, even if some students may not choose to attend college. Thus, the general education phase of the high school curriculum tends to follow a subject matter form that approximates both state graduation requirements and college admission standards. And what is interesting about this pattern is not only what it includes but also what it excludes. One will not likely find, for instance, many requirements for studies in art, music, or vocational education, and only recently have states begun to think about mandating a technology or computer science course requirement. It is surprising to note the scarcity of government and citizenship requirements.

But there are still more curriculum design possibilities for general education in high school. A school with a sense of itself (with a strongly worded mission) might choose to reflect unique patterns of emphasis in its coursework. Because state graduation requirements usually define only a minimum level of achievement, and because college admissions standards are primarily concerned with academic studies, the school's curriculum could specify other types of common experiences. General education in some schools, whether they be comprehensive high school or specialized ones, might require coursework in vocational, citizenship, technological, or sociopersonal domains, for example, none of which might be identified by state requirements or college admission standards. Or, a curriculum might highlight an interdisciplinary course, such as a Problems of Democracy, an issue-centered course on understanding the relationship between science, technology, and society, or a social issues course with a community outreach component. More innovative approaches to general education in the secondary school are more probable in states with fewer and more flexible regulations for graduation. In Iowa, for instance, where the relation between the state and local school districts is permissive, the possibilities for unique and locally inspired general education designs are greater than in more regulatory states, such as Texas or North Carolina.

The balance between the function of general education and specialized education is different at the elementary school level. The elementary school classroom is almost entirely dedicated to general education, meaning that virtually everything taught in the elementary school classroom is appropriate for the education of all youth. But here any efforts to respond to individual differences and needs are largely made in the context of general education, and are left to the discretion of the classroom teacher. This is another way of saying that an effort to respond to individual interests, talents, and needs in the elementary school, is expected to arise not from particularized coursework but from the discretionary judgment of the classroom teacher, usually working in a self-contained setting. Specialized education is therefore embedded in the structure of elementary school general education. Of course, the education of special needs children is an exception to the rule, although the mainstreaming mandate still keeps many children in the general education setting. One could also find specialized pull-out programs for children documented as gifted and talented or for children requiring English-as-a-Second-Language (ESL) instruction. But otherwise, the specialized education function of the elementary school curriculum becomes an instructional and pedagogical matter that resides in the hands of the classroom teacher, who might use ability groupings, special assignments, and self-instructional methods, among other things, to cope with individual student differences.

At the middle school level, however, specialized education becomes a course-level concern. This change has to do with the fact that the self-contained classroom is dropped in favor of separate classrooms compartmentalized by subject areas and taught by teachers with particularized subject-level training. General education also moves into this more subject-centered landscape, where each subject area comprises specific courses and specialized teachers. Thus, in the middle school, the organization of the macrocurriculum's structure has to account for both general and specialized education coursework separately. The latter can be further divided into exploratory studies, which aim to respond to and broaden interest levels, and enrichment studies, which aim to respond to aptitude and achievement concerns. Because middle schools see themselves as designed to be attentive to preadolescent needs, they usually put quite a premium on exploratory studies.

But a middle school's general education design is not as subject centered and requirement bound as that of the high school. One should remember that, unlike the historical junior high school, the middle school typically does not see a place for the ninth grade in its structure. This liberates it from the college preparatory influences and state graduation requirements that accompany ninth grade coursework.

The relation between general and specialized education is most complex at the high school level. First, as mentioned, general education in the secondary school is usually the vehicle used to fulfill core graduation requirements. So, if the school mandates four Carnegie units (four academic years) of mathematics, then the general education phase will likely contain the courses needed to fulfill such a requirement. But just how this takes shape will vary according to the school's conception of general education. A four-year requirement in mathematics might be fulfilled through a menu of ability-grouped mathematics courses, through four levels of a common unified math course, or through some combination of the two. Thus, general education might be viewed as simply representing a set of common skills and knowledge taught in ability-based settings at different speeds (and perhaps with different modes of extension and enrichment) or as a common unified experience highlighting the teaching of common skills and knowledge. This difference in outlook is the difference between conceiving of general education as common experiences and or as common requirements.

Curriculum developers working in high schools, of course, can also get creative with general education and design it in a way that resonates with a unique feature of their mission or in a way that results in interdisciplinary offerings. But the organizational pattern must balance general education with the emergence of the specialized education phase of the secondary school curriculum. Thus, in the name of specialized education, we might find an expansive network of elective courses in the high school expressly designed to meet and expand various individual interest levels. Some of these courses might even be tied to club or extra-classroom activities. A speech and debate course could be tied to participating on the speech and debate team, or an acting course to participating in the school play. Also in the name of specialized education, we might find a network of honors and advanced placement (AP) courses expressly designed to give students with college ambitions (or students with a deeper level of commitment to a particular area of study) a more advanced academic learning experience. Advanced placement courses can be seen as part of the specialized education phase of the curriculum, but because they are sometimes interchangeable with courses in general education (one can fulfill a general education requirement in science with AP biology), one could also categorize AP courses as general education offerings. Hence, we encounter the collision in the high school of the common agenda (general education) with the individualizing agenda (specialized education), which is a design problem requiring some resolution. One way to reconcile the conflict is to identify general education as common experiences rather than as common requirements, making a clear separation between the courses that qualify as general education and those that qualify as specialized education. And specialized education, we must not forget, can also be used to realize a specialized program of studies in vocational education for students who may not have college ambitions.

As Figure 5.2 demonstrates, the relation between general and specialized education changes as students move through the grade-level structure of school

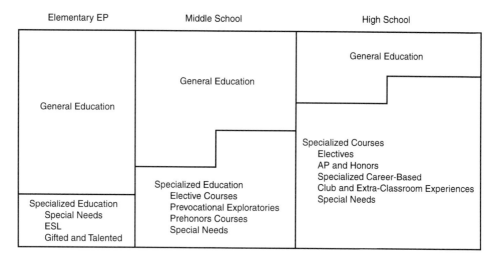

FIGURE 5.2   The Shifting Balance Between General Education and Specialized Education

Source: Adapted from D. Tanner & L. Tanner. (1986). *Supervision in education: Problems & practice.* Upper Saddle River, NJ: Pearson Education, Inc.

systems. In elementary school, general education is essentially the main business of the school. Everything that occurs in the elementary school classroom, with a few exceptions, is conducted in a common place (the self-contained classroom) and in relation to a common basis of skills, knowledge, and values. Where individualizing issues arise, they are placed almost entirely on the shoulders of the classroom teacher, whose job is to react instructionally to a wide range of interest, aptitude, and achievement levels. In the middle school, specialized education becomes more of a structural matter in the curriculum, as it begins to manifest as coursework that aims to offer new exploratory and enrichment possibilities for preadolescent students. Because the pressures of college-admission and state-graduation requirements generally do not apply to the middle school, general education in this setting has its best odds of producing a locally derived vision of a common educational experience. In high school, however, specialized education takes on more prominence. General education still has an important place in the high school curriculum, but the proportion of resources and time given to it begins to diminish because of the growing role of specialization in the curriculum. The need to offer college preparatory coursework and vocational education (for those not destined for college) exerts a powerful specializing pressure, as does the mandate to further extend exploratory and enrichment studies. Even general education tends to collapse into specialized subject-centered coursework that fulfill graduation and college-admission requirements.

HORIZONTAL AND VERTICAL ARTICULATION

Before we begin to put the pieces together for the coursework in the macrocurriculum, we need to reintroduce the idea of horizontal and vertical articulation. The structure of the macrocurriculum represents a kind of sinew in the body of the curriculum that binds experiences across and within grade levels. As a result, the curriculum developer has to make all the coursework fit together and cohere over time. This is known as *articulation*, and we think of it in two ways.

The first has to do with how everything fits together within a grade level, usually over the course of an academic year. Because curriculum developers often use a two-dimensional scheme to organize the macrocurriculum, they identify the act of coordinating intra-grade concerns as a horizontal articulation exercise and place it on a horizontal axis. If we think about scope and sequence as a horizontal articulation concern, we are thinking about how school work done early in the academic year will logically flow into work done later in the year, or about how the behavioral side of our objectives (thinking and so forth) will change over the course of an aca-demic year to reflect increasing developmental capacities. Whenever we think about the order of educational events and the range of expansion on key ideas, concepts, and content taught within a grade level, we are working on the horizontal axis. Horizontal articulation, however, also helps us to manage the obligations that different courses have in relation to the overarching purposes of the school and to consider how the full complement of courses within a grade level is balanced. Thus, from the standpoint of horizontal articulation, we ask how instruction justified as social studies might relate to instruction justified as language arts in a particular grade. In the elementary school, the teacher might very well look to articulate these studies, using, say, literary readings in language arts in relation to a topical area of study in the social studies. Courses in physics and calculus are typically taught in the same grade in high school because they complement each other. If we support the teaching of a certain set of thinking, communication, and inquiry skills, we have to understand just which courses will make a claim to these skills and if the overall composite of courses effectively fulfills the school's mission. All of these matters are articulated as horizontal or intra-grade concerns.

Vertical articulation, conversely, reflects cross-grade concerns. In other words, how does the teaching of math in seventh grade relate to the teaching of math in eighth grade? Vertical articulation build's coherence in students' educational experience over the course of their entire school career, by defining prerequisites, as well as scope and sequence. The science curriculum in an elementary school will certainly utilize key principles and concepts that transcend grade levels. Reading instruction, too, will follow a course of identifiable skills across grades—those related to, say, phonemic awareness, vocabulary development, narratives gauged by readability variables, and so forth.

An interesting feature of articulation in the curriculum is that it mostly refers to content structures. The scope and sequence of the curriculum obviously must account for a changing and developing sense of pervasive skills but much of the organizational structure of the curriculum is built with the brick and mortar of subject matter. In skill-based subjects, such as reading and math, the organizational structure is well delineated and often uses a spiral design, where children return to concepts and skills repeatedly at a higher and higher level of sophistication and abstraction. Tellingly, even content standards in the curriculum often have a sense of scope and sequence to them that can prove quite useful in giving structure to the curriculum.

Posner and Rudnitsky (1997) have identified some organizational principles that can be used to design the scope and sequence of curriculum content. The first, *world-related sequences*, organize the content of the curriculum around the characteristics of space, time, or physical attributes. The use of a chronological sequence, which would likely be favored in a history class, is an example of a world-related sequence because it uses the attribute of time (from earliest to latest) to organize the content. Sequencing content around spatial relations means that the organization of the content can be broached from the standpoint of, say, closest to farthest, bottom to top, or east to west. The vertical articulation of social studies education in the elementary school, for instance, commonly begins with the study of the home in the early grades (drawing on the life experience of the child) and gradually extending the experience outward (as the children grow and mature) into community, town, city, state, nation, and the world. The study of the food chain in science might be approached using a bottom- (of the food chain) to-top sequence and the study of the regions of the United States using an east-to-west approach. Physical attributes, such as size, shape, and range of physical complexity, might also be used. So, in biology class, the study of simple cells could precede the study of more complex ones; the study of elements might be preliminary to the study of compounds in chemistry; the study of the American Civil War can be organized around the size of the major battles; and in geometry, lines might get taught before shapes.

But world-related sequences may not always be desirable. The curriculum developer might find that a more concept-related approach is best (Posner and Rudnitsky, 1997). Here the content is organized around the structure of ideas. Subject matter is sequenced by the use of logical prerequisites, levels of sophistication, and categories of class relations. The logical prerequisite approach is built on the presupposition that some ideas are preliminary to others and need to be taught first. Posner and Rudnitsky give the example of needing to teach the concept of velocity prior to teaching the concept of acceleration, because the latter cannot be understood without first understanding the former. Skill-based content areas, such as reading, mathematics, and foreign languages tend to use this structure because of the highly defined and hierarchical nature of the subject matter.

The content of the curriculum can also be patterned after the principle of sophistication, which gives justification to arranging or sequencing content by using a simple-to-complex or a concrete-to-abstract pattern, both of which demonstrate the idea of using simple tasks as subordinate parts to more complex tasks.

Class relations implies a deductive whole-to-part pattern of sequencing that starts with class characteristics and moves to specific examples of the class. Thus, democracy is studied as a concept and followed by particular examples of working democracies. In science, the classification systems used to organize living things (amphibians, reptiles, mammals, fish, and so forth) might be studied first, followed by examples of animals that represent each system.

All kinds of other organizational possibilities are also in play. And many of the best ones arise from the emergent judgment of teachers and curriculum developers. So, in history class, one creative way to organize to the content might be to go in reverse chronological order, or a social studies class might start with the specific and move to the general (Poser and Rudnitsky, 1997).

Interestingly, content organization is not always a classroom teacher's major concern because it is more often decided by state-mandated content standards, which are often designed with scope and sequence considerations in mind. One of the main vehicles used to cinch the place of content standards in the curriculum is the textbook, which continues to be designed by commercial publishers around state content standards. But for the curriculum developer, content scope and sequence is still a matter that can lead to any number of innovative learning experiences keenly responsive to the school's stated mission and purposes.

What about the behavioral side of our curriculum equation? Do we have to concern ourselves with scope and sequence concerns in the behavioral realm of thinking, communication, inquiring, and studying? Naturally, there are some scope-and-sequence concerns here, but they are largely learner related and instructional in orientation. Developmental differences across and even within grade levels should remind us to reconceive how we might approach the integration of thinking, communication, and other pervasive skills in the curriculum, and will have some effect on the kind of subject matter brought to the classroom experience. But because the conceptual organizer for the behavioral side of the curriculum is really the developmental nature of the learner, we leave much of this to the judgment of the teacher. The main articulation concern pertaining to the teaching of pervasive skills is to properly dispense the responsibilities across the grade levels, so that each subject area understands its role in the matrix of skills the school seeks to cultivate.

ORGANIZING CONTENT AND COURSES

The organization of subject matter in the school curriculum usually defers to traditional subject-matter lines, leaving the content of the curriculum with a familiar subject-centered profile. Math, science, language arts, and social studies are the main bodies in the general education realm. Elective coursework, justified as exploratory study, often is the only place that turns out anything outside of traditional coursework. This, of course, does not have to be the case. Although schools are increasingly under specializing pressures, determining the organizational form of the content and the courses in the curriculum should be a matter of mission and purpose and thus should not always result in the same configuration of content and courses.

The Carnegie units used to dictate most state graduation requirements speak loudly about the organizational form of the school curriculum. Generally speaking, the American high school is still very much loyal to the classical liberal arts model of subject organization. And the trickle-down effect in the curriculum is obvious; even the teachers working in self-contained elementary classrooms often organize their classrooms along subject matter lines resembling the Carnegie units. This subject-centered orientation to the curriculum is, as indicated, encouraged by external factors, including the fact that middle and secondary school teachers are themselves trained as specialists in a disciplinary field. So, much of the content of the school curriculum is logically linked to traditional disciplinary subject-matter divisions. This is an advantage if specialized academic courses need to be taught or if good justification can otherwise be found to organize content along disciplinary lines. Difficulties, however, emerge when the purpose of the school demands experiences that are not easily accommodated by the traditional boundaries of academic subject matter. This could be especially problematic in the design of general education courses that aim to fulfill purposes related to citizenship, personal development, or vocational skill. So, we will explore other ways to organize subject matter.

Patterns of Content Organization

Daniel and Laurel Tanner (1992) have helped to distill several alternatives to the disciplinary organization of curriculum content. They have categorized at least four alternative patterns of organization, known as correlation, fusion, broad fields, and the integrated core (see Fig. 5.3). Each moves in a direction away from disciplinarity, although some of the schemes still retain their traditional subject boundaries. The movement away from disciplinarity, it should be said, is simultaneously a movement in the direction of general education. The models we will be discussing are especially suitable for general education as a designed common experience, although they are not exclusive to them. They sometimes call for a team-teaching arrangement but can also be used in a self-contained classroom or even in a separate specialized classroom, but only with careful articulation agreements between teachers. The intention of the alternative patterns of organization is to try to overcome the limitations of compartmentalization and to allow for a more interdisciplinary and issue-centered

Description	Organizational Scheme
Maintaining discipline-centered lines of organization	DISCIPLINARITY
Combining two or more studies, while still retaining disciplinary lines	CORRELATION
Combining two or more studies into a new synthesis	FUSION
Combining two or more studies into a synthesis across an entire branch of knowledge	BROAD FIELDS
Dissolving subject matter lines in favor of issue and problem-centered focal points of organization	INTEGRATED CORE

FIGURE 5.3 **Patterns of Content Organization**

treatment of subject matter in the curriculum. An interdisciplinary framework is not intrinsically better or worse than a disciplinary framework, but it does provide important flexibility for the curriculum developer who needs to consider a range of ways to organize subject matter in order to match the curriculum experience to school purposes.

One way to begin to break down subject-matter lines in the curriculum is to think about how to develop good horizontal articulation between two or more subjects in the curriculum. The correlated curriculum design does exactly this by seeking some common basis of study between two or more subject areas. In the high school or middle school setting, for instance, some articulation agreement might be made between the teacher of English and the teacher of social studies that results in literary readings associated with topical studies in the social studies. John Steinbeck's *Grapes of Wrath,* for example, might be read in English class while the period of the Great Depression is studied in social studies, or Melba Pattillo Beals's *Warriors Don't Cry* might be correlated with the study of the historical effort to desegregate the public schools in the American south. Great biographical works of key historical figures can be read simultaneously with their treatment in the history classroom, as can other acclaimed nonfictional work, such as *The Diary of Anne Frank.* In the elementary school classroom, teachers, of course, have an ideal opportunity to make such connections themselves because they are responsible for multiple subject areas. They can plan a correlation between language arts and science—or any other subject area—on their own.

Correlations can manifest differently in the curriculum. The *discipline-*centered form matches subject matter deemed essential in one discipline with the study of materials related to that subject in another discipline. So, as we plan to study essential periods of history, we might, as suggested above, ask English teachers to integrate good literary works that parallel these periods. Here the language arts component is correlated to the history component. But we could also, in a less likely scenario, plan to examine certain great literary novels and use history to help explain their importance, focusing on their place in history, on the sociocultural temper of the times in which the works were written, and on various historical conditions that might prevail in the novels. And in this way, two subjects, history and language arts, are correlated.

A unit dedicated to the topical study of crime, economic inequities, racism, environmentalism, or any number of issues could be approached through a correlation. The choice of classroom materials in the separate subject areas would be a reflection of the shared idea being explored. If the topic is racism, we might find ways to design the content so that the English and history teachers alike explore the topic.

When a correlation is brought together under some unifying topic, it usually results in what Daniel and Laurel Tanner (1992) describe as a laminated treatment of subject matter, where each participating subject area has a discrete and independent charge. Rather than bringing some unity of treatment to the topic of, say, environmentalism, each constituent element of the correlation offers a separate unit of experience. So, the student moves from one discrete treatment of environmentalism to another—from the language arts phase, to the mathematical phase, to the science phase, and so forth. Interestingly, some of the earliest efforts at designing interdisciplinary treatments in the curriculum were, in effect, lamination efforts. The American Herbartian movement, for instance, highlighted the importance of singling out a general topic (known as a concentration) on which the entire school, usually an elementary school, would focus its studies. Thus, a school might aim to correlate all of its subject areas to the reading of a single book, such as *Robinson Crusoe*, which was seen, for reasons that are too lengthy to explain here, as the kind of book that could offer something to all subject areas.

The point of the correlated curriculum is to bring together two or more subjects of study into some common contact points. The subject-matter lines retain their place in a correlation but are brought together for a particular time and a particular purpose. In some cases, it can be planned in a team-teaching arrangement or simply be articulated by two or more teachers who share the same students. A correlated curriculum can also be actualized in a block time schedule, which would give more flexibility to the correlation and allow teachers to combine or separate their classes as the educational treatment of the topic might demand.

Whereas the correlated arrangement seeks interrelations between two or more subject areas without losing the distinct elements of the participating subjects, the *fusion* design seeks to bring two or more subject fields (or subfields) together in a way that erases all distinctive lines and essentially merges or blends them into one synthesized subject. So, in a block-scheduled setting, two teachers could combine their resources and know-how in a way that could result in a fused course. The Tanners (1992) use the example of a social statistics course that fuses mathematics with social studies, and brings the study of social problems to light through statistical data that would have to be understood mathematically and that would offer unique possibilities for students to interpret social policy and various social phenomena.

The most common types of fused courses in schools are the ones that unify or blend substudies of a discipline. Thus, we could consider biology a fused course largely because it represents a way to unify knowledge taken from botany, zoology, anatomy, and other subdivisions. A general mathematics course might also qualify as a fused course if it offers an integrated exposure to algebra, geometry, and trigonometry in one continued setting. Language arts in the elementary school is usually approached as a subject area that fuses reading, writing, spelling, speaking, and grammar. And earth science could be seen as uniquely pulling together elements taken from chemistry, geology, and geography. The key to the fusion design is in its unifying structure. If a fused course brings together various elements and treats them separately, the design is not fused. So, if a general mathematics course teaches mathematics, geometry, and algebra as distinctive or self-contained experiences, the course fails to synthesize constituent elements and is better described as the laminated (or layer-cake) approach previously described. The same applies to language arts instruction, which often is approached in a laminated way, with teachers separating instruction in spelling from instruction in grammar and so forth.

Another form of subject organization, known as the *broad fields* approach, seeks an even wider form of integration and synthesis. The broad fields approach projects itself as a way to find some synthesis of content across an entire branch of knowledge. We can find broad fields in any number of configurations in the school curriculum. A course in general science or the social studies certainly qualifies as broad fields. Each brings together a wide spectrum of knowledge from various subdisciplines. The problem is that general science and social studies are rarely taught as singular or unifying courses and are instead often carved into more discipline-centered studies. So, instead of receiving a broad fields exposure to general science, most American high school students take separate courses in biology, chemistry, and physics. And instead of taking a unified course in social studies, most high school students take a range of courses justified as social studies, including history, economics, American studies, and even psychology. In the elementary school, general science and social studies are indeed intended to provide a broad fields treatment of subject matter, but the curriculum sometimes lacks a unifying design that gives way to a laminated approach, so that the various subdisciplines of science are treated as separate and distinctive elements.

The broad fields approach is really a form of fusion that aims across an entire branch of knowledge. But it could also aim to bring together several branches of knowledge. The Tanners cite as an example a course on ecology, one that is organized around subject matter drawn from biology, physics, agriculture, geography, public health, zoology, and others. A course in the humanities might also qualify along these lines because it commits itself to the study of the great achievements of humankind and consequently relates insight and knowledge from multiple studies, including science, literature, art, drama, philosophy, and music. American studies might also be viewed as a broad field that could bring a wide range of studies into a synthesized experience, as the place where music, art, history, science, and literature might all find their way in some combined and coherent form.

Teachers working with a broad fields design must have an interdisciplinary vision. And that is often the very thing lacking in the training of professional educators. Thus, in the middle and high school at least, the broad field design has its best chances of success in a block-schedule pattern, where teachers can work together to find ways to produce a unifying broad fields approach (as opposed to a laminated one). The elementary school teacher, in a way, uses nothing but a broad fields approach. General science, general mathematics, general social studies, and general language arts all pose unique opportunities for broad and integrated coverage of subject matter across an entire branch of knowledge. The reality, however, is that the broad field design in the elementary school often becomes laminated.

Arguably the most radical form of subject organization in the curriculum is known as the *integrated core* curriculum design. The reference to core should make it clear that this is a design especially suited for general education purposes. The core curriculum does indeed target an organization of subject matter that looks to core values and core problems in the living experience of the learner. The effect is that the traditional disciplinary lines of the subject matter are suspended, largely because the problems that take center stage in the integrated core curriculum cannot be logically met by a discipline. The organizational center of the core curriculum transcends subject-matter lines.

In today's climate of mandated content standards, the integrated core is a difficult scheme to justify, mostly because it cannot always align itself with the school's content standards. However, if a school's aim is to offer a general education offering that is patently issue centered, linked closely to the living experience of the children and the community, and committed to engaging some common dialogue on common concerns, an integrated core is certainly viable. Under such circumstances, the school could design a course or set of courses in the general education phase of the curriculum that takes its conceptual lead not from subject-matter coverage needs, but from a commitment to studying common problems and issues. The problems placed on the investigative docket are impossible to know in advance, because they emerge as local concerns. Important topical focal points might include racial and ethnic conflict, immigration, generational poverty, the treatment of the aged, censorship in the community, hunger and homelessness, terrorism (in its varied contexts), public health concerns, consumer judgments, war and peace, drug and tobacco use, environmentalism, housing issues, crime, human rights, the abortion debate, cloning, the ethics of medical decisions, and election-year politics. Some of these concerns might have relevance in the local experience of the children and could be accompanied with an extra-classroom outreach activity or program.

One has to appreciate the fact that, in an integrated core, the teacher does not benefit much from the support of a textbook or even from content standards. The teacher has to go at it alone, with the assistance of curriculum development support, and organize the subject matter in the core in a way that is responsive to the mission of the school and other professional factors. And although the integrated core might sound like something a social studies teacher might do, the idea behind it is to make it a truly integrated experience that all teachers might have a hand in producing. Because the integrated core is built on the premise that general education should offer common experiences, it must be conducted in heterogeneous groups and it has its best chances of succeeding under a block-schedule arrangement that allows for some flexibility in planning and for more intensive investigative pursuits.

Patterns of Course Organization

We arrive at the moment of truth in the macrocurriculum when we begin to structure the nature of the coursework and its inherent subject matter across and within grade levels. The curriculum developer quickly asks what proportion of the school curriculum should be dedicated to general education and wonders whether it should be designed as a common experience or simply as a list of common requirements. And then the question arises of what subject matter to include as common learning and how exactly to organize it. And before long, a cavalcade of other questions follows: Will the general education phase be satisfied with a disciplinary design or will it aim at an integrated core? Will it seek some balance between the two? Will curriculum tracking be allowed in general education? Should a general mathematics course be required, followed by two or three years of more discipline-centered math? And how many years for language arts and science, and will they be taught as broad fields or as separate disciplines? Should foreign language at least become a common requirement? Regarding specialized education, what part of the school curriculum should be openly devoted to exploratory studies, enrichment studies and special programs in vocational education, business education, or technology education? Will the extra-classroom experience be tied into general education and specialized courses?

Time-allocation concerns are, of course, primary to the structuring of coursework. Decisions related to the amount of time given to various subject areas and to the balance of time standing between general education and specialized education coursework are influenced by a wide range of concerns including, especially at the high school level, the presence of mandated content standards, existing graduation mandates, certain textbook adoptions, and general testing pressures. But the curriculum developer's main guide is the mission statement of the school. If the school pledges an educational commitment to citizenship or personal development, then the coursework in the school must, at some structural level, reflect such a pledge. A unique or distinctive mission must reflect a unique or distinctive pattern of coursework.

The Elementary School.   As mentioned earlier, virtually the whole of the elementary school experience is dedicated to general education. Most elementary school classrooms are self-contained, taught by teachers who have multiple subject-area responsibilities and who offer most of their instruction in common learning settings. This is not to say that the elementary school curriculum ignores the needs of individualization. The point is that even the specializing function of the curriculum in the elementary school is actualized in a common learning setting. Structurally speaking, the only specialized education that usually has a separate standing in the elementary school curriculum is tied to special needs instruction, often in relation to students with disabilities, students working in bilingual or ESL classes and less often, students documented as gifted and talented. Everything else commonly occurs in a common general education setting.

Two prevalent concerns have to be managed in the organization of the general education phase of the elementary school curriculum. The first has to do with subject-matter organization. Most elementary schools expose their students to some variation on the traditional four subject areas: language arts, science, mathematics, and social studies. Art, music, and physical education are frequently handled by separate teachers, but with the same common group of students.

As Figure 5.4 shows, the elementary school day can use any number of different schemes to organize the subject area. A broad fields approach in mathematics and science and a laminated approach in language arts allow the teacher to see each area of study widely and to approach the content as a unified branch knowledge. But one could also see that the schedule detailed in Figure 5.4 reflects some effort to offer more integrated and problem-focused opportunities for learning. The reader might notice the strong emphasis placed on socio-civic experiences, which (for analytical purposes) we will say is justified by the school's mission statement. And although mathematics, social studies, language arts, and science are each offered through a broad field or laminated approach—which is familiar (if not traditional) in the elementary school—each also has some involvement with integrating socio-civic causes. An integrated core of studies between math, language arts, and social studies, for instance, generates learning units, such as "School and Classroom Surveys," which is dedicated to the ongoing development, distribution, and analysis of surveys taken by the class on emergent topics related to local, state, and national concerns. The survey instruments used in the course are designed by the students and the data are not only collected but also analyzed and eventually disseminated (and formally presented) by the students. The core also contains a unit titled "Understanding Social Phenomena Mathematically," which uses various sources of graphical and tabular data of various social phenomena to better understand social issues in the community and world. Another block-scheduled unit fuses social studies and language arts. One unit used in this fusion might be titled "Life Writings," which focuses on writing activities built around ongoing relations with pen pals from around the nation and the world, writings about individual living experiences and cultural traditions, active political writing to newspapers and elected officials, and writings to experts in various fields of endeavor. Yet another unit might explore the practice of journalism and seek to produce a classroom newspaper that deals with ongoing problems and issues in the classroom, school, and community. And a third component might be titled "Meet Our Community," which is an ongoing project dedicated to writing the history of the local community and the biographies of interesting local persons. The broad field of general science is also side by side with a period of time dedicated to a fused course on health and nutrition studies, which focuses on the benefits of good eating habits and other healthy practices. Other potential areas for integration in the macrocurriculum include the role the art classroom might play in the design of the classroom newspaper, some correlated arrangement between music and art, and an effort to fuse social studies with mathematics through a series of units

	M	T	W	TH	F
1	General Mathematics				Individualized Math Projects (Remediation and Enrichment)
2	General Language Arts — Laminated — Reading Discussion Groups and Small Group Instruction (Remediation and Enrichment)		Spelling and Grammar	Fused core featuring Math, Language Arts, and Social Studies. Units include: • School in Classroom Survey • Understanding Social Phenomena Mathematically	Language Arts Fused with Social Studies. Units include: • Civic Writing • The Classroom Newspaper • Meet Our Community —Outreach Component—
3	Laminated Social Studies — Laminated — History / Geography		Social Studies Fusion with Math. Units include: • How do banks work and why are they important? • How does the stock market work and why is it important? • Why do sports stars get paid so much?		Art Correlated in Separate Classrooms with Newspaper and Civic Writing
4	General Science				Science Fused with Health Health and Nutrition Studies
5	Physical Education		Music	Art — Correlated — In Separate Classes	Art Correlated in Separate Classrooms with Newspaper and Civic Writing

Pull-out programs for special needs students, including ESL, Gifted and Talented, and Special Education Programs

FIGURE 5.4 Macrocurriculum in Fourth Grade

that examine the economics of banking, the stock market, and the sports industry (perhaps in historical context). One should also notice that the specialized feature of the curriculum is built into the common experience, so that time is allocated to individualized mathematical projects, which could include opportunities for both remedial and advanced work and small-group instruction (from remedial to advanced) in language arts.

The time allocations given to different subject areas are not easy to calculate because of the blending that occurs between subject areas. But if we count each unit period as a single unit and any fused course by the proportional representation of the subject area, the schedule outline in Figure 5.4 approximates the following number of periods per week: mathematics, 5.5; language arts, 5; social studies, 4.5; science, 4.5; health, .05; physical education, 2; music, 1; and art, 2. This is certainly a balanced schedule that, for some schools, may not reflect enough emphasis on reading and the language arts. One should note that, on the average, the American elementary school classroom dedicates approximately 60 percent of its instructional time to the language arts. Our allocation for language arts stands at 20 percent, but the result is that other subject areas notably neglected in the elementary school (science and social studies) get their due. Time allocations should be allocations of mission and purpose, which the curriculum developer must always keep in mind. It should also be said that the aforementioned schedule was made without any contemplation given to state or district mandates pertaining to the content of the curriculum. Thus, decisions regarding content might be more circumscribed than is conveyed here. Nevertheless, one can see that because the elementary school usually operates as general education (a common, heterogeneously mixed experience), it is full of possibilities for an integrated program.

The second concern we need to address in the macrocurriculum is a horizontal articulation matter. The reader might recall from the preceding chapter that the purpose of the school is moved by two key dimensions: subject matter and behaviors/skills. The subject matter is the main focus when organizing the macrocurriculum, but the behavioral component cannot be ignored. So we return to the pervasive skills of the curriculum to remind ourselves of a key articulation concern. Figure 5.5 illustrates the high-priority areas (among the pervasive skills) for the various subject areas used in the example of a macrocurriculum (as illustrated in Fig. 5.4). It is no surprise to see that each of the subject areas, except for physical education and art/music, give high priority to thinking skills. This, of course, does not mean that students do not think in music, art, or physical education class. It does mean, however, that consciousness for thinking skills (as they might be defined in Bloom's taxonomy or in some other design) in music, art, and physical education does not have as much of an instructional priority as in most other subject areas. Communicating skills are also widely embraced as a high priority in the curriculum, while inquiry skills are highlighted as a priority in science, social studies, and fused areas. Interpersonal skills and intrapersonal development are mostly high-priority concerns in language arts, fused areas, and

Subject Areas	Pervasive Skills				
	Thinking	Communicating	Inquiring	Interpersonal Engagements	Intrapersonal Development
General Math (4)*	✓		✓		
General Language Arts (3)	✓	✓			✓
Laminated Social Studies (2)	✓	✓	✓	✓	
General Science (4)	✓		✓		
Fused Core (Language Arts, Math, and Social Studies) (3)	✓	✓	✓	✓	✓
Language Arts and Social Studies Fusion (2)	✓	✓	✓	✓	✓
Math and Social Studies Fusion (2)	✓	✓	✓		✓
Science/Health Fusion (1)	✓		✓		
Art and Music Correlation (2)	✓				✓
Art Correlation (1)	✓			✓	
Physical Education (2)	✓			✓	
Total No. of Scheduled Periods Dedicated to the Skill Area	22	17	19	10	12

* Number of scheduled periods associated with subject area.

FIGURE 5.5 **High Priority Areas for Each Subject Area in the Fourth Grade Macrocurriculum**

art/music. The grid in Figure 5.5 illustrates a way of accounting for the skill-based focal points for each subject area in order to ensure that each area is covered and that teachers understand the expectation of each subject area in relation to the whole curricular scheme. Figure 5.6 displays a "high-priority weight factor" that is given to each skill area in each subject area. This is a simple calculation involving the number of time periods dedicated to each skill area divided by the number of pervasive skills that share the scheduled space. The presumption is that each skill identified as high priority will be treated equally in the subject area. Such a weight factor can help a school achieve a sense of the balance between the skill-based components of the curriculum.

Exactly how we design the general or pervasive skills will have an effect on how the skills might be embraced in each of the subject areas. Nonverbal communication skills, for instance, might have high priority in the art domain, while other skills in the communication category may not prevail as a high priority matter in art. So, the nature of the pervasive skills will have much to do with the nature of their relation to the subject areas.

The Middle School.   The middle school curriculum represents the first effort to structurally define coursework for both general and specialized education. Although general education is still the predominant feature of the curriculum, specialized courses related to the exploratory and enrichment functions begin to emerge. Unlike the elementary school, the middle school is taught by specialized teachers in separate specialized classrooms. In many cases, the middle school offers children their very first experience in between-class grouping, as some attention is given to individual aptitude and achievement differences. Because the middle school usually does not have to worry about college-admission or state-mandated graduation requirements, it is relatively free to experiment with the general education curriculum. But because it has to concern itself with vertical articulation connections to the high school, state and college influences are still felt.

Figure 5.7 (p. 148) outlines the macrocurriculum for the eighth grade. The arrangement for the teaching of mathematics is a departure from the elementary school model. In an effort to respond to individualized differences in mathematics, the curriculum offers its first planned interclass differentiation (using ability and interest levels), by offering a general mathematics course and an alternate accelerated algebra block. The implications of this decision reach outside of the eighth grade because an accelerated track in the eighth grade will require an accelerated track all the way through the high school years. General science, language arts, and American studies are all taught as broad fields and all qualify as common general education experiences. Foreign language is required for all students and qualifies as a common requirement, as several different languages might be available for study. The featured performer in the general education program, however, is the integrated core, which meets once a week in

Subject Areas	Pervasive Skills				
	Thinking	Communicating	Inquiring and Studying	Interpersonal Engagements	Intrapersonal Development
General Math	2	—	2	—	—
General Language Arts	1	1	—	—	1
Laminated Social Studies	0.5	0.5	0.5	0.5	—
General Science	2	—	2	—	—
Fused Core (Language Arts, Math, and Social Studies)	0.6	0.6	0.6	0.6	—
Language Arts and Social Studies Fusion	0.4	0.4	0.4	0.4	0.4
Math and Social Studies Fusion	0.25	0.25	0.25	—	0.25
Science/Health Fusion	0.5	—	0.5	—	—
Art and Music Correlation	—	1	—	—	1
Art Correlation	—	0.5	—	0.5	—
Physical Education	—	1	—	1	—
Total High Priority Weight Factor	7.25	5.25	6.25	3	2.65

FIGURE 5.6   **High Priority Weight Factors by Subject Areas in the Fourth Grade Macrocurriculum**

	M	T	W	TH	F
1	General Mathematics or Accelerated Algebra Track				Integrated Core
2	General Science			Correlated: Music / Art	Integrated Core
3	General Language Arts				Community Outreach
4	American Studies				Community Outreach
5	Foreign Language I			Exploratory (elective) Clubs	
6	Correlated: Physical Education / Health			Exploratory Prevocational Courses	

□ = Specialized Education

FIGURE 5.7 Macrocurriculum in Eighth Grade

a block schedule time, under a team-teaching arrangement, to work on common topical problems related to community, state, and national issues. All of the forces of math, science, language arts, and American studies are brought to bear on the core, but in a way that is issue centered and problem focused (and not laminated). Thus, topics related to personal development (such as understanding one's body, making wise consumer choices, examining various beliefs and superstitions) or topics related to societal concerns (such as homelessness, poverty in the community, war and peace, environmental issues, and understanding local ethnic groups) have center stage in the integrated core. The exploratory function in the curriculum is introduced through a menu of courses that targets some special interest areas. One exploratory space in the schedule is designed around club activities that are designed to have an after-school life and that seek to tie coursework into planned extra classroom experiences. All the familiar clubs might be included (math, speech, debate, chess, and computer), as might less-regular choices, such as an environmental club, a music appreciation club, or a club for move buffs. Because of the exploratory function, these would be seen as short courses that would shift their enrollment every semester or trimester. The other aspect of the exploratory offers a choice of courses from a prevocational list, including, say, introductory courses in carpentry, engines, plumbing, electrical wiring, gardening, landscaping, masonry, or computer repair. These too would rotate to encourage a range of new experiences.

The High School.   As indicated earlier, the macrocurricular arrangement of the coursework in high school is complex because of the growing relevance of the specialized curriculum and the need to balance it with the continuing role that general education plays. Figure 5.8 (p. 150) illustrates the overarching structure as it relates to all four grade levels in high school. One can see that the general education function remains intact for ninth grade, as most of the courses are required and are offered as common (mixed-ability) experiences. The first-year courses in General Math, and Foundations of Science, however, are accompanied with an important change. Simultaneous to the courses in General Mathematics and the Foundations of Science is an honors and AP track for students who desire or otherwise need a more specialized and accelerated experience in math and science. Thus, the conditions for general education in math and science are compromised because they move away from the idea of the common experience. Students enrolled in the honors and AP track will not enroll in the more general math and science courses. This is a trade-off by design, one that accounts for the realities of trying to meet the specialized academic needs of certain students. It also demonstrates the encroachment of specializing education on general education. But the common experience is still retained in some of the other courses. American Studies, Government, and a Problems of Democracy course are all required mixed-ability courses. The social studies strain of common courses is especially well suited for general education because of its association with pervading social issues and problems. Specialized AP courses, however, are available in history,

9th Grade	10th Grade	11th Grade	12th Grade
General Math (Mixed Ability)			
Honors and AP Track: Geometry, Algebra, Calculus			
Foundations of Science (Mixed Ability)			
Honors and AP Track: Biology, Chemistry, Physics			
American Studies (Mixed Ability)	Government (Mixed Ability)	Problems of Democracy (Mixed Ability)	
English I (Mixed Ability)	English II (Mixed Ability)	Honors and AP Track in English	
Physical Education and Health (Mixed Ability)			
Specialized Foreign Language Track: Foreign Language I–IV			
Specialized Vocational Education Track: Vocational Cluster Areas			
Specialized AP Academic Courses in History, Economics, Geography, Computer Science			
Exploratories			
The Fine Arts and Club Activities			

FIGURE 5.8   Macrocurriculum for the High School

economics, and geography, but only as elective or exploratory options. Coursework in English is similarly arranged, starting with a mixed-ability general education requirement for first-year students, and changing to a two-track system that allows students to either continue in English II for another year or to fulfill their English requirements with more specialized English courses or with honors or AP courses. I have also isolated a scheduling space for a specialized track in the curriculum, organized along three main areas, for each of the four years in high school. These include a foreign language education, vocational education, and AP academic specialized track. Students bound for college will likely opt for the foreign language education track and the AP academic track, while those not headed to college will move in the direction of vocational studies. But more than one scheduled space is available for this purpose in the macrocurriculum. In eleventh and twelfth grades, for instance, students (in our example) are no longer required to take general education courses in math and science and could use this open space in the schedule to do more specialized coursework. Students in vocational studies are particularly well served by this because they are less likely to opt for AP courses in math and science and could use the room in their schedule for more intensive vocational studies available through the specialized vocational track. Finally, the exploratory track allows students to pursue their interests in two key areas: the fine arts and club activity. A menu of coursework in the area of music, art, and theater allows students to select these as either exploratory or enrichment courses. The club activity component ties its coursework to extra-classroom activities (theater, speech and debate, the student paper, competitive mathematics, and so forth). And to add to the possibilities, the specialized track might also serve an exploratory function and vice versa—so these two components, from a scheduling standpoint, can be seen as interchangeable.

Figure 5.9 (p. 152) demonstrates the fundamental difference between the ninth-grade and twelfth-grade schedules. Of the several periods available for scheduling in the ninth grade, five are required courses, although two of the five allow for an honors or tracked component. In the twelfth grade, only two courses remain as common experiences: Physical Education and Health, and Problems of Democracy. The open nature of the twelfth grade testifies to strengthening posture of specialized education in the school life of the student. College-bound students will likely use the openness in the schedule to accumulate some AP courses or to otherwise build a course portfolio that will appeal to colleges, which could include certain exploratory and enrichment courses. Students planning to work after high school will likely use the more open plan to focus on core vocational education courses and to also pursue certain exploratories.

THE EXTRA-CLASSROOM EXPERIENCE

The reach of the school curriculum does not, by any means, extend only to the physical limits of the classroom. The activities that the school chooses to sponsor

	9th Grade	12th Grade
1	Required General Math or Honors/AP	Open Selected Math AP Selected Exploratory Selected Specialized
2	Required Foundations of Science or Honors/AP	Open Selected Science AP Selected Exploratory Selected Specialized
3	Required American Studies (Mixed Ability)	Required Problems of Democracy (Mixed Ability)
4	Required English I	Open Selected English AP Selected Exploratory Selected Specialized
5	Required Physical Education and Health	Required Physical Education and Health
6	Selected Specialized	Selected Specialized
7	Selected Exploratory/Enrichment	Selected Exploratory/Enrichment

FIGURE 5.9   **Ninth Grade Schedule vs. Twelfth Grade Schedule**

outside of the classroom are no less important than those within it. Likewise, extra-classroom activities are no less obligated to be educative in nature and carry the same expectation of responsiveness to the macropurposes of the school as any other aspect of the curriculum. This is the main reason why I choose to refer to such experiences as extra-classroom activities, not extra-curricular experiences. Extra-classroom activities generally occur outside of the classroom but they are of (not extra to) the curriculum.

The idea of the extra-classroom experience is one that applies mostly to the middle and secondary school context. This is because extra-classroom activities are strategic to the functioning of specialized education, which itself embodies an effort to broaden and deepen areas of individual interest and aptitude in the curriculum. Although we might have some form of student government in the elementary school (and perhaps even sports teams, hobby clubs, and a school newspaper), such activities have a nominal place in education of elementary school children. Part of the reason for this has to do with the dominance of general education in the elementary school, the wide developmental differences represented in the student population, and the group identification that children have with their classrooms. But when the individualizing features of the curriculum begin to be structurally defined in the middle and secondary school, the extra-classroom experience also increases in visibility and significance.

We could classify the extra-classroom activities of middle and secondary schools in the following way: academic clubs, athletics, newspaper or yearbook, music ensembles, drama, dance and cheerleading, speech and debate, student government, and hobby or vocational clubs. The list does not account for all the possibilities but it is representative of them.

Figure 5.10 (p. 154) gives us a sense of the national participation rates in extra-classroom activities in the twelfth grade (National Center for Education Statistics, 2002). Unsurprisingly athletics is the big winner, with a participation rate of over 35 percent for varsity sports and 29 percent for intramural sports. The remaining areas range from a participation rate of about 10 to about 25 percent. In the middle school, the sports participation rate is even higher (47 percent varsity sports and 42 percent intramural sports), as are the participation rates in musical ensembles, which stand at 40 percent in eighth grade compared to 15 percent in twelfth grade. Participation rate data are important to curriculum developers because they give us a sense of the support for and the popularity of the intrinsic objectives or purposes tied to extra-classroom activities. And by doing so, they tell us something important about what the school is doing. If we used the national participation rates listed in Figure 5.9, what might they say about the school curriculum?

Let's examine athletics first. What school-related purposes can we say athletics fulfills? First, the subject-area linkage to athletics is physical education. Many high schools wisely count participation in school-sponsored sports programs toward the physical education requirement, allowing students room in their schedule to pursue other curricular options or to simply have an open period. But the key areas of learning for athletics are both interpersonal and intrapersonal development. Competitive team sport, for instance, is as much cooperative as competitive in orientation; there is an agreement between teams to compete within the rules as well as a cooperative agreement within teams to work together in preparation for competition. One could also make an argument that, in the context of competing together, athletic teams have a chance to pro-

Extra-Classroom Activities	High School Senior Participation Rate (1992)	Subject Orientation	High Priority Areas				
			Thinking	Communicating	Inquiring	Inter-personal	Intra-personal
Athletics	65%	Physical Education				✓	✓
Musical Ensembles	20%	Music				✓	✓
Drama Groups	15%	English		✓		✓	✓
Speech and Debate	NA	Social Studies/ English	✓	✓	✓	✓	✓
Student Government	15%	Social Studies		✓		✓	✓
Student Newspaper/ Yearbook	18%	English		✓		✓	
Academic Clubs	25%	Varied	✓				✓

FIGURE 5.10   Extra-Classroom Activities

mote the prospects for racial, ethnic, and even religious tolerance (as they help build friendships among team members), while also teaching key values related to perseverance and industry. Of course, whether this is actually the case means that the school would have to evaluate for it, something that it could only do if it upholds such objectives as central to the viability of the athletic program.

The significant number of students participating in music, drama, student government, the student newspaper, and speech and debate programs shows that the subject areas affiliated with these activities get a significant boost in the extra-classroom experience. But each of these areas also has some association with other skill-based areas of learning. Music obviously speaks to several interpersonal and intrapersonal goals, as well as the skill of musical communication. Drama also fulfills various objectives in the interpersonal and intrapersonal domains, while advancing a set of oral communication skills. Speech and debate not only touches on its own unique set of communication skills, but also on various inquiry skills, as students conduct research in preparation for their debates and for the writing and presentation of their speeches. Student government and the student newspaper are loosely affiliated with social studies and English, but are also well positioned to help develop and extend fundamental communication skills. One could see that the set of skills that get privileged in the extra-class experience is different from the set of skills linked to the coursework. And this is as it should be, because one should remember that extra-classroom activities are fundamentally justified as assisting directly with individualization (enrichment and exploration, the two main pursuits of specialized education). We can see from Figure 5.10 that interpersonal and intrapersonal development take a lion's share of the attention in the extra-classroom activities, acting to give them added support.

Finally, it should be noted that the extra classroom is not always extra *to* the classroom. Many of the activities justified as extra-classroom events are linked to courses. Thus, musical ensembles could be structured into the coursework schedule, while also assuming a time commitment outside of the course. The same could be said of drama courses linked with school plays, speech and debate courses linked with competitions, a journalism course linked with the production of the student newspaper, and so forth. Moreover, we might find an outreach or service component in a course justified as general education that could be interpreted as an extra-classroom activity.

SUMMARY

The public school curriculum is essentially reducible to two macro functions: general education (or common learning), often set in common, mixed-ability settings, and specialized education (or individualized learning), which, at least from the middle school on, often results in separate (frequently self-selected) coursework. In the elementary school, general education dominates, largely because the main aim of the school is to work with the normative mandate in a common learning venue. Specialized education in the elementary school is largely an instructional matter that each teacher must self-manage through special assignments, within-class ability grouping, and other tactics targeted at individuals. In the middle school, however, specialized education begins to become a structural concern in the curriculum and surfaces, essentially for the first time, as coursework. Hence, we see efforts in the middle school to design elective (exploratory) courses, honors courses, and extra-classroom outreach. Specialized education continues to grow in significance in the high school, where AP and honors courses must be offered, exploratory options for courses increase, and specialized career-based programs (such as vocational education) begin to take hold.

In thinking about the design of the subject matter for coursework justified in general education or specialized education, the curriculum developer is usually under pressure to embrace a disciplinary scheme. Carnegie unit requirements for graduation and college admission standards (as well as the imposition of content standards) can create a subject-centered climate in the school. The pressures are especially strong in the high school, making the prospects for designing subject matter along more interdisciplinary and issue-centered lines limited.

But alternative ways of organizing subject matter should be used where the mission of the school justifies such a treatment. Thus, rather than seeing all coursework in the general education phases of the high school curriculum as strictly discipline centered, the curriculum developer can begin to correlate courses (giving them some common contact points), to fuse courses (creating a new blend of subject matter), or to reconceive the subject matter altogether around a core of issue-centered focal points. Using these alternative schemes of subject organization allows the curriculum worker more flexibility to design coursework allegiant to the school's mission statement.

In the end, the macrocurriculum has to be well articulated vertically (across grades) and horizontally (within grades), and should demonstrate a balance of experiences in accordance with the school's mission. This includes the management of extra-classroom activities, which have no less of a responsibility to deliver educational experiences in the school curriculum than does the formal coursework.

DISCUSSION QUESTIONS AND SUGGESTED ACTIVITIES

1. Explain how the relation between general and specialized education changes from the elementary school, through the middle school, and into the high school.

2. How can external influences such as graduation requirements, college admission standards, and even content standards and textbook publishers affect the nature of general education in the high school?

3. Why is it sensible to exclude grade 9 from the grade configuration of a middle school?

4. How is specialized education generally handled in the elementary school curriculum?

5. What is the difference between constructing general education in the high school as a common experience as opposed to a common requirement?

6. In what ways do the functions of general education and specialized education clash in the high school curriculum?

7. What are the main things the curriculum developer has to think about when focusing on horizontal articulation issues?

8. How does vertical articulation differ from horizontal articulation?

9. Why is the organizational scheme of the curriculum usually built with the "brick and mortar of subject matter"?

10. What are some examples of a world-related sequencing approach? Compare them to examples of a concept-related sequencing approach.

11. Describe the application of a correlation design in the conduct of a self-contained elementary school classroom.

12. How does a correlation design sometimes lead to a laminated way of organized subject matter?

13. Describe a fused or broad fields design in the macrocurriculum of a middle school.

14. How can block-scheduling assist with efforts to use less disciplinary schemes of organizing subject matter?

15. What are the difficulties in designing and operating an integrated core design in the general education phase of a high school curriculum?

16. How might a curriculum developer begin to understand the horizontal articulation issues involved in meeting key pervasive skills in the curriculum?

17. How might extra-classroom activities be systematically structured into the macrocurriculum of a middle school or high school?

18. How can a curriculum developer use participation rate data in extra-classroom activities to make some judgment about what the curriculum values and what it ultimately aims to accomplish?

NOTES

National Center for Education Statistics (2002). *Digest of Education Statistics*. Washington, DC: U.S. Department of Education.

Posner, G. & Rudnitsky, A. (1997). *Course design: A guide to curriculum development for teachers* (5th ed.). New York: Longman.

Taba, H. (1962). *Curriculum development: Theory and practice*. New York: Harcourt, Brace and Jovanovich.

Tanner, D. & Tanner, L. (1995). *Curriculum development*. New York: Macmillan Co.

CHAPTER SIX

INSTRUCTION AND PEDAGOGY

Mere activity does not constitute experience
—John Dewey

The design and implementation of instruction in the school curriculum is of obvious significance to the curriculum developer. When we begin to discuss matters of instruction and pedagogy, we begin the put an analytical lens on the main interactive point between teachers and students. Concern for the discretionary space of the teacher now becomes a practical reality because, by all measures, instruction (and its partner, pedagogy), belong to the teacher. Together they constitute the essential living condition of the school curriculum experience—the calculated effort to give rise to experiences that fulfill the school's purposes and respond to the emergent condition of the educational situation.

The distinction between the instruction and pedagogy helps us understand the relation between teacher judgment and the curriculum. Instruction refers to a planned course of learning experiences, designed and justified by the teacher, which aims to fulfill the purposes of the school curriculum. A teacher's decision to use methodology x in order to fulfill a set of central purposes or objectives is principally an instructional decision. If, for instance, interpersonal skills were viewed as important ingredients of a history course, an instructional response that favored methodologies suited to such purposes (such as cooperative learning techniques or inquiry-based activities) would logically follow. Similarly, the design of a lesson plan (or any deliberate rationalization for the application of a particular teaching strategy) is also a planned event that qualifies as instruction. Pedagogy, on the other hand, is what actually happens when teachers begin to teach, when they begin to interact with students and conduct or implement the planned instructional experience. Pedagogy is what we might view as the emergent or expressive side of teaching. We witness it in the spontaneous and situationally bound behaviors of teachers. We see pedagogy, for instance, in the nuances of a teacher's questioning techniques, the manner in which feedback is offered to students, the deliberate effort to model certain behaviors, the nature of the conversations had between the teacher and the students, and in the general way that social behaviors are handled in the classroom. Pedagogy is also the very behavior that leads the teacher to embrace what Eisner (1998) calls expressive goals or outcomes in the curriculum. These are the goals and activities that rise up from the experience itself. Expressive goals are met by situational or emergent decisions in the curriculum that, unlike instruction, are generally not preplanned and are mostly impossible to anticipate.

THE BIRTH OF INSTRUCTION

The decision to embrace certain teaching events should be informed by the curriculum's purposes, which can be modestly represented in the two-dimensional matrix discussed in Chapter 4. In other words, when teachers finally design learning experiences, they cannot be expected to make these decisions without some guidance from the curriculum. So, a curriculum that clearly organizes two essential factors—content (or subject matter) and pervasive skills—sends a strong signal to the teacher about what the moving objective of a lesson should be. Remember, the formulation of objectives in the microcurriculum is a teacher decision drawn from broader conceptual directives that are organized as aims or goals (both of which we find in the two-dimensional matrix). The level of specificity desired is a decision largely in the hands of the teachers.

We turn to Figure 6.1 to understand this connection. The directive in the curriculum is to teach identifiable content and to integrate it, as best as one can, with selected skills or behaviors. The teacher's job is to take this directive and translate it into a set of planned learning experiences.

PRINCIPLES FOR SELECTING
LEARNING EXPERIENCES

Although making the connection between experiences and subject matter/skills is an important step in setting the instructional course for the school curriculum, it is not the only one. Other factors also come into play. Tyler (1949), in fact, identified a number of principles (Fig. 6.2, p. 162) that teachers need to keep in mind when rendering instructional decisions.

First, Tyler made it clear that teachers must remember that experiences should result in opportunities to practice the behaviors implied in the objectives. This might seem obvious, but in the world of schools, the purposes and objectives of the curriculum are not always taken seriously and even when they are, they

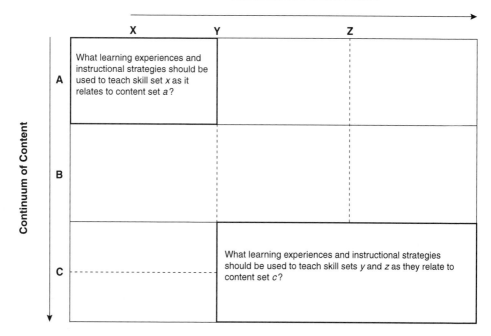

Continuum of Pervasive Skills

FIGURE 6.1   **The Birth of Instruction**

sometimes result in unusual, if not inappropriate, applications. Some time ago, for instance, the Chicago Public Schools advocated the use of a phonics-based (mastery learning) reading program that actually overlooked the need to give children the opportunity to read, opting instead for skill-based workbook exercises. In this example, one could appreciate Tyler's point, which is that the application of instruction must be consonant with the nature of the ends or purposes. No purposes and objectives in the curriculum have relevance unless they result in associated or logically connected activities. Talk of problem solving in the curriculum requires problem-solving activities; a commitment to community service or citizenship skills in the curriculum needs to be reinforced by a community activity (not simply a reading exercise).

Second, Tyler advises that all learning experiences offer satisfying activities that build an appreciation for learning and for the content and skills embodied in those activities. This is another way of saying that when we teach something, we teach not only the content and skills represented in the instructional plan, but also various appreciations and attitudes. Lesson plans and various instructional objectives to teach, for example, mathematical operations cannot ignore the effects that activities might have on student appreciation for that subject. By keeping such a principle in mind, the odds increase that children will encounter satisfying experiences in school.

Principle 1	Experiences must result in opportunities to practice the behaviors implied in the objectives.
Principle 2	Experiences must be satisfying and build important appreciations.
Principle 3	Experiences must be allegiant to the theoretical forces of the curriculum—the learner, the society, and subject matter.
Principle 4	Experiences can be associated with multiple purposes, and multiple experiences can be derived from a single purpose.

FIGURE 6.2   Principles in Selecting Learning Experiences

Third, the selection of learning experiences must be allegiant to the theoretical forces of the curriculum, namely the learner, society, and subject matter. Thus, the selection of learning experiences and their implementation (pedagogy) require the teacher to think about the learner in a way that demonstrates responsiveness to home and community factors, developmental nuances, and individual interests, aptitudes, and needs. Likewise, the teacher must also account for societal factors and ensure that the learning experiences chosen are attuned to the values and aims of democracy, while not neglecting the place of subject matter.

As a final point, the selection of learning experiences should be linked to the overarching purposes and objectives of the curriculum, so that each purpose can yield multiple experiences and each experience can address multiple purposes. This is an important point because it underscores the range of creative expression that a teacher can exercise, and it allows curriculum developers to see the multiple effects of a single instructional experience.

Instructional Models and Approaches

Variation is the key to good teaching. The deeper the reservoir of instructional insight, the greater the possibilities of finding an adequate instructional approach suited to particular curriculum objectives. As indicated, when making a decision on what instructional approach to employ, the teacher obviously has to consider the task demands of the curriculum purpose. Other factors, such as the nature of the educational situation (which includes some consideration of the learner and the society) as well as a consciousness for appreciations in learning also come into play. The possibilities of making good matches between method and purpose are enhanced when the instructional toolbox is full. In this sense, variety is the essence of the instructional side of the curriculum. Pratt (1994) made the same point when he asserted that only "variety can absorb variety," meaning that the action of the curriculum depends on the presence of strategies varied enough to deal with the variety of purposes in the system. A comprehensive school mandate requires a comprehensive instructional response.

Yet, a tendency exists among educators today to declare some instructional strategies as intrinsically good for all children at almost all times and places. Such thinking is flawed because teaching cannot and does not follow a best-method approach. If a best-method approach were used, we would not expect much independent judgment from teachers and could even view teacher creativity and teacher innovation as out of alignment with best methods.

However, it is equally wrong to suggest that any method, if engaged by the teacher and congruent with objectives desired in the curriculum, is as good as any other. Some methods, even in their decontextualized state, are on more solid theoretical ground than others. Most of us would probably agree that some instructional strategies are, by their nature, better attuned than others to the life of the learner and to the kind of society we value. For instance, instructional methods that encourage student discussion and insight obviously have some claim as methods well situated in the lives of learners. Similarly, instructional methods that encourage cooperation, group participation, and group deliberation have some intrinsic resonance with the values and aims of our democracy. From the standpoint of the learner and the society, these are generally sound instructional approaches. Nevertheless, we should remember that instructional judgments are made primarily in the interests of achieving specified aims, goals, and objectives in the curriculum. Thus, we cannot sensibly pursue instructional strategies that are good without also contemplating what they are good for. And, in the end, even a discussion-based instructional model (or one that values group deliberation and discussion) can be perverted and thereby lose its educative value.

One can classify instructional methods in any number of ways. What follows is a broad outline of various instructional techniques: discussion-based, inquiry-based, and independent and individualized instruction. These are, by no means, mutually exclusive and in no way represent the entire instructional repertoire. In fact, many teachers have idiosyncratic and personalized ways of offering instruction that often encompass multiple methodologies.

Direct Instruction.   Direct instruction is familiar to most of us. It is the traditional form of teacher-initiated and teacher-directed instruction. It usually takes on the form of lecture and demonstration and is followed by some schedule of practice and review. It is usually targeted at the whole class, with a built-in provision for questions, guided and independent practice, and the employment of corrective measures. The aim of direct instruction is to help students achieve mastery of key ideas, facts, or skills. Direct instruction starts with a teacher presentation (lecture or demonstration), is followed by some experience in guided practice, and then shifts to the provision of feedback and corrections. Independent practice activities and ultimately demonstrations of mastery complete the procedure (see Fig. 6.3, p. 164).

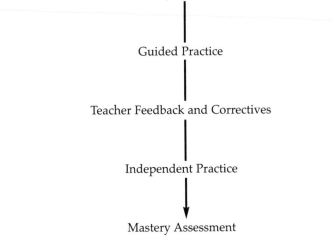

Teacher Presentation by Demonstration or Lecture

Guided Practice

Teacher Feedback and Correctives

Independent Practice

Mastery Assessment

FIGURE 6.3   Features of Direct Instruction

Lecture or demonstration is probably the most commonplace instructional approach used in the schools. Interestingly, many educators are heavy handed in their criticism of the lecture method, equating it unreasonably with bad instruction. Their thinking is that bad instruction always prevails wherever teacher-talk dominates and student discussion opportunities are limited. But, lectures can be thrilling learning experiences, and can accomplish certain purposes more effectively than other methods. Of course, they can also be misused, overused, poorly conceived, or poorly conducted.

The lecture method is best suited for older children. We know from a developmental standpoint that asking children to sit and listen attentively to what often amounts to an exposition of ideas and facts is not a wise way to teach children who have not yet achieved formal operations and whose attention spans are still relatively short. This cautionary point is an example of what we mean when we say that the instructional strategy must be attuned to the nature of the learner. But, absent any learner limitations, if the exposition of various facts, ideas, and skills is a key component to a curriculum purpose, a lecture method might prove to be a useful strategy. It is, after all, an effective way to transmit knowledge, especially if the teacher has good lecturing skills. Lectures can also prove to be useful where note-taking, listening, and thinking skills take a prominent role in the instructional strategy.

Lectures, moreover, should be viewed as something more than a person talking. Lectures are perforce pedagogical acts that bring together an array of skills related to the use of voice, inflection, drama, emotive language, rate of delivery, and conceptual structure. A lecture is not only given to an audience but can and should be developed with an audience. Far from being strictly expository, the lecture method can be a fluid experience that responds to the vagaries of the audience. Thus, lectures can become active events for the students, clarifying information or bringing forward student points of view. Visual computer technologies, such as Powerpoint, give the teacher the opportunity to further concretize an abstract idea, offer visual documentation, and work through various data sets.

In direct instruction, the teacher-presentation phase is followed by guided practice in which the teacher tries to distill the lecture or demonstration into some identifiable form of facts, skills, or knowledge that can, in effect, be practiced or otherwise manipulated for an educational effect. Guided practice is not independent work, but work done under the watchful eye of the educator, who uses it as an opportunity to check for understanding and to correct or remediate any emergent problems. The focus on feedback and correctives comes into play as the educator works on individual cases.

The very last steps of the direct-instruction model include a phase for independent practice (seatwork or homework), and then some form of assessment. One can see that direct instruction is not suited for every objective in the school curriculum. It is, in fact, best equipped to handle objectives that target skill-based needs. This makes it a good candidate for reading and mathematics instruction and also potentially for discipline-centered instruction such as science, where particular mechanisms, skills, and processes need to be learned. But direct instruction does not have a monopoly on skill-based objectives. Remember that multiple instructional approaches can be used to achieve singular objectives. And because the teacher ultimately puts instructional plans into action, the presentation phase of direct instruction does not always need to be followed by any of the review and practice mechanisms described here and could instead lead to discussion-based or inquiry-based instructional approaches, which could serve as practice and review opportunities.

Discussion-based Instruction.   The use of discussion in class is closely related to the purposes of exploring, extending, probing, analyzing, clarifying, and evaluating. Discussion-based instruction obviously requires small student groups to enhance the prospects for individuals to discuss, share, and otherwise engage each other at a level of intimacy not easily accomplished in the larger group setting. As a result, discussion-based instruction is a more likely choice for curriculum objectives that stress oral expression, social mutuality, critical-mindedness, and the development of various social skills.

Whereas the orientation of direct instruction is teacher demonstration and student practice, the orientation for discussion-based methodologies is teacher facilitation and student discovery. In other words, most discussion-based models try to limit teacher-talk and instead encourage meaningful conversational engagements between students and between students and teachers. Direct instruction offers teacher knowledge, while discussion-based instruction challenges the student to contextualize and converse about the knowledge. And because discussion is influenced by the student perspectives on matters (student interests, aptitudes, and questions), it works in the interests of developing important appreciations.

Multiple options are available to the teacher who is interested in bringing discussion-based instruction into the classroom. Some options, such as the Socratic questioning method, still very much depend on teacher direction, but most of the others simply try to find a way to offer students an idea-oriented context within which they can pursue questions and problems that will require informed conversation and the active exchange of viewpoints and insights. Here are four general approaches to discussion-based instruction.

Role Playing.   Role-playing activities attempt to get the students to psychologize the main features of what they are studying. The technique demands an emotional and cognitive involvement with the assigned role. This is an approach that is especially useful in the study of history, contemporary social problems, and—with younger children—in the examination of human relations problems, including interpersonal conflicts, intergroup relations, and individual dilemmas (Joyce and Weil, 1986).

A role-playing activity requires the application of a wide range of skills, including dramatic presentation, memorization, some empathetic attachment to the role, and possibly even the physical construction of the stage or scene. The educational benefits of a role-playing activity, however, do not cease with the presentation or performance. Because role playing is viewed as discussion-based instruction, its primary educational benefit is rooted in the debriefing session that follows the presentation. This is where students can ask questions, seek clarifications, offer opinions, and suggest improvements.

The use of role playing in the classroom is yet another reminder of the importance of keeping the conception of the learner in mind when we make instructional selections. If, for instance, a role-playing activity requires the student to perform a racist, sexist, or bigoted role, the teacher, before proceeding, should account for the age and the maturity levels of the learners, as well as address any ethnic, racial, or religious sensitivities. Asking a Jewish child to play the role of Hitler, or an African American to play the role of a slave may not be a prudent decision. Similarly, teachers need to be keenly aware of the language used in the role activities produced, and decide whether the use of language is appropriate, given the sensitivities of the student and community population.

Simulations and Games.   The intention of simulations is to replicate the real-life conditions of a particular situation or event where key decisions need to be made. This is quite useful when the pervasive skills of problem solving or decision making are featured in the curriculum. An educational game, on the other hand, has no designs on simulating reality, and can integrate any number of other purposes, including drill practices and knowledge acquisition. Because games (and sometimes simulations) involve a competitive task structure (tasks or activities that require students to compete against each other), they should be used judiciously, especially in settings that attach great importance to cooperative activities.

Because simulations attempt to replicate real-life situations, the student's encounter with the simulation is itself educative. History is learned in historical simulations, and knowledge of government is learned in simulations featuring the work of legislative government. In most cases, teachers use the simulation as an application and synthesizing activity that helps to bring together the content of the curriculum into a working reality-based scenario. And again, especially in the case of the simulation, much can be gained from a debriefing session that follows the conclusion of the simulation. This allows the teacher to put an analytical lens on the simulation itself, giving students the opportunity to discuss and reflect upon what they learned and to draw connections to subject matter. If we look at the simulation as the journey, the discussion that follows is the destination; it is the place where the activity culminates in a well-regulated and a sharply analytical debriefing experience.

The very definition of game implies fun, so there is a tendency to equate the application of games in the classroom with fun-filled experiences that could build important appreciations. Although all games are not created equal (and many are about as much fun as watching paint dry), the appeal to the idea of playing games, especially to young children, cannot be denied. This gives the game strategy an important advantage in assisting with the development of appreciations. Teachers sometimes recognize this and use games to compensate for activities that may not have much of an intrinsic appeal to students.

Cooperative Learning.   Cooperative learning is often seen as a reprieve from the traditional whole-class and individual seatwork model that still dominates the classroom. It is an especially attractive instructional option in any classroom that values the development of social skills and that aims to encourage problem-solving and inquiry skills as well as the development of prosocial behaviors.

Cooperative learning often involves small groups, put together by the teachers, that perform a task requiring a cooperative group effort and ultimately some group consensus. The task could be something as simple as getting together to brainstorm on a topic or as sophisticated as pursuing a specific research question that calls for a lengthy and nuanced (and well-researched) group response. Often cooperative groups are limited to a heterogeneous mix of four or five students, with each participant taking on a specific role in the group process. The idea is for the group to organize and manage itself, to have an opportunity to engage in discussion and debate, to find ways to reconcile internal differences of opinion, and to ultimately offer a single group product. The actual task structure of the group assignment is central to the success of the cooperative group. The approach to the task not only has to be organized conceptually but also in terms of labor allocations. So, if the assignment is to evaluate the application of a new proposed law or to write and dramatize a play depicting an important historical event, some group structure (roles and functions) should be in place to handle the task structure. Johnson and Johnson (1991) suggest, at least with younger children, that the cooperative group can be best managed by identifying seven key functions: summarizing, checking, researching, running, recording, supporting, and troubleshooting. These roles could be appointed to individuals or to subsets of the group.

The cooperative learning experience is monitored closely by the teacher, who has some obligation to be sure that the group is on task and to otherwise assist the group with advice on both practical and conceptual concerns, including problems that might surface from social frictions. And as with the other discussion-based approaches mentioned, the cooperative learning experience also undergoes a debriefing session that allows the groups to discuss how well everything has functioned, to distill and summarize the key ideas taken from the different groups, and to reflect on what exactly made some groups more effective than others.

Socratic Questioning. Socrates subjected his students to a carefully tailored sequence of questions that encouraged clear thinking and expression, as well as conversational repartée. The nature of the Socratic exchange is tutorial, or one-on-one. But used in a seminar setting it can generate important conversational events instrumental to the development of thinking and communication skills. Socratic questioning techniques actually aim to cultivate the act of conversation itself. In a way, the questioning techniques point to a way to have a conversation.

The Socratic dialogue generally starts with the student supporting (or being asked to support) some proposition or declaration. This sets the instructional problem by putting the teacher in the spot of deliberately subjecting the student's position to a rigorous questioning technique, using an array of conflicting possibilities, analogies, counterarguments, and various turns of logic to evaluate the student's position. The purpose is to get the student to begin to doubt or question the original position and to test it against alternatives and counterexamples, all in the hope of leading the student to a reconstructed and improved position.

Socrates, of course, had a great mind with a great store of knowledge to bring to the classroom. Not all teachers might be able to explore an argument's contours with Socrates' intellectual veracity, but they can certainly learn something important from the orientation of his method. The teacher should aim to test central propositions studied in class and subject them to a questioning routine designed to create doubt as a precondition to more nuanced insight.

The Socratic style of questioning can be confrontational and off-putting. Because it almost takes on the character of an interrogation, it has to be used carefully, with particular attention paid to its effect on appreciations and its suitability for certain age groups. The Socratic method is an especially useful technique for training in debate, where students might be forced, as an analytical exercise, to speak for or against a particular resolution, using evidence, logic, and good language to make their case. It obviously requires the teacher to be a fully informed expert on the studied topic. And although much of the Socratic method is pedagogical in nature, the teacher should be prepared to pursue certain analytical avenues. In other words, there is an instructional planning side to the method that amounts to some predesigned ideas on how to counter certain positions.

Inquiry-based Instruction.   Inquiry-based instruction involves putting the student into the role of researcher. Rather than being the receiver of knowledge from the teacher, the learner is more like an explorer guided by the teacher's map. The use of an inquiry-based strategy is obviously appropriate if the pervasive skills of inquiry take center stage in the curriculum. If skills related to observing, measuring, predicting, inferring, interpreting data, evidence collection, hypothesis formation, and experimenting are at all a part of the curriculum plan, then inquiry-based instruction will likely have a place in the microcurriculum.

Dewey (1933) believed that the main effect of inquiry was reflective thinking, which led to minds that were best prepared to lead an informed and intelligent life. An individual skilled in reflective thinking, for instance, is skilled in perceiving problems analytically, in treating problems as opportunities for improvement, and in applying knowledge and evaluating evidence. All of this, in the end, produces individuals who have the skills to control their destinies with quality judgments and enlightened behaviors.

The processes of inquiry are put into motion when events need to be addressed or when problems need to be resolved. So, inquiry-based instruction is simultaneously problem-based or problem-driven instruction. The creation of what some educators call cognitive dissonance, initiates inquiry-based instruction. This can be a "what if?" problem or a real-life school or community-based problem; it can be an ethical dilemma or question that asks the student to evaluate or analyze ideas and topics.

The task of the teacher is to supply an experience that allows the learner to become better acquainted with the problem to be studied. This could result in independent research work, various reading requirements, and structured discussion groups. An important feature of this part of the instructional process is for the student to collect relevant evidence and to evaluate it, looking with a critical eye at the nature and credibility of the source and other factors attesting to the veracity of the evidence. This phase of the inquiry process also provides a context for the learning of the subject matter.

After all the evidence is collected and evaluated and the nature of the topic is understood from its context in the subject matter, the inquiry process turns to addressing possible solutions, explanations, or hypotheses (depending on the nature of the problem). Obviously, good communication and debating skills are required. The inquiry process finally comes to a close with an illustration of conclusions and implications, which summarize what was learned and what else might now be pursued to further the line of inquiry initiated.

Inquiry-based instruction obviously makes use of other instructional models. Direct instruction might play a role in helping to explain the problem, small discussion groups might be at the core of the research and data-gathering stage, and cooperative learning might very well be the best way to forge and test hypotheses.

Independent and Individualized Instruction.   Much of the work done by students in class is accomplished without the direct assistance of the teacher. The logic of the classroom points to the need for children to often be working independently, if only because their teacher simply cannot be beside them at all times. Independent work is an important part of the instructional repertoire, so much so that we find it built into other instructional approaches. One might recall, for instance, that the last phase of direct instruction involves independent practice activities and that much of cooperative learning also relies on independent social and decision-making interactions.

Independent work also possesses the advantage of individualization. That is, it makes room for pacing differences and other forms of differentiation related to aptitude, achievement, and interest levels.

Some instructional approaches toward individualization do little more than set different paces or speeds for learning. Mastery learning programs, for instance, allow children to work through a common series of self-instructing workbook exercises at different rates of speed. This is not the most dynamic form of instruction, but it does have some limited place in the classroom, as long as it can fulfill the demands of the selection criteria detailed in Figure 6.1. We might, for instance, consider it as a reinforcement strategy for certain skills or as the independent practice feature of direct instruction.

A more progressive concept of independent and individualized instruction is embodied in the idea of the project method. Project-based learning has a long history in the elementary school of providing students with an idea-oriented and problem-focused project. Projects extend into any number of subject areas, reinforce numerous pervasive skills, and develop important appreciations for what is being learned and how it is being learned.

The project method was first popularized by William Kilpatrick, whose 1918 treatise on the topic served as an impetus for a progressive new movement toward active and experience-based learning. The idea of the project method was partly designed to counter the established mentalistic conventions of schooling. Rather than engaging in learning that was book-bound and rooted in the disciplinary traditions of the formal subjects, Kilpatrick's method was active and aimed to explore problems and ideas that transcended the formal subject-matter lines. The method's strength was its capacity to bring any number of different activities to the classroom. Drawing, constructing, reading, and viewing, for example, could all become part of a project. The intention was to make schooling coterminous with life itself.

The project method gives the teacher enormous flexibility in responding to individual differences and desires because it expects students to pursue purposeful activities independently. In fact, the key feature to the project method is self-initiation—what children want to do in school is a big factor in deciding what they do in school. (This idea has some child-centered and romantic overtones.) One, however, can still appreciate how expressive goals might very much be behind the use of the project method, as the teacher decides to follow up on and reinforce emergent interests and purposes. But the project method's strength is that it has no real methodological profile. Activities that create something, cultivate an appreciation, rectify some intellectual problem, or that develop some degree of skill or knowledge could all qualify as projects (Kilpatrick, 1918).

PEDAGOGICAL ISSUES

As mentioned, the act of teaching comprises both instructional and pedagogical concerns. Good teachers have a strong sense of what they need to accomplish and how they might begin to select learning experiences. These are largely instructional decisions. At the same time, good teachers also have a strong sense of the emergent condition in the classroom and are able to think and act on their feet in accordance with the objectives of the curriculum and the best interests of the learner. These are largely pedagogical judgments. Curriculum design speaks mostly to instructional decisions, but the implementation of the curriculum (its very life in the classroom) is a pedagogical matter.

The way teachers teach is, needless to say, crucial to the success of the curriculum. By examining the levels of curriculum performance in the classroom, we can see how a good curriculum relies on the professional discretionary judgment of the teacher.

Levels of Curriculum Performance

Teaching can be categorized into three main levels of performance. According to Tanner and Tanner (1995), these are actually levels of curriculum performance (see Fig. 6.4, p. 172). Level I, known as *Imitative-maintenance,* is the most simplistic. It is marked by routine and adoptive practices. Activities are essentially scripted by teacher manuals, closed instructional systems, or a "teaching to the test" mentality. The notion that learning is based on emergent conditions is not part of the instructional calculation. Level II, known as *Mediative,* registers at a higher

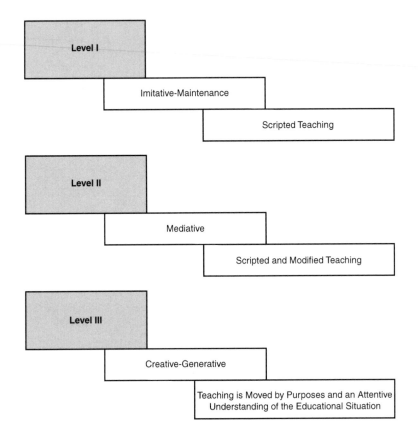

FIGURE 6.4   Levels of Curriculum Performance

professional scale because it represents a movement away from simple maintenance and adoption and a movement toward refinements or adjustments in practice based on some awareness of the uniquely dynamic condition of the classroom. Level II, in essence, is an acknowledgment that teaching is not solely a prefashioned affair that leaves the teacher with little more to do than to follow someone else's instructional plan. Finally Level III (*Creative-generative*) is the highest ideal of professionalism because it upholds teaching as a problem-solving process that requires teachers to make judgments based on the widest school purposes and the evaluation of learning needs.

It is important to note that these levels are not necessarily developmental ones—no professional growth theory points to the conclusion that teachers must start at Level I, and with experience, move to Level III. All teaching professionals, novices and veterans alike, should be working at Level III, but various factors related to school policy and experience will determine how successful a teacher is at working at this level. Still, the curriculum relies on a Level III teacher. Because the curriculum only has relevance as it exists in the main interactive circle of teacher and student, the teacher has enormous power over curriculum implementation and its overall effects on the lives of the learners.

Imitative-maintenance. Teachers who work at this level usually see the classroom in pure management terms. Reliant on routine activities that keep the children busy, Level I teachers readily used pre-made commercial materials in the interests of keeping good classroom order. Because of the concern for smooth operations, the classroom experience is largely reduced to lower-level exercises and a lower level of skill development. Problem-focused inquiry and idea-centered learning pose methodological concerns to these teachers because they require some assessment of the classroom condition and some imaginative planning that goes outside the lines of the textbook or workbook.

Teachers operating at Level I are quasi technicians, whose main function in the classroom is to carry out the instructional directions of a prescribed system of learning. The dominance of competency-based instruction, mastery learning, teacher-proof materials, and programmed instruction testifies to a Level I condition. Such instructional systems tend to reduce the teacher's role in the classroom to its most rudimentary and routine elements: clerical acts, handing out worksheets and exams in proper sequence, documenting the results, and keeping the children on task. Under these conditions, the teacher clearly has a limited instructional and pedagogical role.

Level I teachers are also more prone to teach to the test than are teachers working at a higher level of professional development. Any teacher inclined to engage in the most blatant form of teaching to the test (taking past exam items and teaching them directly) is operating at Level I. The use of reflective intelligence in the classroom to make adjustments in teaching based on interactions in the curriculum and on emerging knowledge of the learner does not exist at Level I. Classroom assessments that diagnose learner weaknesses (with the presumption of making instructional corrections) essentially do not exist either.

Mediative. Level II represents some professional awareness of the situational context of the classroom. It is a considerable jump up from Level I, but teachers at the mediative level only make partial use of their classroom awareness, limiting their decisions to certain refinements and adaptations. Thus, one could find, among Level II teachers, some of the very instructional strategies used at Level I, but with some adaptations that show an understanding of the situational context. A reliance on a competency-based method of learning, for instance, might exist, but with some refinements; Level II teachers might skip certain sections of the curriculum, add supplementary materials here and there, or decide to use another instructional approach together with the competency-based approach. Thus, one cannot expect any grand innovations in the curriculum from the teacher at Level II, but certain modest changes, justified by some consideration of the learner, will likely occur.

Many teachers working at the mediative level are held down by poor curriculum design. This is especially the case if a school district and certain super-ordinates in a teacher's professional life require the use of a closed and instructionally prescriptive curriculum. Burdened with a curriculum that constricts judgment, teachers can only, at their best, make some alterations or perhaps find the time to offer some alternative instructional approaches. Pressures to teach to the test, use certain textbooks, and engage in instructional techniques favored by in-service training programs could have the same effect.

Creative-generative.   Level III represents the highest standard of professional actualization. At this level, teaching is moved by the widest educational purposes of the school, not simply those that have priority on standardized tests or that are conveniently encapsulated in competency-based learning systems. Hence, classroom activity has a wide-ranging quality to it, finding itself concerned with not only academic and intellectual skills but also socio-civic attitudes, individual interests and talents, an array of thinking, communication, and inquiry skills, constructive attitudes toward learning, and so forth. Activities in the classroom are problem focused and idea centered, and are planned and operated through the creative judgment of the teacher, whose thinking is always inspired by some regard for the nature of the learner, the values of the society, and the knowledge embodied in the subject matter. The curriculum is organized in any number of ways but often reflects interconnections between ideas and between disciplines, and shows good articulation between grades or age levels.

The Level III teacher is fundamentally a diagnostician, who reflects on the classroom in ways that draw from a wealth of instructional and assessment strategies. The idea of assessment is especially important because it demonstrates that attention is being paid to whether instructional strategies are resulting in the kinds of effects desired. If they are not, the teacher (using experience, theory, and research) will make changes that will ultimately be retested in the experience of the classroom. Thus, the teacher at Level III must be a consumer of research and must have the authority to exercise independent judgment in selecting materials and methods. Teaching to the test does not exist here because no test could possibly privilege everything that the teacher seeks in the education of the learner. Competency-based systems also go against the grain of Level III because of their narrow skill base and their prescriptive instructional nature.

The Latent Curriculum

The curriculum development process is mostly concerned with manifest purposes, with manifest actions that bring life to these purposes, and with manifest ways to understand whether such actions fulfill expressed purposes. Curriculum development, in this sense, is mostly an explicit matter, marked by publicly acknowledged and publicly rationalized events.

But the implementation of any curriculum also carries various latent or implicit meanings that teach children crucially important things. So, as we teach something like multiplication skills, we also might be teaching children something about liking or disliking math and learning, or even perhaps something about what it means to work hard, have patience, and be honest. It is unlikely that any teacher would design lessons dedicated to making children more honest, for instance, but it is likely that many aspects of the school experience will communicate latent messages to children about honesty. Such messages can be transmitted to the student in multiple and highly nuanced ways—in the rectitude of the teacher's own behaviors (both inside and outside of the classroom), in the manner in which teachers respond to student questions and concerns, and in the general interactive pattern between teachers and students (tone of voice, style of body language, language used and favored in the classroom, forms of affection, if any, and so forth). We call this the *latent curriculum*, also sometimes known as the implicit, covert, or hidden curriculum. The latent curriculum lives in the thousands of interactions that occur between teachers and students each school day.

The idea of the latent curriculum has fascinated curriculum scholars for many years because it widens the sense of the school experience by looking beyond traditional concerns about meeting behavioral objectives, covering content, keeping order, and raising test scores. Because the early progressive movement in education took part of its identity from a commitment to broadening the curricular focus of the school (in a way that accounted for the development of various habits, attitudes, and dispositions rarely acknowledged as relevant to the curriculum development process), the latent curriculum became a front-and-center concern for progressives. Consequently, new and provocative questions about curriculum development followed. What effect, for instance, did schools have on the student's disposition to enjoy learning, derive pleasure from inquiry, and be practically empowered by the wider world of knowledge brought forth in the school? What did the schools do to construct the self-esteem of youth, influence their leisure-time habits, and sway their attitudes and actions toward community, society, and government? Referring to the latent curriculum as collateral learning, John Dewey (1938) wisely understood the power of implicit lessons taught in school. "Perhaps the greatest of all pedagogical fallacies," he wrote, "is the notion that a person learns only the particular thing he is studying at the time. Collateral learning in the way of formation of enduring attitudes, of likes and dislikes, may be and often is much more important than the spelling lesson, or lesson in geography or history that is learned" (p. 48).

The latent curriculum is important to the curriculum developer because it shapes important values and outlooks, including critically important values related to independent learning and independent thinking. Learning to read, for instance, is undeniably important, but it is essentially a lost cause if the learner who can read ably actually hates to read altogether and rarely engages a book independently. The latent curriculum is the main influence in producing the kinds of values and outlooks (negative or positive) we embrace toward schooling and learning. What schools teach implicitly can also strongly influence the makeup of the cultural norms conveyed and reinforced in the school, sending signals about what is worthy to know, read, and do, as well as indirect lessons about various common values and mores. The latent message of a reading list in English class that includes only the work of white, European men may not be one that a teacher wants to send.

The latent curriculum is largely in the hands of a teacher's pedagogy. If a teacher of English, for instance, regularly uses writing assignments to punish poor behavior in class, a latent curriculum is very much at work, sending a less-than-constructive message to the student about the act of writing. If a teacher can always be seen reading in the library after school hours and is known for having read every book on the *New York Times* best-seller list, an important pro-reading message is sent. If the social studies teacher gives an unpopular viewpoint in class the same level of critical respect and appreciation that popular views enjoy, an important message about critical consciousness and dissent is conveyed. If an unpopular and socially clumsy student receives the same degree of respect from the teacher as does a popular sports star, a latent social lesson is communicated. If disrespect, dishonesty, shoddiness, and laziness are treated with consistent intolerance by the teacher, again the latent lessons are clear. And in none of these cases was there ever a need to design a lesson plan; the teaching was in the subtext of the interactive pattern between the teacher and the student.

From the standpoint of the curriculum, it is important to be conscious of the presence and the possibilities of the latent curriculum, and for educators to try to think deliberately about how their behavior results in offering latent lessons. The other important key is to valorize the latent curriculum by privileging its effects in the evaluation of the curriculum, so that all of the attitudinal factors that play into the latent curriculum make their way into the evaluative mechanism, something I will discuss in more detail in the next chapter.

Expressive Goals

Everything that is worth doing in a school does not have to emerge from a plan. Eisner (1998) articulated the idea of expressive goals to describe events in the classroom that have no explicit or manifest plan or objective. The term *goal* is slightly confusing here because of the convention of equating the idea of a goal with a preplanned event. We must try to imagine a teacher embracing new and unanticipated goals as they materialize in the midst of classroom action, usually in response to a particular situation. The decision to take a student, or more generally an entire classroom, in an unforeseen teaching direction can be influenced by a teacher's intuition, by some felt need to shift course, by a desire to remedy an emergent problem, or by an effort to attend to interest levels. The intention of expressive goals is to inject something valuable in the experience that was not part of the preplanned sequence of instructional events.

Expressive goals are important to the curriculum development process because they give the school experience important flexibility while also honoring the professional judgment of the teacher. They are the main ways that teachers can honestly respond to the particulars of their classroom situation. To have expressive goals is to have a classroom whose teachers are on the lookout for what some people might call a teachable moment, a point in time that surfaces in the classroom and presents itself as worthy of continued discussion and examination. Expressive goals can also manifest as efforts to individualize the school experience for children, rationalized by an understanding of individual needs and interests (as they express themselves in the life of the classroom). The pedagogy of the teacher is very much shaped by expressive goals, by decisions to venture from routine (or from some other preplanned event) in order to pursue something that is viewed as educative. A creative-generative teacher very much relies on expressive goals because of the demand to diagnose classroom problems and convert them into problem solutions. Conversely, a classroom that shuns expressive goals is, in effect, asking the teacher to perform at the very lowest level of professional judgment.

Consider a teacher of high school history who decided to pursue, say, a role-playing activity in class. After the students set out to write their scenarios, the teacher discovered that the students were having an especially difficult time writing dialogue. At such a point the teacher could go in any number of directions: drop the assignment and go forward with the rest of the preplanned agenda; decide to not worry about the poor writing, knowing that problem will be attended to later by the English teacher and again go forward with the rest of the preplanned agenda; or exercise an expressive goal that goes after the problem, perhaps asking the English teacher to join in a week-long collaboration. It is not likely that writing dialogue is part of the original purpose of history class, but it could become one if the teacher sees the opportunity to pursue it. These are precisely the kinds of twists and turns that teachers encounter, requiring them to respond to goals arising from within activity.

The idea that goals can be derived from activity is one that has been with progressive thinkers for some time. Dewey, who understood the influence of goals in directing experience, also spoke of the possibilities of goals emerging from experience. Aims, he declared "are not strictly speaking ends or termini or action. . . . They are terminals of deliberation and so turning points in activity" (p. 223). This was Dewey's way of saying that teaching should not be viewed as simply the means used to fulfill and complete ends. Teaching is indeed guided by goals, but it also produces its own goals. Goals derived from within an activity are closely associated with the particulars of the learner and the wider educational situation, and offer important continuity to the school experience. So, although objectives fundamentally act as directives, they can be produced by activities, which give birth to subsequent experiences.

The exercise of expressive goals does not give the teacher a free reign over the curriculum. The normative agenda of the curriculum, as articulated in the manifest curriculum, cannot be denied and any decisions to pursue goals derived from within activity must be professionally defensible, meaning that they must be suited to the age and maturity level of the student, the values of our society, and the general mission of the school. In other words, expressive goals are not simply willy-nilly decisions. They are justified by a teacher's nuanced understanding of the learner, and may stem from a hope to correct a misunderstanding, to broaden an experiential horizon, or even to simply have fun.

SUMMARY

The design of learning experiences is naturally at the core of the curriculum development process. The preliminary work of forming purposes and organizing the macro features of the school gets us to the point of contemplating the selection of learning experiences. Although such selections spring from the defining elements of our purposes (pervasive skills and content), other principles also come into play. These include a demand to select experiences that build important appreciations and that retain some identity with the nature of the learner and the values of the society. Curriculum developers should also be sure that selected experiences are congruent with core purposes and safeguard against the segmental treatment of purposes and experiences.

The distinction between instruction and pedagogy defines the limits of the planned instructional experience. Even if the curriculum's purposes are dynamic and enlightened and the planned instructional response is consonant with those purposes (and with a sense of what is best for the student population), those plans still have to be realized in the life of the classroom. And an understanding of pedagogy is necessary for that to happen. Pedagogy is simply the curriculum in action, as it truly exists in the circle of engagement between students and teachers. The discretionary power of teachers resides in their pedagogy, in their ability to account for the unique factors of the classroom and the many dimensions of the learner's situation. The exercise of expressive goals or outcomes relies on teacher judgment—a decision to go forward with a course of activity that was not preplanned but that arose from within an activity and that ultimately promised to deliver something meaningful and educative to the learner.

Because the curriculum should not script instruction, it depends on a teacher who can exercise informed independent judgments in the classroom. Such teachers operate at the creative-generative level of curriculum performance. They can diagnose problems and account for various situational factors in their classroom decision making. They also understand the importance of the latent curriculum by trying to be conscious of the implicit effects that the school experience has on various attitudes and appreciations.

DISCUSSION QUESTIONS AND SUGGESTED ACTIVITIES

1. What is the distinction between instruction and pedagogy and why is it helpful to understand the curriculum development process?

2. The selection of learning experiences is rooted in its connection to purposes. What other factors are also required to secure wise instructional selections?

3. How might one argue for or against the idea that variance is the key to good teaching?

4. What is meant by the argument that one cannot pursue instructional strategies that are good without contemplating what they are good for?

5. How might one argue that the criticism against the lecture-demonstration method has been somewhat unfair and heavy-handed?

6. Describe what a direct instructional lesson might look like in a third-grade mathematics classroom and in a high school algebra or science classroom? What might be the likely pervasive skills covered in a lesson and how might the content of the lesson be approached?

7. How is role-playing a discussion-based instructional approach and what are some of the cautionary points to consider with a role-playing strategy?

8. How is inquiry-based instruction related to reflective thinking?

9. Describe a classroom run by a teacher who is operating at the Imitative-maintenance level of curriculum performance.

10. How is good curriculum development dependent on a teacher who is operating at the creative-generative level of curriculum performance?

11. What is the latent curriculum? Describe examples of how implicit messages or meanings are taught to children through the latent curriculum.

12. Describe a classroom scenario in which a teacher makes use of expressive goals.

NOTES

Dewey, J. (1922). *Human nature and conduct.* New York: Henry Holt.
Dewey, J. (1933). *How we think.* Boston: D.C. Heath.

Dewey, J. (1938). *Experience and education.* New York: Macmillan.

Eisner, E. (1998). *The educational imagination.* New York: Macmillan Co.

Good, T. & Brophy, J. (1991). *Looking in classrooms.* New York: Harper Collins.

Johnson, D.W. & Johnson, R.T. (1991). *Learning together and alone.* Englewood Cliffs, NJ: Prentice-Hall.

Joyce, B. & Weil, M. (1986). *Models of teaching.* Englewood Cliffs, NJ: Prentice-Hall.

Kilpatrick, W. (1918). The project method. *Teachers College Record XIX* (September, No. 4), 319–335.

Pratt, D. (1994). *Curriculum planning.* New York: Harcourt Brace.

Tanner, D. & Tanner, L. (1995). *Curriculum development.* New York: Macmillan Co.

Tyler, R. (1949). *Basic principles of curriculum and instruction.* Chicago: University of Chicago Press.

CHAPTER SEVEN

EVALUATION

Where there is reflection, there is suspense
—John Dewey

We evaluate or otherwise try to understand our world as we live in it. Our abilities to pass thoughtful judgments, to draw reasonable conclusions, to establish a sense of what is worthwhile, and to understand what needs to be changed (as well as conserved) are all rooted in the act of evaluation. To evaluate the world means to think actively about it and to ultimately problematize it in a way that sets the conditions for its progress. Evaluation, in effect, allows us to know what we have done well and to find a way to convert what we have not done well into corrections and improvements. It is the feedback loop in the design of the curriculum—which is to say the procedure we use to note whether certain purposes have been achieved. But it also involves other curriculum-based factors, such as individual student performance, teacher performance, and other quality concerns related to the organization and mission of the school.

The idea of evaluation is uniquely positioned in the process of curriculum development. The overarching question is whether the curriculum has produced experiences that have attained the main purposes of the school. As Tyler (1949) put it, "the process of evaluation is essentially the process of determining to what extent the educational objectives are actually being realized by the program of curriculum and instruction (pp. 105–106). So, the question is not whether evaluation will play a role in the curriculum. At some level, it must. The question is more about what its nature shall be.

THE IDEA OF EVALUATION

The term *evaluation* means something distinct from other terms (such as *testing, measurement,* and *assessment*) with which it is often associated. Ralph Tyler claimed to have coined the term in the context of the school curriculum, and he gave it a meaning and a function that is characteristic to the act of curriculum development.

Tyler hit on the idea of evaluation because of his frustration with the use of tests as single-point appraisal mechanisms. The early development of testing in the public schools was accompanied by a tendency to reduce the judgment of the curriculum to a single test score. Tyler saw this as a dangerous misuse of testing— one that threatened to distort the nature of the school curriculum itself. Today, of course, the problem is still with us. The handiwork of our failure to make any good distinction between testing and evaluation has given rise to what Popham originally called high-stakes testing: tests that are linked to high-stakes events, such as graduation requirements, grade-retention decisions, enrollment in various curriculum tracks, and even the use of special classifications, such as gifted and talented. When testing has this kind of influence in the curriculum, the consequences are predictable in that we can expect the test to displace the core purposes of the curriculum as the driving factor in the development of the curriculum.

Tyler's idea was to link evaluation to purposes and to devise a way of determining effects of the curriculum that transcended the idea of the test. Tyler suggested using a variety of strategies to document some judgment of what students have learned. In other words, Tyler constructed evaluation as an evidence-collection process that made use of many appraisal tools relevant to the curriculum's main purposes. Thus, if we consider core purposes x, y, and z and provide responsive instruction to x, y, and z, we inevitably also have to look for ways to evaluate x, y, and z, which means that we must look for the appropriate evaluation tools. Rather than use only a test for such a task, we might instead embrace any number of devices, including observational data, interview data, behavior inventories, rating scales, student products, and any other possible range of tools that teachers (or school-wide authorities) might find (including, of course, tests). Tyler (1949) spoke directly to the features of this evidence collection:

> Since evaluation means getting evidence about behavior changes in the students, any valid evidence about the behaviors that are desired as educational objectives provides an appropriate method of evaluation. This is important to recognize because many people think of evaluation as synonymous with the giving of paper and pencils tests. . . . However, there are a great many . . . desired behaviors which represent objectives that are not easily appraised by paper and pencil devices. . . . Observations are useful to get at habits and certain kinds of operational skills. Another method which is useful in evaluation is the interview, which may throw light upon the changes taking place in attitudes, in interests, in appreciations and the like. Questionnaires sometimes serve to give evidence about interests, about attitudes and about other types of behavior. The selection of actual products made by the students is sometimes a useful way of getting evidence of behavior. (pp. 107–108)

So, the curriculum developer should first understand that evaluation is a process that includes any number of evaluative methods. Second, evaluation is designed to look for group effects—specifically, the appraisal of curricula and programs. In other words, evaluation "grades" the curriculum; it is only indirectly involved with grading or judging students (Madaus and Kelleghan, 1992). It goes without saying then that tests could be used as evaluative components, and that measurements (quantitative gauges), interviews, surveys, and observations could be part of the school's evaluative profile. And in each case, we look to see how well each tool produced helpful information on aggregate (group) effects in the curriculum, looking particularly at evidence for the fulfillment of purposes.

At the microcurricular level, however, the teacher is also involved in an appraisal process that affects student grading and other judgments of individual performance. This process of appraisal is known as *assessment*. To put it simply, assessment is designed to show what a *person* knows or can do (Maduas and Kellaghan, 1992). Because of the focus on the individual, assessment is largely a classroom-based concern. But assessment and evaluation walk hand-in-hand in the curriculum. If we aggregate assessment data, for instance, they can be used as evaluation, and in this sense, might even be considered part of an overarching plan for evaluation. Moreover, the instrumentation of assessment itself could become the subject of evaluation (Madaus and Kellaghan, 1992). Although I will be discussing, more often than not, the construct of evaluation, the reader should understand that assessment components are entwined with evaluation.

THE INSTRUMENTATION OF EVALUATION

The evaluation of the school curriculum is mostly a matter of discerning what has been learned as a function of what has been taught. But the instrumentation used in an evaluative design also has to worry about validity and reliability concerns. That is, curriculum developers have to be sure that the methods they use to discern effects are valid (meaning that they actually give the evidence that they are designed to produce) and are reliable (meaning that the evidence collected is consistent internally and over time). Some instruments of evaluation, such as achievement tests, might be compromised by validity issues, especially if they are not appropriate to the age and maturity level of the child or if they test something that the teacher has not even taught. On the other hand, reliability concerns are likely to threaten observational data, producing fundamentally different results based on who is doing the observing. Of course, to the extent that some components of evaluation are not valid, they will also likely be unreliable, and vice versa. I will talk about these matters in more detail as they apply to specific instruments.

The traditional way to look at evaluation is to see it as a summative phenomenon, as something that occurs at the logical conclusion of a unit, chapter, or semester. The purpose of a summative evaluation is to get feedback on the curriculum experience at the completion of some logical phase of instruction. Summative evaluations are important precisely because they provide us with a completed sense of the curriculum experience. But no evaluation should become an exclusive, one-time-only procedure that occurs at the end of a program. Hence, curriculum developers should see evaluation as a process that also has a formative point of reference. Formative evaluation is what we call ongoing evaluation. It might be given before the start of a new chapter, unit, or semester (possibly to be used to gauge growth over time), or at any other time during the instructional phases. Formative evaluation gives the curriculum a way to negotiate changes and to appraise emerging problems, deficiencies, and strengths. Pedagogical decisions and the formation of expressive objectives very much rely on formative evaluations and assessments.

Before moving forward with the discussion of the actual instruments of evaluation, I would like to underscore three principles that apply to the entire evaluation design—ideas that I adopted mostly from the work of George Madaus (1999). These principles are relevant to the curriculum designer, who should keep them in mind when contemplating the evaluation features of the school curriculum (see Fig. 7.1). First, in approaching the design of evaluation, the curriculum developer should protect the school experience against the fallibility of all appraisals used in the curriculum by not depending on any one particular appraisal. No single test or single appraising event can effectively capture the comprehensiveness of the school's mandate. To the extent that we allow ourselves to reduce the appraisal of the school curriculum to a single experience, we make ourselves vulnerable to considerable validity and reliability problems and to the high-stakes testing distortions that occur when we unreasonably heighten the stature of the appraisal mechanism in the instructional experience. Second, the curriculum developer should understand that the evaluation of x endows x with considerable instructional authority. This is another way of saying that whatever gets evaluated in the curriculum usually gets taught in the classroom. The failure of the curriculum developer to reflect all of the curriculum's core purposes in the evaluation of

Principle 1	The curriculum developer should protect the school experience against the fallibility of all appraisals used in the curriculum by not depending on any one particular appraisal.
Principle 2	The curriculum developer should understand that the evaluation of x endows x with considerable instructional authority; said another way, whatever gets evaluated usually gets taught.
Principle 3	The curriculum developer should understand that assessment treatments in the classroom reflect the wider design of the evaluation, so that whatever is honored in the evaluation will also become an assessment concern and whatever is ignored in the evaluation will likely be ignored in assessments.

FIGURE 7.1   Principles for Curriculum Evaluation

the curriculum underscores the inconsequentiality of those purposes left behind. If democratic attitudes, love of learning, moral behaviors, thinking skills, and research skills are all viewed as important to the mission of the school, they must also be viewed as important to the design of the evaluation. Finally, the curriculum developer should understand that assessment treatments in the classroom reflect the wider design of the evaluation, so that whatever is honored in the evaluation will also become an assessment concern and whatever is ignored in the evaluation likely will be ignored in assessments. This is a variation of the second principle. Because assessment decisions are made in the classroom, they are an especially important concern in the conduct of the curriculum. Teachers will be reluctant to overlook anything in their assessments that is valued in the evaluation of the curriculum. Assessments, in this sense, solidify the strength of both the instructional experience (if one appraises it, one has to teach it) and the actual evaluation (if one assesses it, one provides data to the evaluation).

Tests

Few things are more ubiquitous in the school experience than the phenomenon of testing. Most tests aim to "measure" performance through the use of either selected-response items (multiple choice, true-false, matching, and other one-answer choices) or constructed-response items, which include written short answer and essay responses. Other testing possibilities include oral examinations, which are rare in the American schools, and authentic performance exams that ask students to engage in specific tasks that coincide closely with real-life tasks. A driver's exam that requires a student to demonstrate various maneuvers with the car to the satisfaction of an observing judge is a type of authentic performance assessment. For our purposes, we will be discussing the most obvious and omnipotent form of testing in the school curriculum—what Tyler called pencil-and-paper exams.

   The curriculum developer needs to recognize the two main forms of tests typically used in the school curriculum: norm-referenced and criterion-referenced exams. Because the orientation of norm-referenced exams is to assess the performance of an individual relative to the performance of other individuals, they are popular in schools. Norm-referenced exams feature what are known as relative measures, which means that an individual's score on the exam is relative to the scores of other individuals. In this way, the norm-referenced test is designed to produce a distribution of different scores that allows the school to judge higher and lower performers. The results of norm-referenced exams are sometimes converted into percentile rankings and are ideally used when there is a need to make some judgment based on comparability, such as (at least arguably) assigning student grades. For the curriculum developer, the important point to remember is that norm-referenced exams are designed to produce variance, so that if any item on a test does not contribute to the cause of variance it becomes a candidate to be excluded from subsequent exams. If all the students get a test item right or, as the case might be, all get it wrong, the item is not likely to survive for long on a norm-referenced exam. This could be a source of frustration with some teachers because test items that reflect well-taught concepts that all students have learned will inevitably be dropped from a norm-referenced exam. Criterion-referenced exams, on the other hand, attempt to ascertain a learner's performance against a predetermined task or criterion. They are sometimes known as absolute measures of performance. Criterion-referenced exams are not driven by a desire to compare performance between students but by an effort to subject performance to a reference standard or criterion of proficiency. Often this includes an effort to signify whether a student has met a rudimentary performance standard, which all children are expected to master, or a more advanced performance standard. On a criterion-based exam, it is desirable for all the test items linked to the rudimentary domain to be answered correctly. This would signify universal mastery at the most basic or rudimentary level.

One could appreciate how the norm-referenced exam might be valued in an evaluation or assessment plan. If the school wants to identify the most meritorious in a particular area of study or to use a grading system in the classroom that is moved by a norm-referenced spirit (which means that a grade of *A* is an *A* relative to how well the other students do), then norm-referenced exams will have a place in the assessment scheme. Norm-referenced testing certainly has a more prominent place in the high school than in the elementary school, mostly because of the pressures that high schools are under to identify exceptional precollege candidates. But it might also have a purpose in helping to identify students for special instruction (enrichment to remedial) and in placing students into different within-class and between-class ability groups. Having said this, however, it is also important to note that norm-referenced exams represent single-event appraisals and, like all appraisals, are fallible. A classroom teacher who assesses performance using only one norm-referenced exam is violating the aforementioned important principle of variety in technique. A school-wide evaluation that uses only, say, the Iowa Test of Basic Skills (ITBS) to appraise the curriculum perpetrates the same principle and likely distorts the curriculum because it would probably fail to reflect the standing of purposes not covered by the ITBS.

The design of tests, for either evaluation or assessment purposes, always poses a number of validity concerns. There are some obvious considerations in this regard, such as ensuring that all tests contain clear directions, provide adequate time limits, avoid ambiguous statements, and properly match the age and maturity level of the student. But to determine the nature of the validity issues, one must also know the specific intent of the tests. Is the intention to show achievement? If so, our validity concerns will revolve around demonstrating some link between what was taught and what was tested. This is known as content validity, which is an especially important factor in achievement, because achievement is, as indicated, a matter of having learned what one has been taught. Thus, if at the conclusion of a botany course, a student is given a test on auto mechanics, obvious content-validity problems will prevail. Or if a teacher spends five weeks working on the textbook's Chapter Five and only one day on Chapter Six, only to reflect an equal number of test items associated with each chapter (with equal valuative weights), we might again argue that a content-validity problem is at work. The interesting problem here, at least at the evaluation level, is that if all teachers working at the same grade level actually used the same standardized test, content-validity problems would be almost inevitable. Differences in the textbooks used by the teachers, in the topical range of their courses, and even in the manner in which they emphasize or de-emphasize certain content knowledge and skill usage, could all potentially contribute to a content validity problem. That is why, generally speaking, teacher-made assessments run less of a risk of harboring content-validity problems than do standardized tests, assuming the teacher is aware of the link between what is taught and what is tested. If a teacher makes a test deliberately linked to what was taught, accounting for the nuances of the classroom instructional exposure, then the prospects of finding the test out of alignment with what was taught are less great than if the test is standardized. This partly explains the popularity of curriculum standards, which represent an effort to coordinate the curriculum in a way that ensures more standardized exposures to the content and skills advanced between classrooms and even schools.

If we expect our tests to predict future success or even some future behavior, then we face another kind of validity problem that revolves around the issue of demonstrating some association or link between doing well on the test and performing a particular behavior. If, for instance, we want the test that we use to assess civic knowledge to also predict civic behavior (say, as measured by community volunteerism and voting habits), then we would have to be able to show some correlation between success on the test and actual acts of community volunteerism and voting. This is known as predictive validity. Such tests might be used in the schools if the actual behavior sought in the evaluation were not easily observed in the educational situation.

And if we expect our test to speak to a general construct or characteristic (such as thinking skills, problem solving, or democratic attitudes), we face a validity concern in demonstrating how our test can be interpreted as a meaningful measure of our construct, which is a problem known as construct validity. Concerns over predictive and construct validity can be partly handled by adopting commercial tests that have pre-established validity and reliability ratings. This allows the school to offer a test that targets any number of constructs relevant to the school's mission (thinking, problem solving, self-esteem, social tolerance, democratic attitudes, scientific thinking, and so forth) and to use them as a component of the evaluation.

The issue of reliability is also fundamental to the construction and use of tests. Reliability refers to the nature of consistency in an appraisal instrument. Someone concerned about reliability will ask, if test x was used today with group z, will it yield the same effects if it is used with the same group tomorrow? What if another teacher gives the exact test to the same population, will it produce the same results? This kind of consistency is known as stability consistency, or test-retest reliability (Popham, 1999). Teachers will not likely have the occasion to use a test-retest procedure for their own tests, mostly because it is not a very practical thing to do in the classroom, but most standardized tests will subject themselves to stringent test-retest procedures. The ideal is for the test to have good consistency over time and a good positive correlation between the original test and the retest would indicate a strong degree of consistency.

Another kind of reliability refers to alternate forms of the same exam. Some teachers have a bank of test items from which they draw to make different equivalent forms of the same test. But if different forms of the test are to be used, one has to be sure to get consistent results between the different tests. One test cannot be easier or more difficult than the other. To be confident of alternate-form reliability, we would expect significant positive correlations between the paired items used on the different forms of the exam (the sets of items used to assess the same material) and between the overall scores of the two exams, assuming that our test groups are equal.

Reliable tests need to also consider internal consistency performance, which refers to the extent to which the items on a test are functioning in a consistent and homogeneous manner. Hence, if our test purports to measure x, then every item on the test should be making some contribution to measuring x. Internal consistency is sometimes measured with what is known as a split-half correlation, where the scores for a random sample of one half of the exam are correlated against the scores of the other half. If we have a significant positive correlation, we can be fairly certain that our internal reliability is pretty good. Obviously, in all the cases discussed, good clarity in the questioning routines, in the criteria used to score the tests, as well as in the directions and administration of the test help the cause of reliability.

Written exams or tests with constructed response items are especially problematic from the standpoint of reliability. How do we know, for instance, that teacher a is consistent with teacher b when scoring the same written exam? One of the best ways to attend to this problem is to subject the test to the judgment of independent and similarly qualified professionals, and to determine if the judgments are consistent, a process known as inter-rater reliability. This is no easy matter for classroom teachers who typically do not have the opportunity to have other teachers independently grade their student's work, although this certainly would be a productive activity for a curriculum-evaluation design to sponsor.

At the evaluation level, if the school is interested in offering a way to evaluate student writing or if it is asking more complex and open-ended questions in various subject areas (such as history, social studies, or even mathematics), an inter-rater reliability mechanism will probably have to be integrated into the design. The inter-rater mechanism correlates the independent judgments of different scorers. If the correlation is strong enough to indicate a consistency of response from one rater (or scorer) to another, one could say that the grading between the raters is reliable. If it does not produce a good positive correlation, one would need to have the scorers revisit the criteria used to make the score and to articulate the reasoning behind their judgment so that subsequent rating efforts might be more consistent.

Scoring guides, or rubrics, play an important role in tests that use constructed responses. Rubrics describe the things we are looking to find in a response. If these descriptors are clear and unambiguous, they are less likely to give us reliability problems. So, if we want to use rubrics to grade a written essay, we would want to use ones that offer us fairly specific descriptions of what we see as desirable (high-achieving) essays and what we see as undesirable (low-achieving) ones. The orientation of the rubric can be holistic, meaning that it simply aims to give a general assessment of quality without specifically aiming to judge any of the constituent elements of writing (a holistic score range of "excellent, very good, good, limited, or poor") or it can be analytic, which aims to offer some judgment of quality against named specifics (Popham, 1999). Analytic rubrics allow us to assess specific factors in the curriculum.

Popham (1999) designed an analytic rubric for the skill of oral communication, which is a pervasive skill in the curriculum (see Fig. 7.2). The rubric clearly gives the teacher a way to get a profile of the attendant subskills of oral communication. The main conceptual criteria to the evaluation include a rating for the delivery, organization, content, and language used in the student's oral performance, with each rubric area offering language detailing what the evaluator should try to find. Now contrast Popham's analytic rubric to the holistic rubric on oral communication depicted in Figure 7.3. The benefits that accrue from the analytic rubric

---

Task

During regular class sessions, students will be required to present a specified oral communication (namely, an impromptu, extemporaneous, or extensively prepared speech) to their peers.

Evaluative Criteria

Each oral communication will be judged on the basis of four evaluative criteria—namely, *delivery, organization, content,* and *language*. Each evaluative criterion is based on two or three factors that are considered when the criterion is applied. These factors are identified below (and explained, if necessary) for each evaluative criterion.

The stringency with which these criteria are applied should vary depending on the nature of the oral communication involved (e.g., lower expectations would be employed when judging impromptu speeches than when judging extensively prepared speeches). Consideration should also be given to the age of the students involved.

FIGURE 7.2   Analytic Rubric for Appraising Oral Communication Skills

Source: From W.J. Popham. *Classroom assessment: What teachers need to know,* 2d ed. Published by Allyn & Bacon, Boston, MA. Copyright © 1999 by Pearson Education. Adapted by permission of the publisher.

(continued)

When considering each evaluative criterion's factors, the notions of "adequate" and "superior" performances should be used. *Adequate* student performance refers to a level of quality consonant with what would be expected of a student who is making suitable developmental or instructional progress. In a sense, therefore, adequate performance on any factor signifies, roughly, that the student is performing at grade-level expectations. *Superior,* then, means the student's performance is clearly at a level of quality higher than grade-level expectations. For each of the four criteria, 1 to 3 points can be awarded. Any given speech, therefore, can receive a total score of 4 to 12 points. Although intended to be used analytically, the rubric can be employed holistically by disregarding per-criterion point allocations.

Delivery

The delivery rating for an oral communication is based on the following three factors: *volume, rate,* and *articulation* (that is, pronunciation and enunciation).

- In *advanced* speeches (3 points), all three delivery factors are at least adequate and two or three factors are superior.
- In *proficient* speeches (2 points), all three delivery factors are at least adequate.
- In *partially proficient* speeches (1 point), fewer than three delivery factors are adequate.

Organization

The organization rating for an oral communication is based on the following two factors: *sequence* and *relationship* among ideas in the communication (that is, the clarity of the order and connection among the speech's points).

- In *advanced* speeches (3 points), both organization factors are superior.
- In *proficient* speeches (2 points), both organization factors are at least adequate.
- In *partially proficient* speeches (1 point), fewer than two organization factors are adequate.

Content

The content rating for an oral communication is based on the following three factors: *amount* of content, *relevance* of the content to the assigned speech topic, and *adaptation* of the content to the listeners and situation.

- In *advanced* speeches (3 points), all three content factors are at least adequate and two or more are superior.
- In *proficient* speeches (2 points), all three content factors are at least adequate.
- In *partially proficient* speeches (1 point), fewer than three content factors are adequate.

Language

The language rating for an oral communication is based on the following two factors; *grammar* and *word choice.*

- In *advanced* speeches (3 points), both language factors are superior.
- In *proficient* speeches (2 points), all three content factors are at least adequate.
- In *partially proficient* speeches (1 point), fewer than three content factors are adequate.

FIGURE 7.2   Continued

5—Excellent	The student clearly describes the question studied and provides strong reasons for its importance. Specific information is given to support the conclusions that are drawn and described. The delivery is engaging and sentence structure is consistently correct. Eye contact is made and sustained throughout the presentation. There is strong evidence of preparation, organization, and enthusiasm for the topic. The visual aid is used to make the presentation more effective. Questions from the audience are clearly answered with specific and appropriate information.
4—Very Good	The student describes the question studied and provides reasons for its importance. An adequate amount of information is given to support the conclusions that are drawn and described. The delivery and sentence structure are generally correct. There is evidence of preparation, organization, and enthusiasm for the topic. The visual aid is mentioned and used. Questions from the audience are answered clearly.
3—Good	The student describes the question studied and conclusions are stated, but supporting information is not as strong as a 4 or 5. The delivery and sentence structure are generally correct. There is some indication of preparation and organization. The visual aid is mentioned. Questions from the audience are answered.
2—Limited	The student states the question studied but fails to describe it fully. No conclusions are given to answer the question. The delivery and sentence structure are understandable, but with some errors. Evidence of preparation and organization is lacking. The visual aid may or may not be mentioned. Questions from the audience are answered with only the most basic response.
1—Poor	The student makes a presentation without stating the question or its importance. The topic is unclear and no adequate conclusions are stated. The delivery is difficult to follow. There is no indication of preparation or organization. Questions from the audience receive only the most basic or no response.
0	No oral presentation is attempted.

FIGURE 7.3 Holistic Rubric for Appraising Oral Communication Skills

Source: Adapted from G. Wiggins. 1998. *Educative assessment*. Copyright © 1998. This material is used by permission of John Wiley & Sons, Inc.

become fairly obvious. In the example offered in Figure 7.2, the rubric gives us data that might be useful to the improvement of instructional practice. The four elements of the rubric could help to indicate where we might be falling short. The holistic rubric, on the other hand (Fig. 7.3), gives us an idea of how things generally stand with oral presentation skills, but not much more than that. So, unless other data were collected, the holistic rubric would be of limited use.

Observations

Schools do not typically see classroom observations as forms of curriculum evaluation. Observations rarely make it into the documentation used for the evaluation of the curriculum, although they do have some status in assessment. In at least the younger grades, for instance, student report cards sometimes do reflect insights and generalizations (usually concerning classroom behaviors) drawn from teacher observations. And educators today are still expected to observe the children in their classrooms so that they could note concerns and strengths that might, in the end, allow them to make improvements and adjustments to the educational situation. This is, in fact, the essential process we witness in the creative-generative (Level III) teacher, who uses a form of diagnosis drawn from multiple sources (but taken heavily from observations of children in school) to adjust and attune the school experience to the nature of the learner. Part of being a professional educator means to make evaluative observations of children.

Teacher observations are largely anecdotal, emergent, and unstructured. They are usually made with assessment purposes in mind, meaning that they are often targeted at individuals. But teacher observations can also be more structured and can produce group-effect data. We can look to the purposes of the curriculum for some clues on how to structure such efforts. If the pervasive skills of the curriculum represent some range of commitment to thinking, communicating, and researching, as well as certain civic behaviors, we might very well ask the teacher to keep an ongoing observational eye on these traits as they manifest in the conduct of the students in the classroom. This can be done using conceptual rubrics that give the teacher a good sense of where to focus her attention. So, if cooperative behavior is an important component to the mission of the school, the teacher should take some time to observe and appraise for cooperative behavior (see Fig. 7.4); if inquiry skills have some standing in the educational mission, then the teacher should again seek some way to understand whether such skills are in evidence in the workaday world of the classroom (see Fig. 7.5, p. 194). And in each of the two examples just mentioned, the observational record could be documented and eventually used in the evaluation of the curriculum. The use of structured teacher observations can be part of a formative evaluation, an ongoing and periodically employed method that reminds the teacher of the importance of some of the purposes in the school curriculum that are typically not tested but are nevertheless evaluated. We should remember one of the earlier principles of evaluation: to evaluate x means to give instructional authority to x. If used in the evaluation of the curriculum, structured observations that focus on the presence of various skills or behaviors in the classroom will potentially have the effect of giving them some value in the instructional experience.

The use of observational accounts by people outside of the classroom is also an overlooked mechanism in curriculum evaluation. Yet there is a tradition in the school of using outside observers to appraise and supervise teacher performance

Use: Whenever students are working without the teacher.

    1   Strongly Evident
    2   Some Evidence
    3   Little or No Evidence
    4   Evidence to the Contrary

_____ The nature of the interactions between the students is friendly and helpful.

Observational Remarks: _____

_____

_____ Students use each other to gain clarifications and insights.

Observational Remarks: _____

_____

_____ Personal views are balanced against group views. Compromise and adjustments to thinking occur.

Observational Remarks: _____

_____

_____ Differences in viewpoints are handled constructively. Belittling, sarcastic, and other hostile remarks are avoided.

Observational Remarks: _____

_____

_____ Efforts are made to include all participants and to seek multiple perspectives on matters.

Observational Remarks: _____

_____

FIGURE 7.4   Observational Rubric for Cooperative Behavior in the Classroom

in the classroom. Most of us who have taught school probably remember being observed by principals and district supervisors who would, based on two or three different visits, write an evaluative account of what they witnessed. The very same idea can be applied to the evaluation of the curriculum. An evaluation design can try to make use of outside observers who would look for evidence of certain factors in the classroom experience. This might be done with an outside team comprising some combination of consultants, principals, and fellow educators, or

Use: Whenever students are working without the teacher.

1 Strongly Evident
2 Some Evidence
3 Little or No Evidence
4 Evidence to the Contrary

_____ Students are involved in idea-oriented and problem-focused studies in the classroom.

Observational Remarks: _____

_____

_____ Student work requires some data collection of facts.

Observational Remarks: _____

_____

_____ Student work involves using library and reference sources.

Observational Remarks: _____

_____

_____ Student work is associated with some ongoing project that results in some presentation of findings.

Observational Remarks: _____

_____

_____ Students can discriminate between dependable and undependable sources, between fact and opinion.

Observational Remarks: _____

_____

FIGURE 7.5   Observational Rubric for Inquiry in the Classroom

with a team of professional researchers. The use of an observational team that is trained to identify factors fundamental to the mission of the school could generate essential data on what is happening in the classroom. Hence, if thinking skills have a place in the curriculum, an outside team of observers might try to examine the patterns of instructional interaction between the teachers and the students, looking particularly for some evidence of thinking. When the teacher asks questions in class, do the students always answer with a recall of facts, or do their answers involve also applying facts, making hypotheses, and interpreting data? When teachers make statements in class, are their statements principally factual, or are they phrased as problems, criticisms, hypotheses and so forth? Such data could give us a revealing picture of the opportunity to think in the classroom.

Eisner (1998) sees the idea of using observers to describe and appraise classrooms as contributing to a more artistic vision of evaluation, one that gives us a better sense of what the school experience is actually like. The questions Eisner wants asked in the evaluation of the curriculum are ones that can only be answered by observing the classroom. As he put it: "What is Mrs. Jones' classroom like? In what sorts of activities have the children engaged? What does Mrs. Jones provide that is uniquely hers? What is the character of the school day for children in her class? What are the children deriving from her class that is not likely to be revealed by standardized testing?" (p. 185). If we are serious about wanting to know if the classroom is operating in a way that resonates with the mission of the school, we will have to employ some observational methods. How can we know, for instance, if the classroom functions in the spirit of cooperation and mutual respect between teachers and students, and among students, if we do not observe it and systematically evaluate for it? How can we know if independent thinking and social responsibility are being advanced in the school experience if we do not try to find evidence of it? How can any of the pervasive skills that we might see as essential to the school experience ever be understood without making some effort to understand how they are integrated in the classroom?

The interesting effect of the observational tool is that it could yield a written descriptive account of the classroom that has the chance of being a richly nuanced interpretation of instructional and pedagogical events. It also is the kind of evidence that peels away at some of the layers in the curriculum development process and reveals insight essential to the task of curriculum improvement. If we know, for instance, that the teaching of inquiry skills is flawed from the perspective of test scores, we can only begin to guess where the problem might exist. But if we know that the teaching of inquiry skills is flawed from the perspective of our observational data, we can begin to target changes in the classroom. So, it is important to note that when we expand our sense of evaluation we are also expanding the power of the data to affect curriculum improvement efforts.

Observational data can also be based on structured frequency-counting systems, or coding systems. If a particular set of behaviors is viewed as especially desirable in the experience of the school, a good evaluation seeks to determine whether such behaviors are at all prominent in the classroom. Let's say we want to examine the incidences of cooperative behaviors in the classroom. An unstructured way to tackle this problem would be to simply ask outside observers to look for evidence of cooperative behavior in the classroom, but a more structured way to do this might be to ask the observer to scale and count particular behaviors drawn from our sense of what it means to be cooperative and uncooperative. Is there evidence that students work together without constant teacher supervision? Negatively stated, is there evidence that students refuse to listen to one another, interrupt one another, and ignore requests for information and assistance? Is there evidence of poor peer relations? Are the conversations between the students marked by sarcastic and belittling comments? Or positively stated, do the students provide helpful feedback to each other? Do they independently ask and receive help from each other? Is the nature of the conversations friendly, constructive, and marked by mutual respect? To look at such behaviors using a frequency-counting system allows the evaluation to get a gauge of how often such behaviors prevail in the classroom and to come up with a quantifiable metric against which future observations can be compared. Reliability issues require us to be sure that the raters are employing a consistent method of counting, something that will require training and authentication through inter-rater reliability measures.

Interviews

Sometimes the best way to understand the effects of the school experience is to ask its main participants. Although interview data can be unreliable, what students, parents, and teachers have to say about the process of schooling cannot be undervalued and represents a very real and important contribution to the curriculum-evaluation process.

Imagine if the reading program in an elementary school wanted to collect data on attitudes toward reading. Given the importance of teaching good reading habits, the school might want to collect data on the recreational reading habits of children and various other attitudes related to the act of reading. So, how does one begin to get such data? One method might begin by sitting down and discussing key questions about reading with children and parents, using an interview protocol that raises questions in areas of particular interest to the curriculum. Questions might include How often does the child read at home? What kind of genre of writing does the child seem to most enjoy? What factors might interfere with reading at home? Is it too much homework interfering with the time to read independently? Are the students making poor choices at selecting books at an appropriate reading level? These are data that might prove to be helpful. But because these kinds of questions begin to touch upon family conditions, one must understand that the disclosures emerging from the interview may not be reliable.

The same kind of interview techniques might be used with children for assessment purposes. I can recall a time when I interviewed a sample of sixth-graders at the conclusion of an instructional unit in health that dealt with the topic of cigarette smoking. When I asked them to verbally explain what lung cancer was, I was surprised to find that many students had only the vaguest sense of the disease and what it actually did to the lungs. I also discovered, through the interviews, that resisting the opportunity to smoke was most difficult for these preadolescents when it involved peer pressure situations, especially those that included their closest friends. But these were exactly the kinds of findings that I could use to improve my subsequent teaching efforts. So, the next time around, I arranged to have a medical doctor come to class and to discuss the specifics of lung cancer. He even brought samples of diseased and healthy lung tissue. I also tried to highlight peer pressure situations, using a simulation technique that allowed the students to begin to find the language and the social skills that they might use to resist smoking.

Although oral examinations are not, strictly speaking, interviews, they are a form of oral questioning that can generate very useful and often penetrating insight for the curriculum. It is not a coincidence that the tradition of oral examinations exists at the highest level of educational attainment. Graduate students in various disciplines often have to take oral examinations to complete their education. The reason such exams exist at this level is because they allow students to offer fully developed and carefully nuanced answers to various complex questions and problems. One-word answers or bubble fill-in test forms will not do here. And because of this, the questions themselves can be much more interesting and intricate. Using oral examinations to keep assessment data on individuals is a time-consuming process. It certainly is not something that many schools embrace and is not likely to surface as an important ingredient to evaluation, mostly because of the logistical difficulties of providing oral examinations to an entire student population. But good things do not always come easily. In some European academic high schools, the oral examination is organized as a culminating activity for graduation and is viewed as an important rite of passage for the graduating senior. Faculties get together, mostly in their subject units, and design questions that are given to individual students who must offer oral responses to a panel of faculty. The questioning routines could get into details and implications in a way that simply would not be possible on any pencil-and-paper test. The difficulty here is finding a rubric that can be used by the faculty to grade the response. Analytical rubrics, attesting to the accuracy of factual details used in the response, to the overall persuasiveness of the response, and to the student's ability to handle follow-up questions, might be a good starting point.

Surveys

The use of surveys or questionnaires in the school is usually a helpful way to sample the various concerns, attitudes, values, and beliefs of the main involvement groups associated with the school (students, parents, citizens, teachers, and other school personnel). Surveys are typically constructed with rating scales that try to represent degrees of intensity in the response. Although less popular, ranking scales are also sometimes used, especially if there is some need to get feedback on priorities (what is most important, second most important, and so forth).

Surveys clearly have their place in the evaluation scheme but they have their problems too. Because surveys are self-reported, they have some built-in validity and reliability problems. What people self-report may not always square with reality. If the school, for instance, was interested in getting data from parents on home literacy conditions, the data will not likely reflect realities in the home that might cast a cloud on the family. Likewise, if teachers wanted to get data from students on attitudes toward school, the student responses, even if anonymous, could simply reflect what the students think the teachers want to hear, with the presumption being that children (especially young children) will try to do what they can to please their teachers. With older children, the opposite effect could be at work, as they try to "get back" at a teacher for a poor grade or some other problem by using the survey to convey only negative feedback. The actual language used in the survey is also crucial to validity. Imprecise or leading language could wreak havoc with surveys. An alteration of simply one word in an item could fundamentally change the nature of the response. And surveys that use rating scales sometimes create what we might call artificial variance, meaning that although there is a quantitative difference suggested between, say, a rating of good and excellent, there may in fact be little difference between the two because of subjective differences how the respondents define those terms. This is absolutely a problem with ranking systems also, which force variance because the respondents have no option but to prioritize (or rank) items, even if they feel the items should be equally ranked.

How does one decide what to evaluate with surveys? It depends on the nature of the purpose being evaluated, how effectively survey data may contribute to the understanding of such purposes, and how effectively other instruments might play into the process. I'll use the example of reading again. Figure 7.6 represents a survey that could be used to gauge the extent to which children are reading recreationally and to identify what they might be reading. These surveys could be conducted anonymously but any survey given by teachers to students, especially elementary school children, will likely be viewed as a tool used to gratify the teacher. So, our items cannot simply ask children if they like to read, or if they like school. The results will be predictable. Instead, the survey asks more particular questions about behaviors and habits and tries to elicit short constructed responses to help verify answers. The survey in Figure 7.6 asks students about recreational reading habits, but requires most of the responses to be verified with examples. So, if students claim to read often, we ask them to give examples of the books they read as well as a short description of the books. When we ask for feedback on their least and most favorite book genres, we ask for similar verification.

Surveys have been especially popular when it comes to judging attitudinal factors in learning. Even with younger children, surveys have been used to try to determine how children feel about various matters pertaining to school, or in more specific cases, how they feel about particular lessons or units or other specific events experienced in school. The survey could aim to get a self-assessment of how interesting the lesson or unit of study was, whether the lesson was understood, whether the lesson aroused continued interest in the topic, and even whether the lesson was interesting enough to make its way into family discussions (Wulf, 1984). The survey could be used to produce aggregate evaluative data

1. How often do you read books at home?

_____ Every day
_____ Three or four times a week
_____ Only on weekends
_____ Seldom or never

What are the names of two books you read recently?

Describe in a sentence or two the plot of two books you read recently:

2. Name 3 books you have recently checked out of the library:

3. What books have you read or are you reading that you or your parents have recently purchased?

4. What kinds of books do you most like to read?

5. Have you ever read and enjoyed any of the following types of books?

My least favorite   *My favorite*
  1...............................2...............................3...............................4...............................5

Science Fiction Books: 1   2   3   4   5

Name one you've read: _____

Books about Sports: 1   2   3   4   5

Name one you've read: _____

Adventure Books: 1   2   3   4   5

Name one you've read: _____

Mystery Books: 1   2   3   4   5

Name one you've read: _____

Humorous Books: 1   2   3   4   5

Name one you've read: _____

FIGURE 7.6   **Recreational Reading Survey**

(continued)

| Comic Books: | 1 | 2 | 3 | 4 | 5 |

Name one you've read: _____

| Non-fiction History: | 1 | 2 | 3 | 4 | 5 |

Name one you've read: _____

| Non-fiction Science: | 1 | 2 | 3 | 4 | 5 |

Name one you've read: _____

| Plays: | 1 | 2 | 3 | 4 | 5 |

Name one you've read: _____

| Poetry: | 1 | 2 | 3 | 4 | 5 |

Name one you've read: _____

Other:

6. What do you like to do when you have free time at home?

	Never	Sometimes	Almost Always	Always
Read books:				
Watch TV:				
Play video games:				
Play with friends:				
Listen to music:				
Go on the Internet:				
If it's something else, tell me:				
_____				
_____				

7. Do you think you have enough free time at home to do the things you like to do?

8. If not, what would you change to give yourself more free time?

FIGURE 7.6 Continued

that might contribute to some idea of general strengths or weaknesses in the curriculum, or to produce individual assessment data that might help the teacher to work with particular children.

Portfolio Assessment

Among the least appreciated sources for evaluation is the display of the actual work accomplished by students during their time in school. Artists display their handiwork and skill by keeping a portfolio of their work that gives others the opportunity to appreciate their renderings. The very same idea can be applied to the classroom. Teachers could encourage students to keep a portfolio of their work as a way to testify to the quality of their experiences in school. We sometimes call this portfolio assessment. In the elementary school, this is often done by the teachers themselves, who keep an ongoing folder or record (from September to June) of the work accomplished by the students. The intention is to provide object examples of just how far the students have grown in one academic year. Contrasting the work done in the latter parts of the academic year with the work done in the earlier parts can indeed be an impressive way to show discernible improvements.

The structure of most portfolio assessments is often dependent on what the individual students select for inclusion in their portfolios. But exactly what gets included in a portfolio can, of course, also be influenced by teachers, who might want to examine examples of work that touch upon some of the fundamental purposes of the curriculum. An example of a speech, a research project, a persuasive essay, a poem, or some nonverbal mode of communication can all be structured into the guidelines of a portfolio. If each of these enclosures is also offered as a representation of the student's best effort, the portfolio even can begin to take some place in the evaluation scheme of the curriculum, because the teacher (or some team of evaluators) can subject the portfolios to a systematic appraisal that uses rubrics to score for evidence of, say, thinking, communication, and inquiry skills, and general understanding of content. Aggregate data compiled from such an effort might reflect something important about the school experience.

REVISING THE CURRICULUM

Thus far, the discussion of evaluation has focused on the variety of instruments we could use to determine whether our purposes have been fulfilled. The nature of this very act is to provide feedback on changes that might be needed. But if test scores reveal low achievement in mathematics, or if observational data show little opportunity to learn inquiry skills, or if interview and survey results indicate that children do not enjoy school, how would anyone know what to do with these data to initiate reforms?

Clearly, something in the design of the evaluation has to go beyond the question of meeting purposes. What is needed is a comprehensive evaluation, which means not only looking at whether purposes have been met, but also examining whether the purposes themselves are even realizable, whether the qualifications of the teachers are up to par, whether the evaluation design is in alignment with the rest of the curriculum, or whether facilities problems or instructional technique might be throwing a wrench into the system. The fact is that curriculum evaluation also needs to direct some attention to the elements of the curriculum that affect its implementation.

Appraising Purposes

We have made much of the importance of purposes in the design of the curriculum. So, it should not be much of a surprise to see the evaluation of the curriculum turn to the idea of appraising purposes. If purposes drive the curriculum, then there has to be some consensus on their importance and some way to evaluate their continued relevance in the school.

Understanding how widespread the commitment is to certain purposes is an important factor in the appraisal of purposes. If the evaluative data show that certain purposes are not being met, one reasonable way to interpret this problem is to speculate that those purposes may not be viewed as very important to teachers or their supervisors. Another possibility is that many teachers may not even be aware of certain purposes or simply do not have the materials, time, background, qualifications, or resources needed to achieve them. Additionally, it is possible that school purposes are too ambiguous or vague to give any real direction to the teacher. To understand whether any such conditions apply, some evaluative instrument (mostly likely a survey or structured interview) can go out to teachers and other key curriculum participants. The survey depicted in Figure 7.7 is a holistic appraisal of the school mission. It gets at questions about the clarity, meaningfulness, awareness, and implementation of the school's mission. Feedback on this form could later become the basis for a detailed follow-up survey or for analytic interviews of teachers. In fact, the structured interview depicted in Figure 7.8 (p. 204) concentrates on specific purposes identified as problematic through other evaluative means. Data taken from the structured interview should give us the kind of feedback that speaks directly to revisions in the curriculum.

The appraisal of purposes can also focus on what the school chooses not to do, what Eisner (1998) calls the null curriculum. We could ask, "Is there something important and overlooked that needs to be included in the mission of the school? Is there evidence of a problem in the school or the community that requires the school to rethink what it does"? If there is evidence, for instance, that high school students are harassing gay and lesbian students, the curriculum should consider making some change that deals directly with the issue. To the extent that the school curriculum keeps its ear to the ground and notes problems and issues in

For each statement, select one of the following responses:

1	2	3	4	NA
strongly agree	agree	disagree	strongly disagree	not applicable/ don't know

Clarity
1. I easily understand our school's mission statement.   1 2 3 4 NA
2. The students easily understand our school's mission statement.   1 2 3 4 NA
3. The local community at large easily understands our school's mission statement.   1 2 3 4 NA

Meaningfulness
4. I am committed to the goals and mission of our school.   1 2 3 4 NA
5. My beliefs are reflected in our goals and mission statement.   1 2 3 4 NA
6. Parents are committed to the goals and mission of our school.   1 2 3 4 NA
7. The beliefs of the community are reflected in the goals and mission statement.   1 2 3 4 NA

Awareness
8. Our mission statement is displayed prominently.   1 2 3 4 NA
9. My colleagues and I agree on the meaning of our school's mission statement.   1 2 3 4 NA

Implementation
10. Our school's goals are reflected in our school plans.   1 2 3 4 NA
11. Our school's goals are used to establish priorities in the school budget.   1 2 3 4 NA
12. Our discipline practices reflect our school's goals and mission.   1 2 3 4 NA
13. Our school's goals and mission are reflected in classroom practice.   1 2 3 4 NA

Long-Range Focus
14. Our school's goals encourage a broad range of student achievement (beyond the intellectual-cognitive area).   1 2 3 4 NA
15. Our school's goals emphasize developing student commitments to lifelong learning.   1 2 3 4 NA
16. Our school's goals emphasize developing citizenship.   1 2 3 4 NA
17. Our school's goals emphasize development of self-worth.   1 2 3 4 NA
18. Our school's goals emphasize developing life skills.   1 2 3 4 NA

FIGURE 7.7   Holistic Survey of the School's Mission

Source: Adapted from K. Leithwood & R. Aitken. *Making schools smarter: A system for monitoring school and district progress*, pp. 163, 169, copyright © 1999 by Corwin Press, Inc. Reprinted with permission of Corwin Press, Inc.

	Specific Problematic Purposes				
	x	y	z	a	b
1. How important do you think this purpose is to the school?					
2. How important do you think this purpose is to your classroom?					
3. How aware were you of the fact that this is a purpose in our school?					
4. How much time do you dedicate to this purpose?					
5. Would you like to dedicate more or less time to it?					
6. Do you have the training you need to fulfill this purpose?					
7. Do you have the materials you need to fulfill this purpose?					
8. Should we consider changing or getting rid of the purpose?					

FIGURE 7.8   Analytic Interview of Teachers on the Topic of School Purposes

the community, it can affect changes in its mission. But the effort to think about ways to modify and revise the curriculum can also be a more systematic affair, part and parcel of a regularly scheduled periodic review of the school's mission. The school can find a compelling rationale to modify the curriculum in light of feedback from a deliberative body of professional educators, students, and community members.

Appraising the Macrocurriculum

Another area of concern for the evaluation of the curriculum has to do with the macrocurriculum, which encompasses the totality of the coursework, services, and extra-classroom events provided by the school experience. The main targets for the appraisal of the macrocurriculum include the actual design and implementation of particular courses (or in the elementary school, various organizational features of the self-contained classroom), some investigation of vertical and horizontal articulation issues, the effectiveness of various school-wide services (counseling programs, homework assistance centers, library and media services) and the effectiveness of extra-classroom programs (sports, music, clubs, student government, and so forth).

The natural starting point for macrocurriculum appraisal is the overall structure of coursework organized in the school. This is easy to see in a high school or middle school, where teachers are assigned to teach actual courses. In the elementary school, the targets of investigation are the various content-related features (science, math, reading, and so forth) of the self-contained classroom. The point here is to look for evidence of whether the coursework is attendant to its expressed purposes, in order to be sure that the content and the pervasive skills assigned to each course (or organization unit in the elementary classroom) are indeed being taught. This is, in effect, an effort to find the places in the curriculum where important purposes are inadequately reflected in practice, with an eye on determining why this might be. Elementary school teachers, for instance, are notorious for giving short shrift to the elementary science curriculum. If observational, survey, and interview data demonstrate that the content and the pervasive skills associated with the science curriculum are only being partially taught, a redesign of the macrocurriculum might be needed. Perhaps a correlation design between the teaching of social studies and science might be explored. Although this would affect the social studies course, it might create a more provocative and attractive option to the teachers. Or perhaps the macrodesign of the science curriculum should shift its focus toward a different set of pervasive skills, highlighting perhaps language-related skills, which elementary school teachers tend to value. Maybe a whole new set of topical units need to be developed by the teachers themselves, perhaps within grade levels, in order to create better teacher ownership of the science curriculum. Of course, various other solutions can also be explored that have little or nothing to do with the macrocurriculum, such as giving teachers more training in science, buying new science textbooks, or making the teaching of science a priority in the teacher's annual evaluation.

Appraisal of how well coursework fulfills its purposes is important because it speaks directly to opportunity-to-learn (OTL) factors. The macrocurriculum is a framework of coursework and services that is designed to produce a general educative effect linked to the comprehensive mandate of the school. If it fails to operate on all of its cylinders, as it were, some students will likely be deprived of something they should be learning. And the logic of OTL extends beyond the coursework because we set certain educative expectations for extra-classroom experiences too, as well as for school-wide services. If the OTL factors associated with participating on the football team are not met (which might include learning about team work, building physical strength, enjoying a sporting interest), then the sport itself should be redeveloped in the curriculum or even arguably eliminated. The bottom line is that the appraisal of the macrocurriculum should consider holding sports, music, student government, club activity, other extra-classroom events accountable to the educational mandate that justifies their place in the schools.

The tricky part of appraising the macrocurriculum is trying to separate the curriculum itself from its implementation. If a course fails to meet its expectations of purposes, is the fault fundamentally with the way the course is designed or with the way the teachers implement it? There is subtlety here because implementational problems can be rooted in poor design. As Eisner (1998) put it, "A teacher might do a brilliant job of teaching, but the ideas or skills being taught might be trivial, biased, or invalid. Conversely, a teacher might be using a faultless curriculum with respect to its intellectual merit and its appropriateness both developmentally and experientially for students, but that teacher might be teaching so poorly that only confusion and frustration result for the students" (p. 179). What seems clear is that the appraisal of the macrocurriculum must be accompanied by an appraisal of teaching or instruction, so that the findings that emerge can be compared. If a course, for instance, is found to be less than successful (using student outcome data as they relate to purposes), irrespective of who is teaching it, this might point to a systemic design problem. If the course has wildly different outcomes based on who is teaching it, further exploration into the instructional differences between the courses might be revealing.

Finally, it is important to emphasize the fact that changes in the macrocurriculum can also be influenced by modifications in the mission of the school or by articulation concerns caused by other changes. New courses might be included in the curriculum simply because there is a desire to reflect new priorities. If a high school wanted to get more serious about its civic education mission and offer a general education course dedicated to the topic of American citizenship or the problems of American democracy, such a decision will likely have ripple effects in the macrocurriculum. If such a new course is moved into the curriculum, will another one be moved out? Will this course require some prerequisites? Does the new course deal with certain content and pervasive skills that overlap with other courses? What are the vertical articulation issues?

Appraising Instruction and Pedagogy

If the school curriculum fails to achieve the kind of success it expects with certain purposes, it will not take long for much of the blame to be directed at the classroom teacher's instructional and pedagogical conduct. This might be slightly unfair because so many other factors are also at work, but it is logical because, as indicated earlier, the implementation of the curriculum is embodied in instruction—in the planned teacher-student interaction. When we appraise instruction and pedagogy, we are in effect appraising the way the curriculum is implemented.

Data on student outcomes are, of course, the key to all evaluation. They tell us where our problems and where our strengths might be. Say there is some good evidence that reading achievement at an elementary school is not at an acceptable standard in the upper grades, that student interest in reading is low, and that writing skills are deficient. Can teachers and instruction be blamed? The short answer is maybe; the long answer is tied to the overall design of the evaluation.

Achievement deficiencies, of course, could be associated with all sorts of different factors, including ones that exist outside of the school. If a school, for instance, has recently experienced a major shift in its demographics, perhaps inheriting a large proportion of low-income and limited English-proficient (LEP) students, achievement declines could almost be expected. But when we start to look inside the school for answers, we should not hesitate to go directly to the classroom itself. Observational teams can be deployed to appraise the kind of instructional strategies being used in the classrooms. Is there good instructional variance in the teaching of reading? Are different ability groups receiving different qualities of instruction? Are the students on task during their independent work time? Is the climate of the classroom one that encourages a love for reading? What are the teacher's questioning skills like? What is the nature of the seatwork assigned to students?

Figure 7.9 (p. 208) itemizes several important features of the teacher's instructional repertoire. The items are part of a survey that can go out to students, parents, or even the teachers themselves, but they also represent focal points for the continued evaluation of teachers and their instructional decisions. What is the evidence, for instance, that teachers in the school are using a large repertoire of instructional strategies? Are student needs, interests, and experiences being integrated into the learning experiences? What kinds of methods are most popular in the classrooms and are they congruent with the purposes undergirding the lessons. Such questions, of course, should be broached with more than survey data. Along these lines, Daniel and Laurel Tanner (1987) offer a troubleshooting checklist to supervisors that get at many of the key variables in the classroom (see Fig. 7.10, pp. 209–210). The use of such a checklist in the observation of teachers can be helpful in identifying general areas of weakness and strength.

Teaching methodologies also have to account for variations in the content taught and purposes embraced. If a particular set of thinking skills is given priority in the science curriculum, then the science teacher's instructional methodologies should reflect this major concern. Because different purposes are assigned to different grade levels and different subject areas, we can expect teachers working in these different subject areas to reflect different profiles of instruction. We

For each statement, select one of the following responses:

1	2	3	4	NA
strongly agree	agree	disagree	strongly disagree	not applicable/ don't know

Instructional Strategy Appropriateness

1. Teachers in our school are becoming skilled in the use of a large repertoire of instructional strategies.   1 2 3 4 NA
2. Students are given the opportunity to determine their learning activities.   1 2 3 4 NA
3. My instructional strategies enable students to construct their own knowledge.   1 2 3 4 NA
4. I take students' interests, needs, and experiences into account when planning learning opportunities.   1 2 3 4 NA
5. My classroom is a comfortable learning environment with minimal distraction from instructional purposes.   1 2 3 4 NA

Instructional Strategy Use

6. My curriculum makes meaningful linkages between learning opportunities and our students' lives and experiences.   1 2 3 4 NA
7. My curriculum stresses learning skills and applications that connect with the world beyond the school.   1 2 3 4 NA

Instructional Time

8. Time lost to student absenteeism and lateness is minimized.   1 2 3 4 NA
9. I always begin my classes promptly.   1 2 3 4 NA
10. I manage student behavior in a way that minimizes disruptions during class.   1 2 3 4 NA

FIGURE 7.9   Survey Related to Instructional Decisions

Source: Adapted from K. Leithwood & R. Aitken. *Making schools smarter: A system for monitoring school and district progress*, pp. 184–185, copyright © 1999 by Corwin Press, Inc. Reprinted with permission of Corwin Press, Inc.

might, for instance, expect proportionally more demonstration lessons from science teachers, more lecture-style methods from history teachers, and more cooperative learning methods from social studies teachers in the high school. The point is that we judge instruction against the purposes accorded to the classroom.

The focus of evaluation can also target factors more identifiable as pedagogical in nature. This might include giving some attention to the social and learning atmosphere of the classroom or the actual manner in which the teacher provides

Factors Influencing Learning	In Evidence	Not in Evidence/ Needs Attention
1. Quality of teacher's explanations		
(a) Teacher describes specific strategies to be employed	_____	_____
(b) Teacher asks students how they got a particular answer	_____	_____
(c) Teacher helps students make interconnections between and among the various subjects	_____	_____
(d) Subject matter is related to life experiences of students	_____	_____
2. Receptivity to students' ideas and contributions		
(a) Students initiate thought questions	_____	_____
(b) Teacher poses thought questions	_____	_____
(c) Teacher encourages students to ask questions, with emphasis on thought questions	_____	_____
(d) Teacher integrates students' questions and contributions into the class discussion	_____	_____
3. Quality of questioning procedure		
(a) Teacher poses thought-provoking questions	_____	_____
(b) Teacher provides time for student to think and vocalize response	_____	_____
(c) Teacher poses new questions and/or clarifies original question when student is unable to respond effectively	_____	_____
(d) Emphasis is on ideas and problems	_____	_____
(e) Factual information and skills are applied to ideas and problems	_____	_____
4. Selection of teaching methods		
(a) Method is determined by purposes and the subject matter	_____	_____
(b) Variety of methods used in illuminating ideas and problems (projects, themes, panel discussions, etc.)	_____	_____
(c) Emphasis given to student inquiry	_____	_____
(d) Cooperative-collaborative learning methods utilized	_____	_____
5. Quality of interactions with students		
(a) Teacher gives students recognition (including praise) for work	_____	_____
(b) Pupil mistakes regarded as fruitful opportunities for learning	_____	_____
(c) Teacher functions as a guide in helping students improve in their work	_____	_____

FIGURE 7.10   Some Examples of Factors for Educational Troubleshooting: Supervisor's Checklist

Source: Adapted from D. Tanner & L. Tanner. (1986). *Supervision in education*: *Problems & practice*. Upper Saddle River, NJ: Pearson Education, Inc.

(continued)

Factors Influencing Learning	In Evidence	Not in Evidence/ Needs Attention
(d) Teacher provides encouragement and enlists attention of all (rather than some) students	_____	_____
(e) Teacher communicates high and realistic expectations to students	_____	_____
6. Atmosphere of the classroom		
(a) Climate is cooperative-collaborative	_____	_____
(b) Mutual respect between teacher and students	_____	_____
(c) Mutual respect among students	_____	_____
(d) Cooperative-collaborative learning methods (students encouraged to help one another)	_____	_____
7. Quality of student activity		
(a) Activity is purposeful	_____	_____
(b) Students are developing increased self-reliance and responsible self-direction	_____	_____
(c) Discipline is creative rather than restrictive or coercive	_____	_____
(d) Students exhibit responsibility for consequences of own actions	_____	_____
(e) Students exhibit a sense of controlling their own destiny	_____	_____
(f) Learning activities appropriate for student developmental levels	_____	_____
(g) Time allocation is flexible to allow continuation of exceptionally productive activities	_____	_____
(h) Resources and facilities appropriate for learning activity	_____	_____

FIGURE 7.10 Continued

feedback to student questions and responses. It might also mean taking a closer look at the questioning routines of teachers. Because we should expect good questioning routines, a positive classroom environment, and effective feedback to be given to all students (irrespective of the purposes of the school), these targets for evaluation should be part of some regularly scheduled routine. In most cases, the data would be derived from observations. Data taken from these kinds of observations could eventually be used to isolate critical factors in the classroom, giving the school the chance to offer a remedy in the form of inservice training, supervisory recommendations, and so on.

Students, of course, can also prove to be valuable in making revisions in instruction. The role of student feedback on teachers is well established in the higher education, but it still has only a small and limited place in the high school, middle school, and elementary school. Holistic surveys can be used to look at the classroom widely, in the interests of helping to show general signs of weakness that could be probed more precisely with other evaluative instruments. Thus, a student survey that asks students to answer general questions about their attitudes toward school, their impressions of teachers, and their views on the nature of their school work could all give us a sense of where we might look to find general deficiencies in instructional practice (Fig. 7.11).

For each statement, select one of the following responses:

1	2	3	4	NA
strongly agree	agree	disagree	strongly disagree	not applicable/ don't know

Views on Atmosphere for Learning

1. Most of my classes are well organized.   1 2 3 4 NA
2. Most of my teachers go out of their way to help students.   1 2 3 4 NA
3. I feel that I "belong" at this school.   1 2 3 4 NA
4. Most of my teachers are interested in me as a person.   1 2 3 4 NA
5. My teachers frequently discuss my work with me.   1 2 3 4 NA
6. Most of my teachers treat me the same as other students.   1 2 3 4 NA
7. Most of my teachers are willing to spend extra time with me.   1 2 3 4 NA
8. Most of my teachers expect me always to do my best work.   1 2 3 4 NA
9. Most of my teachers make me feel comfortable in class.   1 2 3 4 NA
10. I have come to know other students in our school really well.   1 2 3 4 NA
11. I get along with most other students I have met in my school.   1 2 3 4 NA
12. My teachers spend time just talking with me.   1 2 3 4 NA
13. Most of my teachers seem to understand me.   1 2 3 4 NA
14. I get along with most of my teachers.   1 2 3 4 NA

Views on My Schoolwork

15. I am able to understand most of the material covered in my classes.   1 2 3 4 NA
16. I feel confident that I will be successful in school.   1 2 3 4 NA
17. I am learning a lot at school.   1 2 3 4 NA
18. I am satisfied with my marks.   1 2 3 4 NA

FIGURE 7.11 **Survey of Student Views of School Experiences**

Appraising Appraisal Systems

Finally, we cannot forget about the all-important task of appraising the appraisal instruments we use to evaluate the curriculum. The instrumentation of evaluation obviously has an obligation to give us the kind of data that will allow us to judge the full effects of the school experience with an eye toward making well-reasoned revisions. For any of this to happen, we must find a way to ensure that the appraisal systems we use are working the way we expect them to work.

Validity and reliability concerns have already been discussed, mostly in the context of test development. But because these concepts are so fundamental to the health of an appraisal system, they deserve some extra attention. Each aspect of the evaluation design should undergo some periodic review related to validity and reliability concerns. This could include checking for any gaps between what is evaluated and what is given priority in the school experience itself. In other words, are the content and the pervasive skills that are given priority in the instructional experience given the same priority in the evaluation design? If there is a gap, the appraisal system will be compromised with content validity problems. The evaluation will not mirror what actually is occurring in the school experience.

But the appraisal of the evaluation design can also be examined from the standpoint of the school's main causes. Schools, in fact, often prove to be deficient in this regard by articulating support for certain purposes while completely failing to design any substantive evaluation that targets them. Most schools, for instance, will have something in their mission statements about the importance of civic behaviors and attitudes. Yet how many schools take serious steps toward designing an evaluation of civic behaviors and attitudes? Virtually all schools openly tout the virtues of teaching critical thinking skills, social tolerance, creativity, and traits related to honesty and hard work (to name just a few), but how many reflect these concerns in the design of their evaluations? The discrepancy that usually exists between the substance of evaluation and the substance of the school's stated purposes is an ongoing curriculum problem. And where such a discrepancy exists, the odds are quite good that a parallel gap will exist between the school's purposes and the nature of instruction, meaning that if the school does not privilege the place of certain purposes in its evaluation it is not likely that purposes will affect the nature of instruction either.

A comprehensive evaluative design not only means that the scope of the evaluation should cover the school's manifest purposes and objectives, but also that the instrumentation used in the evaluation should represent different appraisal methods or approaches. Recall that one of the key principles to evaluation is to take advantage of the full instrumentation available and not be too dependent on any one tool. The curriculum developer should be aware of this principle and conduct a kind of audit of the instrumentation used. Are multiple means being used in the evaluate scheme? To the extent that this kind of audit is conducted, one can identify the high-stakes testing factors in the curriculum.

All instruments used for evaluative or assessment purposes should also be regularly revisited. All test items, for instance, should be monitored. The language used on the tests, the effectiveness of the distracters, and the general reliability of the scoring system all require ongoing review. These reviews could be inspired by statistical reviews and by feedback drawn from both teachers and students.

One especially important principle to understand in this regard is an item analysis method known as item discrimination. I remember giving an exam once to college students in an Educational Foundations course. During the exam session, many students approached me with questions about some of the vocabulary words used in a few of my test items. The words were not technical words rooted in the subject matter of Educational Foundations, but were simply words that many of the students never encountered previously. Enough students were puzzled by some of the vocabulary words that I asked myself whether the items in question had lost their construct validity? Did I inadvertently convert elements of a test on Educational Foundations to a generic vocabulary exam?

Because my exam was norm-referenced (individual achievement is relative to how well others achieve), I took a closer look at the discrimination levels of the items in questions. Item discrimination tells us how well a test item does with the highest-performing students on the exam. A positive discrimination, which is desirable, means that the students who got the item right were, generally speaking, the students who had the highest overall scores on the exam. Popham (1999) describes a quick and easy way to calculate a discrimination index. Rank the overall scores on the exam from highest to lowest and then divide them into a high and a low performing group, with equal numbers in each group. Then simply determine the number of the students in the high group who got the item correct and divide that number by the number of examinees in the group. Do the same for the low group. Then subtract the low group number from the high group number. Anything lower than 0.2 probably needs to be redone; anything between a 0.2 and 0.4 is (more or less) adequate and anything above a 0.4 is quite good. But remember this applies to a norm-referenced exam that seeks to make discriminations between students. When I subjected my problematic items to a discrimination test, it confirmed my suspicions. The index was right around zero. The items simply were not discriminating between high and low achieving students. It was time to redo the test items and to replace some of the vocabulary words with more accessible and clear language.

Discrimination indices can also be calculated on the distracters (the wrong answers) used in selected response items (Popham, 1998). If correct answers should have a positive discrimination index, then wrong answers naturally should have a negative one, which means that the students who chose the wrong answer should be those who scored lowest on the overall exam. If we find positive discrimination numbers associated with distracters (wrong answers), we know that higher achieving students were falling for them. This might require a better look at the distracter. Perhaps there is a subtlety to the distracter that only the better students were picking up on? We might also find that some distracters are not doing anything at all on the exam. Either no one was selecting them or they demonstrated no good negative discrimination. Again this might be a flag for closer inspection. Items that did not discriminate well could be pulled from the exam and become subject to more detailed feedback from students, so that we might get an idea of how to remedy them.

Criterion-referenced exams can also employ an item-analysis method, but one that is different from the discrimination index just described. Because we do not expect criterion-referenced exams to produce the kind of variance we expect from norm-referenced exams, the issue of discrimination is less relevant. Criterion-referenced exams try to show achievement along certain established domains of learning, so the item analysis on criterion-referenced exams goes to the issue of whether the items were sensitive to instruction. Commonly, the best way to do a discrimination analysis of the items of a criterion-referenced exam is to compare the achievement of the students who have been instructed on the material against those who have not. In other words, we could know that the instructed group has met certain domains of achievement by comparing their performance against the uninstructed group, as long as the two groups were matched by key demographic factors (income, race, language facility, special education designations, and so forth). The discrimination is a straightforward calculation of finding the average score of the uninstructed group for each item (the average of correct answers divided by the overall number of examinees in the group) and subtracting it from the same calculation of the instructed group. The resulting number can be interpreted in the same manner as the norm-referenced discriminations just described.

Finally, all appraisal systems should be periodically subjected to some feedback from both students and fellow teachers. Test items with poor discriminations, for instance, can be pooled together and given to students or fellow teachers for feedback. Is there anything in the language, the instructions, or the layout of the test items that is confusing? How might the items be improved? In regard to interview and survey data, feedback from teachers and students might find a bias in phrasing or certain ambiguities in language. The reliability of the rubrics used in constructed-response tests or of observations can be tested by involving some fellow teachers in a mock scoring session. Similarly, the grading of portfolios and other student products can benefit from bringing another pair of professional eyes to the assessment table.

SUMMARY

The evaluation of the curriculum is an evidence collection process. It should not be dependent on any one appraisal mechanism and should find a way to bring an array of data to the question of whether the school experience has attained its core purposes. Evaluation concerns itself with group or aggregate effects that offer feedback on the processes of the curriculum. This makes it distinct from appraisals targeted at individuals, such as grading practices, which we classify as assessments. The distinction between evaluation and assessment, however, is not always obvious because assessment data can be used for evaluative purposes and the nature of the evaluative design will likely affect assessments.

The key to good evaluation is comprehensiveness in outlook and comprehensiveness in instrumentation. This means that the curriculum developer should design an evaluation that uses a wide variety of strategies to cover the full range of purposes embodied in the school's mission. Any reliance on a single appraisal will subject the evaluation to validity and reliability vulnerabilities and will likely distort the nature of instruction by giving too much standing to a single appraisal mechanism. What we look for in an evaluation design is a wide instrumentation of approaches (including tests, interviews, observations, surveys, and portfolios) not because such instrumentation is intrinsically desirable but because it provides different slants of data representation for different purposes.

Validity and reliability concerns prevail with all forms of evaluation and assessment. Content validity, construct validity, and predictive validity are all important considerations. Content validity has an especially important role to play in assessment because it is so fundamental to making good measurements of achievement. Reliability refers to the stability of intruments over time and in alternative forms. But it also refers to the internal consistency of instruments so that when a constructed-response test is graded by teacher *a*, we could expect the same essay to receive the same grade from teacher *b*.

Finally, the evaluation of the curriculum not only needs to speak to whether key purposes have been met, but also needs to give the curriculum developer some handle on how to make adjustments or improvements to the curriculum. Thus, we should find some elements of evaluation that look at ways to appraise the main processes of the curriculum. This usually takes the form of some periodic review that reconsiders the purposes of the school, the nature of instruction and pedagogy, the overall macrodesign of the curriculum, and the actual appraisal systems themselves.

DISCUSSION QUESTIONS AND SUGGESTED ACTIVITIES

1. What is the fundamental distinction between evaluation and assessment, and how are they related?

2. What is meant by the reference to evaluation as "an evidence collection process"?

3. How is formative assessment a key to good teaching?

4. How might you respond to a principal who claims that the school relies on the ITBS to evaluate the curriculum?

5. How can evaluation positively affect the nature of instruction?

6. What is content validity and why is it so important to achievement?

7. What is the difference between norm-referenced and criterion-referenced exams?

8. Why is reliability an especially important concern on constructed-response exams?

9. What is the difference between a holistic and an analytic rubric?

10. What are some of the advantages and disadvantages of using interview data in evaluations?

11. How might you begin portfolio assessments for evaluative purposes?

12. Detail a strategy to appraise the purposes of the school curriculum.

13. Give an example of an evaluation that targets the appraisal of the macrocurriculum.

14. How might you begin to appraise pedagogy, as opposed to instruction?

15. What is a discrimination index on a norm-referenced exam and how can it help teachers improve their tests?

NOTES

Eisner, E. (1998). *The educational imagination*. New York: Macmillan Co.

Good, T. & Brophy, J. (1991). *Looking in classrooms*. New York: HarperCollins.

Madaus, G.G. (1999). The influence of testing on the curriculum. In M. Early & K. Rehage (Eds.), *Issues in curriculum*. Chicago: National Society for the Study of Education.

Madaus, G.F. & Kellaghan, T. (1992). Curriculum evaluation and assessment. In P. Jackson (Ed.), *Handbook of research on curriculum*. New York: Macmillan Co.

Popham, W.J. (1999). *Classroom assessment*. Boston: Allyn and Bacon.

Tanner, D. & Tanner, L. (1987). *Supervision in education*. New York: Macmillan Co.

Tyler, R. (1949). *Basic principles of curriculum and instruction*. Chicago: University of Chicago Press.

Wiggins, G. (1998). *Educative assessment*. New York: John Wiley & Sons.

Wulf, K. (1984). *Curriculum design: A handbook for educators*. Glenview, IL: Scott Foresman.

CHAPTER EIGHT

IMPLEMENTATION

Action, when directed by knowledge, is method and means, not an end
—John Dewey

The concluding chapter of the book examines the processes by which curriculum developers might be able to better secure the highest purposes of the curriculum in its actual operation, focusing on the methods and strategies that go into building ownership in the school mission and transforming school purposes and school problems into actionable curricular responses. This process is known as curriculum implementation. Simply put, implementation refers to the means that we use to get the curriculum to do what we want it to do (Beauchamp, 1975). Throughout the book, I have portrayed the design of the curriculum as a point of departure for instruction, as a way to set the table for a particular school agenda. At some point, of course, the design of the curriculum leaps off the paper and takes on a life in the school. This is the implementational point of the curriculum, "the spacetime," as Beauchamp put it, "representing the merger of the curriculum system with the instructional system" . . . when "the curriculum becomes a working tool for teachers as they develop their instructional strategies" (p. 164). Just how good the coordination is between the design and the practice of the curriculum will say a lot about the curriculum itself.

THE PROBLEM OF IMPLEMENTATION

With curriculum implementation there are two main concerns: the need for congruence between purpose and action and the need for teachers to apply what we might call sound curriculum knowledge. The first is the more obvious one. When we define the purposes of the curriculum, we are engaged in the process of building the engine that will drive the curriculum. But, to extend the metaphor, there must be a driver in the seat. The teacher is the only one who can transform purposes into action, so we must be concerned about whether the teacher is doing this effectively. As curriculum developers, we want our curriculum to be honest to its design and to be recognizable in practice. Second, irrespective of purposes, the implementation of the curriculum has to go forward with confidence that the teacher's selection of learning experiences will be responsive to what is consciously rationalized as sound instructional and pedagogical judgment. Because good curriculum design is a point of departure to the teacher, we should like to see it operate in a way that allows for the full and complete exercise of teacher perspicacity. Implementation, in other words, is not simply a matter of teacher compliance, or of getting teachers to do as they are told, but one of encouraging teacher ownership of the curriculum and supporting the exercise of professional discretionary judgment in a way that keeps the school experience tied to what the teacher believes is best for their students within the limits of the school's mandate.

Snyder, Bolin, and Zumwalt (1992) describe the main distinctions between three different perspectives on implementation. The first, tellingly known as the fidelity approach to implementation, is concerned strictly with the degree of exactitude that exists between the planned curriculum and the implemented experience. Those who embrace a fidelity perspective interpret any departure from the originally planned experience as a shortcoming, as an example of an unjustified action. This obviously makes the fidelity approach an imperfect model for implementation. If strict fidelity is the ideal, then the use of expressive goals in the curriculum and the general commitment to the emergent professional judgment of the teacher (and any other unplanned feature of the curriculum) are necessarily denied in the school experience. Additionally, the fidelity perspective implies that the curriculum is a script for teachers to follow, one that could even include instructional prescriptions. Such a view of curriculum implementation goes hand in hand with the old-world view of telling teachers what to do and how to do it.

Another approach to implementation, known as mutual adaptation, essentially represents the kind of curriculum development work described in this book. Mutual adaptation stands by the notion that curriculum development is an interplay between the design of the curriculum and the practice of the curriculum. Unplanned adjustments and changes to the curriculum are not viewed as deficiencies or irresponsible drift, as they might be under the fidelity approach, but as decisions made in the interests of the learner within clearly established normative parameters of operation. Under mutual adaptation, the very nature of instruction is obliging to the teacher, whose instructional decisions are influenced by the expression of purpose and not by any imposition of method. Mutual adaptation has literal meaning here. The teacher has an obligation to the design of the school experience—to account for the normative features of the school mandate—but the design of the school experience also has an obligation to the teacher, providing direction while also acceding to the teacher's emergent professional judgments.

The last perspective on implementation, known as curriculum enactment, represents the polar opposite of the fidelity approach. It puts a great deal of priority on the classroom-based (microcurricular) moment in the school experience. Implementation is viewed as a matter of giving teachers the independence to create experiences that may or may not have any link to normative standards or purposes. In effect, teachers working with the students become the designers and the implementers of the school curriculum. They are under little or no constraints other than what we might interpret to be professionally defensible behavior. Curriculum enactment certainly has a role in a mutual adaptation strategy because we expect teachers to show a high regard and concern for each individual in the classroom in a mutual adaptation strategy. But because the curriculum enactment approach does not make the same demand on the teacher to be responsive to the normative mandate of the school, it represents an unrealistic approach to the school curriculum.

So, the problem of curriculum implementation is not a matter of measuring or being concerned about teacher compliance. Rather it is a matter of attempting to ensure that the full dynamics of the school mission are given life in all aspects of the school experience, without telling teachers how to teach. Fundamentally it is a matter of balancing the concerns of the normative against the concerns of the emergent, of being sure that all children are provided with the opportunity to learn what the school mandates as essential while also being sure that all children are provided with a learning experience sensitive to their particular needs and problems. The normative is largely structured in the purposes of the school and the emergent is largely dependent on the situational judgment of the teacher.

FEATURES OF EFFECTIVE IMPLEMENTATION

A curriculum that operates by mutual adaptation is one that is observant about building teacher and community ownership in the mission of the school, that acknowledges certain political and fiscal realities, and that bases changes on revelations drawn from the evaluation of the curriculum. Effective implementation, as defined here, requires the main agents of the curriculum to be in general agreement with the normative tasks at hand. But it also means that the main agents need to have the resources, time, and insight to complete their work, while also understanding that their work is rooted in an ongoing evaluative effort to improve the school experience.

Group Deliberation

I have made repeated references throughout the book to the *curriculum developer,* implying perhaps that curriculum development work is conducted by a single individual who has command and control over the entire schooling enterprise. The only individuals who even come close to this mark are classroom teachers, who have an opportunity to exercise a great deal of curriculum authority in their classrooms, mostly because they have direct interaction with students and are the main agents of curriculum implementation. But as we learned, even classroom teachers do not have free reign in the curriculum and are circumscribed by wider concerns and mandates. The fact of the matter is that curriculum development is a group exercise, involving various participants who each make some contribution to the overall structure and operation of the school experience. Curriculum developers have some leadership role in organizing and managing the overall project, but they are not the sole decision makers.

Schwab described a process of group deliberation for the design of the curriculum whereby various participants in the operation of the school are involved in ongoing discussion and debate over what needs to be done. He put a premium on the idea of deliberation, which means to ponder and reflect, in order to make the point that the curriculum should not be viewed as a technocratic process that reduces itself to a manual of instructions (often written by agents outside of the school community and the educational situation). Because the curriculum is implemented by teachers according to the wishes of a societal and a professional rationale, it should be nothing less than a local event that makes good use of the groups most intimately associated with the school. Curriculum, says Schwab, "arises at home, [is] seeded, watered, and cultivated by some or all of the teachers who might be involved in its institution" (Schwab, p. 258). The advantages of curriculum making through deliberation are obvious. Where group deliberation prevails, the curriculum is necessarily kept specific to the needs of the local situation. Group deliberation also pays a democratic dividend and gives the curriculum the benefit of drawing ideas from multiple perspectives of expertise and experience. Additionally, the key players in the curriculum development process, most notably the teachers, take practical possession of the school curriculum because of their part in determining it.

Schwab advised that a work group be formed to help manage the deliberative process—a work team of about ten members, half of whom would be teachers and the other half comprising some combination of a principal, student representatives, a school board member and perhaps, depending on the situation, an expert consultant or two. The group would be led by a chairperson whose main responsibilities are to direct and manage the group's proceeding in a way that helps the team arrive at warranted decisions. The work team is expected to identify problems in the curriculum and to find consensual problem solutions—an important point because deliberation not only looks to solve problems but also to identify them. As Reid observed, "deliberation is the practice of the identification and resolution of curriculum problems." Thus, the planning group might find itself involved in deliberations over the school's core purposes or philosophy, the macrocurricular design of the school, the selection of content, or some perception of failure in design or practice. And the deliberative proceedings themselves would shape the curriculum by creating a climate where a diversity of views is exchanged in a way that might reshape the future views of the group members.

The idea of bringing involvement groups together to tackle and otherwise rethink various dimensions of the curriculum development process is not a very complicated idea, but it is nevertheless a departure from the conventional view of having teachers implement, sometimes down to explicit instructional detail, what others have fashioned for them. As Fullan (1982) observed, "One of the basic reasons why planning fails is that planners or decision-makers are unaware of the situations which potential implementers are facing. They introduce changes without providing a means to identify and confront the situational constraints and without attempting to understand the values, ideas, and experiences of those who are essential for implementing any change" (p. 83). Group deliberation acts as a foil to such a circumstance—if teachers and other key determinants in the curriculum have some part in fashioning the curriculum, they will obviously be more inclined to support it. At the same time, the curriculum itself will be more sensitive to the local conditions and the educational situation because of their involvement. If we are going to take the idea of mutual adaptation as our guideline for implementation, we must look for ways to actualize a heady dialogue between design and practice.

But the curriculum does not have a requirement stipulating that everyone needs to be involved in every decision. The fact remains that much of the content curriculum is inherited from state requirements, and many of the core purposes of the school are normative to the society. This is a reality with which teachers, principals, school board members and students have to live. Furthermore, instructional decisions are the domain of classroom teachers. Some value could be gained in subjecting them to some group thinking process, even involving people who have never taught school children, but the process would have to be careful to avoid lapsing into the role of offering instructional prescriptions. Still, every aspect of the curriculum discussed in this book can be approached with a group dynamic in mind. The targets of deliberative group proceedings go to the formation of purposes, the organization of experience, the formation of a school-wide evaluative strategy, and to general policy concerns affecting the practice of the curriculum. These are the elements of the curriculum that direct and color teacher judgment without casting it in one form.

So, in contemplating the role of involvement groups in the curriculum, curriculum developers should think in terms of making the individual school the main unit of participation, thereby keeping an intimacy of association with the local situation. They should try to secure a wide participation base, and find a way to offer an ongoing reflective discussion about what is wrong and what is right with the school, which should, in the end, produce specific strategies for maintaining or resetting purposes, experiences, and evaluation.

Inservice Programs

The conventional wisdom of inservice programs is to use them as training programs for teachers, often for the purpose of helping to improve upon basic instructional and pedagogical skills. Because teachers are the main implementers of the curriculum, this is an understandable convention. Some programs, as indicated earlier, go too far and seek to install new instructional methods in the classroom. But rarely do inservice programs take the opportunity to try to exploit teacher judgment for the widest benefit of the curriculum. Teachers, after all, could be used as means for the broader improvement of the curriculum, rather than ends in and of themselves. Thus, we might find an inservice program functioning to identify problems of common concern in the curriculum or supporting the formation of groups working on particular tasks, such as identifying, organizing, and writing the content goals and core pervasive skills of one or many grade levels. In this manner, the inservice program becomes part of a true mutual adaptation approach toward implementation, where teachers not only change according to new design considerations but where design considerations change according to teacher involvement in deliberative discourse.

The nature of inservice work is logically connected to identifiable concerns in the curriculum, and as such, should be a function of the evaluation of the curriculum. Thus, start-up strategies for inservice are often visible in the evaluation design, in observational data, test scores, and other forms of data representation. So, if we find identifiable problems with the mission of the school, the task of the inservice could be in the direction of re-examining or redeveloping the mission; if the problems are in the direction of classroom discipline or poor test design, again the nature of the inservice shifts accordingly. This becomes an implementational issue because any effort to identify a problem in the curriculum or to pose a solution to it becomes in effect an implementation problem.

Social and Political Realities

Deliberation and group work in the curriculum recognize that curriculum development should arise from the prerogatives of the local educational scene, and that good implementation integrates the voices of key participants, keeping the main mechanisms of curriculum development in mind. But like it or not, various social and political winds blow in and around the school community, and sometimes these forces grab hold of the curriculum in a way that limits the range of expression that can emerge from local deliberative judgments.

Historical examples include the powerful influences exerted by national events on the school curriculum. The most obvious example centered around the 1957 launching of the Soviet Union's *Sputnik*, which was the first satellite to orbit the earth. Cold War anxieties were dramatically heightened with the launching of *Sputnik*, creating a nationwide call for improvements in defense-sensitive fields, including primarily the sciences, mathematics, and foreign languages. The practical effect was the creation of a well-financed group of discipline-centered curriculum programs—designed by scholar-specialists far removed from the local educational scene—that were widely adopted in American high schools.

Today sociopolitical conditions continue to have their effect on practice. Federal legislation embodied in the bipartisan No Child Left Behind Act, for instance, carries with it very particular demands on the states, and by implication, the schools. Among the more visible demands is the priority that the legislation puts on testing programs. In some cases, the effect is that the very worth of a school is judged by how well its students do on a set of statewide standardized tests. The problem, of course, is that the test may not, and probably does not, effectively represent the purposes and the operational nature of the school experience. It usually just represents a selective slant on the school experience, often reading and math achievement. So, here is a sociopolitical reality that may very well undermine the implementational efforts. What's a school to do?

This is an especially difficult spot for struggling schools that inherit a disproportionately large low-income population because they will feel the pressure of this kind of political reality more so than schools with more privileged student populations. Can a school community under this kind of pressure legitimately bow to it and say that the school mandate should be reducible to what the state is testing? Certainly, if this were to happen, the school curriculum would be compromised by a weak theoretical base. It would not be able to make much of a case for itself from the standpoint of the learner, the society, and the subject matter. The real question becomes whether the school can effectively fulfill its obligations to the state (and its tests), while still carrying out a wider, locally derived agenda? This is the unsatisfying reality of the matter. One can try to change the legislation, but short of that, the task facing the design of the curriculum is to find a way to fulfill all of the requirements embodied in the purpose of the school, including those that come down hard from the state.

Sometimes local political realities also affect the implementation of the curriculum. Most of us would probably agree that the role of the school is to challenge and extend local traditions, but this is sometimes easier said than done. Controversial inclusions in the curriculum may not have the support of the local community and might have a hard time on the way to the classroom, meaning that teachers might not be inclined to implement them. Obvious examples consist of curriculum inclusions in sex-education courses—such as the teaching of contraceptive use or the acknowledgment of homosexual relations—or in history teachings that include a less-than-complimentary view of U.S. policy or action, or, for that matter, the teaching of any politicized views. Other problem areas might include efforts to try to integrate the role of religion in the curriculum, especially in contexts of history and politics. And what does one do with an accusation, say, from local minority groups, that Mark Twain's *Huckleberry Finn* should not be taught because of its casual use of racist language? The key to this problem is balance, as teachers should be aware of the fact that they cannot politicize their classrooms or condone any form of religious doctrine. The processes of deliberation could also help by bringing concerns out into an arena of open dialogue. But the point is that if we take deliberation seriously, we might find the curriculum delimited by the exercise of local political views that have their way in the deliberative process.

Time and Resources

Society relies on teachers to implement the curriculum, sometimes without thinking about whether they have the time and the resources to do everything that is expected of them. Teachers are busy people and they often cite shortage of time and paucity of resources as barriers to the implementation of the curriculum. Over the years, I have periodically found myself rushing through important material in the curriculum order to satisfy a content-related mandate in the curriculum. I simply didn't have the time to give proper instructional exposure to all of the content required by the curriculum. And time is not the only factor. Problems with resources are also at play. Requirements to teach x and y obviously cannot be fulfilled unless the school has the available materials to meet the requirements.

Comparing the time allocations given to particular courses and classrooms against the realities of classroom is certainly a profitable undertaking. This might be a component feature in the design of the evaluation. Is there a way, for instance, to find out if too much is being expected from some courses? What are the actual instructional-time realities for each of the key content areas and pervasive-skills areas attached to each course or classroom? Might ability-based grouping assist with meeting content and skill commitments by eliminating the inefficiencies of trying to meet all learning needs in one setting? Is there a way to reorganize courses in the macrocurriculum so that a more efficient coordination exists between purpose and action? Might a block-schedule pattern that uses a team-teaching strategy provide an opportunity to do this? Is there unnecessary duplication in some of the things that teachers do in the curriculum? Might more teacher preparation time give teachers the opportunity to better plan their instructional engagements in a way that could result in better time management? Each of these questions also has to consider side effects. Opting for ability groups using a time-efficiency argument does not account for the potential side effects on the quality of the instructional experience. So, as we look at time and resources, we should not lose sight of the fact that it is the quality of time dedicated to teaching and learning that is most important. It could just be that the best teachers (who are potentially the most inclined to use expressive goals in the classroom and to make emergent detours from the planned curriculum) will be those who are least likely to implement the entire curriculum.

Setting Direction and Purpose

If purposes and goals drive the curriculum, then the work of setting clear and useful purposes is a natural factor in good implementation. But by now the reader should know that I am not saying that purposes should be prescriptive. As indicated, implementation by mutual adaptation cannot be successful without a give and take between design and practice.

It is important to note that the task of setting direction and purpose in the curriculum has more to do to with just the nature of the objectives themselves. One crucial and often overlooked factor has to with the ability of the principal or the curriculum leader to solidify the school community's support for the mission of the school, from which its direction and purposes are set. How many teachers truly have a sense of mission in their work, derived from a unique and special sense of what their schools represent? Imagine the boost given to implementation if teachers were truly dedicated to the school's mission.

This is precisely the kind of project that suits group deliberation so well. The possibilities are interesting. Deliberation could lead to the identification of a uniquely local outlook on schooling or to the handling of particular local problems in the curriculum. Concerns about an increase in the dropout rate, an achievement gap between children from low-income and middle- or high-income families, palpable gender bias in the curriculum, or evidence of drug use among tenth-graders, can each lead to new formations and approaches in the design of the curriculum. The curriculum becomes a ground for problem-solutions, which certainly contributes to its sense of mission and purpose.

But none of this is likely to occur unless some leadership guides the process, ascertaining facts about school community problems and transforming them into workable ideas for the design of the curriculum. The skills needed are those used in facilitating intragroup processes, communicating ideas to all involvement groups, diagnosing sources of weakness in the curriculum, using evaluative data and designing evaluative tools for the betterment of the curriculum, and exercising creative judgment for the redesign of the curriculum.

EXERCISES IN DESIGNING SOLUTIONS

Several years ago, I was asked by a member of a school board to offer an opinion on the topic of all-girl classrooms in high school math and science courses. Apparently, some educators in the school district felt that girls were being shortchanged in such courses and decided to take matters into their own hands, asking the school board for approval to proceed with experimental girls-only classrooms in math and science. Despite the possibility that such classes represented a violation of Title IX, the school district was willing to consider the idea and build a case for an exemption. Given these circumstances, the board wanted to know what I had to say about the idea.

The first questions I asked were what evidence the school had collected to demonstrate that the girls' education in math and science was indeed less adequate than the education received by the boys. Were the GPAs of the girls lower? Did the enrollment patterns in the advanced science and math courses demonstrate a disproportional advantage to boys? Were boys who graduated from the high school selecting math and science majors in college more so than did girls who graduated? Were good observational data on the nature of math and science instruction in relation to girls and boys collected and analyzed? Was there palpable bias in the textbooks used? Were surveys or structured interviews taken to get the apparent problem seen by the local educators? As it turned out, the school had no answers to these questions. The single factor at work was a petition, by two or three educators, that was based on their individual perceptions.

I also asked about the appropriateness of the curriculum response. If the evidence pointed to the conclusion that the education of girls in math and science was deficient, was the necessary response all-girl classrooms? Could such a response produce its own negative by-products? Was there a better way to proceed?

The teachers, and in turn the school board, had put the cart before the horse. They were asking a programmatic question before considering the dynamics of the educational situation. Although one could argue against all-girl classrooms from legalistic and philosophical grounds, the real issue was gender equity in the math and science classrooms. If one started with the question of equity, and continued along with an evidence-collection process, one could very well go down a very different programmatic path.

In every school, various problems will appear that have important consequences for the education of the school children. Identifying these problems and finding a way to use them as working material for the improvement of the school experience is a vital and important function of the curriculum. I have thought of a few scenarios, most of which are taken from my own experience with schools, that might be useful in giving the reader some practice in the skill of designing solutions through the curriculum. I also suggest a process, detailed here, that might help with the task in the context of a deliberative work group.

The initiating event in the process is fairly obvious: identifying the problem. Next, the various sources that can be used to get a better handle on the nature of the problem must be considered. Such sources include specialists (in a subject area, instruction, research, and so on), students (current students, graduates, future students, dropouts, perhaps students in a particular program area), parents, teachers, employers, and community and government leaders. Existing data sources should also be examined. School records, demographic data, census-type data, data from other schools and communities, and national data might be on the list. Ways of producing new data that might speak to the problem (a research effort, an experiment, a survey instrument, observations, and so forth) should be explored, and ways of responding to the findings of such inquiries should be determined. The response can deal with any and all aspects of the curriculum. This includes the actual coursework, inservice training needs, community outreach programs, after-school programs, extra-classroom activities, and classroom-based adjustments. Time and resource limitations, social and political realities, and other such constraints must be acknowledged in order to keep the response reasonable. Here are a few examples of what I have in mind.

Scenario 1: Weighted Grade Point Averages

The local parent association is troubled over the manner in which grade point averages are calculated in your high school. They say students who take advanced placement and honors courses are punished because the grades given in these difficult courses are not weighed more heavily than courses in, say, the vocational arts or other nonacademic and nonadvanced coursework.

The problem.   Do students who take AP or honors courses suffer some disadvantage or inequity because their courses carry the same GPA weight as non-honors and non-academic courses?

What we need to know about the problem.   Are AP or honors courses more severely graded than other non-academic courses? Are the prospects of getting into college negatively affected by such a policy? What is the overall effect on the college-bound GPA? What are the parents' and teachers' views on this matter? If the policy is changed to a weighted system, will it generate another kind of problem or negative side effect? How do other schools handle the situation?

The results and the response.   If the findings show that hyper-inflation of grades is occurring in the AP or honors courses, and that it is, in effect, easier to get a high grade in such courses than in so-called non-academic courses, the argument for weighing the GPA is not as strong. Conversely if the data show a ferociously difficult grading distribution, the argument for weighing might be a good one, as it would be if there was evidence that the prospects of the college-bound students are being hurt by the lack of a GPA weight, or that the teachers who teach the non-academic courses agree that such a weighting mechanism should be used. On the other hand, teachers might argue that many of the honors students simply would not be able to excel in a woodworking or vocation-oriented class, and that seeing such classes as easy is a misperception and little more than an elitist bias.

Scenario 2: Attitudes toward Math and Science

The achievement data in mathematics and science in your school are very positive, the highest they have ever been. But only a few high school graduates have opted to take a college major in math or science over for the past three years, a drop of about 60% from the previous three-year average. One parent recently told the school board that the math and science teachers in the high school do a very effective job of teaching math and science but they also do a very effective job of teaching students to hate math and science.

The problem.   Is the nature of high school math and science education having a negative influence on student attitudes toward student math and science and on student career interests in math and science?

What we need to know about the problem.   Is the reported interest in math and science relatively lower than the reported interest in other academic areas? Do observational classroom data suggest a lack of idea orientation or poor teaching strategies in the math and science classes? Can the lack of interest in math and science as a career or a college major be attributable to some factor outside of school? Is the drop in appreciation for math and science a logical and even acceptable consequence of higher overall achievement?

The results and the response.   If survey and observational data suggest that something in the nature of the math and science classroom is failing to inspire students to pursue math and science careers, the logical place to look for reforms might be with the materials and teaching techniques used in the classroom. Simply raising consciousness among the teachers about the problem might also be helpful in bringing forward changes in pedagogy and in sociopersonal engagements in the classroom. This could be done by taking a dramatic stance about the importance of encouraging student appreciations for math and science in the design of the curriculum's purposes. If the dramatic drop is attributable to other factors, such a precipitous increase of interest in business majors or simply a change in the demographic character of the population, then another tack might be taken.

Scenario 3: No Pass, No Play?

The superintendent of the school district is getting a lot of pressure to adopt a "no pass, no play" policy. "If kids cannot or will not do school work," she states, "then maybe we shouldn't let them play football or any other sport." As someone who is involved in curriculum development, what is your advice to the superintendent?

The problem.   Should the school adopt a "no pass, no play" policy and what might be the overall effect on the curriculum?

What we need to know about the problem.   What percentage of the student population might be affected by the adoption of such a policy? What does the educational literature say about the effects of such policies? What do student and parent surveys indicate? What are the educational effects emerging from the sports programs? Do these effects stand on their own merit?

The results and the response.   If the data indicate that the sports program satisfactorily fulfills its own educational agenda, say, perhaps that it provides the only outlet available for athletic aptitudes, it enhances social interaction as well as harmony across races and ethnicities, and it helps to make adolescents physically healthy and strong, then one conclusion might be that it stands on its own as an educational feature of the school and should not be viewed as some kind of luxury that goes only to those who do well in academics. If it does not fulfill its educational mandate, then that is another problem altogether. Do parents and teachers support the policy? If only a very small percentage of students is affected by the policy, could another tactic be used to deal specifically with some of the students in question? If it affects a huge percentage of the population, might the school find its own sports programs undermined?

   Now it is your turn. The following case descriptions give you the opportunity to think about ways to use the curriculum to solve budding problems in the school. After reading each, try to isolate the nature of the problem. Then describe the kind of data that you would like to collect to find out more about the problem. Formulate some working hypotheses that might explain why the problem exists and ask yourself what you might need to know to verify or reject the hypotheses. Speculate about the curriculum response you might advocate if one of the hypotheses you formulated were confirmed. Which of the four questions in Tyler's rationale might be a good starting point for developing a curricular remedy to the problem? How might the three factors play in this process? Describe the process you use.

1. A group of adolescents from your school was caught spray painting racist remarks at the local park. This is the fourth incidence of this type since the beginning of the school year. You sense growing racial tensions in your high school.
2. You have noticed that admission to the gifted and talented program in the elementary school is based on aptitude tests that have little validity for young people. You also noticed that the few kids who are admitted to the program do not reflect the racial or socioeconomic characteristics of the district.

3. You looked over your list of students documented as having a learning or behavioral disability and found something unusual. Ninety percent of the children on the list were boys.

4. Ninety percent of the students from the upper-quartile incomes in your high school go to college while only five percent of students from the bottom quartile of incomes go to college. This gap has never been wider in the history of your school and is wider than any other high school in your district.

5. Your school has recently been subjected to a lot of graffiti and defacement. The cost associated with clean-up and increasing monitoring of school grounds is hitting the budget hard.

6. A group of parents, mostly Russian immigrants, is insulted at the school's failure to be sensitive to the group's cultural and linguistic heritage. They want Russian history and Russian culture taught in the high school and Russian language classes for all of their children. They claim that multicultural education has to celebrate their background and help to maintain their language. First-generation Russian-Americans represent about thirty percent of the school population.

7. Forty percent of the students enrolled in the low-track English and math classes in your school are from a minority group. Yet only ten percent of the student population comprises minorities.

8. Some parents approach you with their concern about a perceived increase in the number of preadolescent smokers in your middle school. One parent, a medical doctor, shows you national data that demonstrate that about one half of all smokers start their habit at around age 14.

9. The dropout rate in your high school has shown little signs of improvement. Although the dropout rate in your school is no worse than that of other schools in your area, you notice that Hispanic children drop out at a rate three times greater than that of white and black children enrolled in your school.

SUMMARY

The nature of curriculum implementation is not about finding ways to get teachers to comply with orders emerging from command and control. Rather, curriculum implementation is a matter of mutual adaptation between the factors of design and the factors of practice. It holds to the notion that good implementation must be allegiant to the design of the curriculum and that the design of the curriculum might recognize the authority and the importance of the emergent condition in the classroom.

Curriculum development is, at its very core, group work, involving the participation of various key players in the educational situation. Because of this reality, the curriculum developer should take advantage of strategies that bring involvement groups together to identify and solve problems in the planning process. The group deliberation process discussed by Schwab is one way to begin to tap this important source of information. Group deliberation, in fact, helps to build widespread ownership and involvement in the design of the curriculum, which naturally assists with implementation. Other factors that contribute to good implementation include using inservice programs to not just train teachers, but to also exploit their insights for the wider service of the curriculum. Time, resources, and sociopolitical realities also have influence.

Finally, good implementation is always served when the curriculum is responsive to emergent problems in the school community. When we use the curriculum to help solve identifiable problems we are engaged in a task of notable importance because we are rethinking not only what we are doing but why we are doing it.

DISCUSSION QUESTIONS AND SUGGESTED ACTIVITIES

1. Explain how curriculum implementation is more than about teacher compliance to design.

2. Contrast the fidelity approach to implementation to the mutual adaptation approach. How are expressive goals treated in each approach?

3. What makes the curriculum enactment approach to implementation problematic in a public school setting?

4. What are the advantages of group deliberation as they relate to curriculum implementation?

5. Describe how group deliberation might work in the context of a curriculum development project.

6. What did Schwab mean when he wrote curriculum "arises at home, [is] seeded, watered, and cultivated by some or all of the teachers who might be involved in its institution"?

7. Describe how inservice programs could be used to help carry out a strategy of mutual adaptation toward curriculum implementation.

8. How do sociopolitical realities factor into the implementation of the curriculum?

9. How are time and resource realities factors in implementation? How might a school conduct a study of time and resource allocations to get a better handle on their influence in the curriculum?

NOTES

Beauchamp, G. (1975). *Curriculum theory.* Wilmette, IL: The Kagg Press.
Fullan, M. (1982). *The meaning of educational change.* Toronto: Ontario Institute for Studies in Education Press.

Reid, W.A. (1993). Does Schwab improve on Tyler? *Journal of Curriculum Studies, 25*(6), 499–510.

Schwab, J.J. The practical 4: Something for curriculum professors to do. *Curriculum Inquiry, 13,* 239–265.

Snyder, J., Bolin, F. & Zumwalt, K. (1992). Curriculum implementation. In P.W. Jackson (Ed.), *Handbook of research on curriculum.* New York: Macmillan.

THE VOCABULARY OF CURRICULUM DESIGN

aims, goals, and objectives   hierarchical levels of purpose in curriculum design. Aims represent broad targets for the curriculum. They are not specific enough to direct instruction, but they form the general outline for more specific targets. Goals represent as intermediate level of specificity and objectives the most precise and instructionally sensitive targets in the curriculum.

assessment   appraisal process that affects student grading and other judgments of individual performance. This process of appraisal is known as assessment. Assessment is principally designed to show what a *person* knows or can do.

broad fields, as a pattern of content organization   an approach to the organization of subject matter that seeks to synthesize content across an entire branch of knowledge.

Carnegie unit requirements   a measure used to represent a 120-hour instructional obligation of time to a subject area over the course of an academic year. Most states retain course area requirements for high school graduation. The states usually stipulate an exposure requirement to a number of core subject areas (commonly the language arts, social studies, mathematics, science, and physical education/health) for graduation. These are typically expressed as Carnegie unit requirements.

comprehensive school mission   comprises four main categories for the mandate of the public school: personal-individual development, socio-civic development, academic-intellectual development, and vocational development. These can be used to begin to broadly frame a comprehensive school mission.

content, levels of   Taba described four levels of organization for the content of the curriculum: (1) specific facts and processes; (2) basic ideas; (3) concepts; and (4) discipline-centered thought patterns and methods of inquiry. These levels can be used as building blocks for the organization of the content in the macrocurriculum.

content standards   standards that simply outline and organize what should be taught in the curriculum from the standpoint of subject matter. They are sometimes accompanied by performance standards that describe how students will demonstrate that they achieved the content standards, and by proficiency standards that provide criteria to scale or measure the degree of progress on the performance standards.

correlation, as a pattern of content organization   an approach to the organization of the subject matter that brings together two or more subjects of study into some common contact points. The subject matter lines retain their place in a correlation but are brought together for a particular time and a particular purpose. In some cases, it can be planned in a team teaching arrangement or simply articulated by two or more teachers who share the same students.

criteria of good aims   three criteria articulated by Dewey used in constructing purposes. First, the formation of aims had to rise up from the educational situation. Second, aims need to have a tentative and flexible character to them, allowing for some range of interpretation as well as some flexibility in shifting course, as circumstance dictates. Finally, aims should produce a freeing or releasing of activities in the curriculum, not a tight constricting or narrowing of experience.

criterion-referenced tests   used to ascertain a learner's performance against a predetermined task or criterion. Such tests are sometimes known as absolute measures of performance. Criterion-referenced exams are not driven by a desire to compare performance between students but by an effort to subject performance to a reference standard or criterion of proficiency.

currere   Latin derivative of the term *curriculum,* associated with the idea of running a racecourse.

curriculum enactment perspective, on curriculum implementation   a perspective on curriculum implementation that puts a great deal of priority on the classroom-based (microcurricular) moment in the school experience. Implementation is viewed as a matter of giving teachers the independence to create experiences that may or may not have any link to normative standards or purposes.

curriculum performance, levels of   three teaching levels of performance. Level I, known as imitative-maintenance, is marked by routine and adoptive practices. Activities are essentially scripted by teacher manuals, closed instructional systems or a teaching-to-the-test mentality. Level II, known as mediative, represents a movement away from simple maintenance and adoption and a movement toward refinements or adjustments in practice based on some awareness of the dynamic condition of the classroom. Level III, generative-creative, stands as the highest ideal of professionalism, because it sees teaching as a problem-solving process that requires the teacher to make judgments based on the widest school purposes and the evaluation of learning needs.

deliberation   a group method used to identify and resolve curriculum problems. A deliberative planning group might find itself involved in deliberations over the school's core purposes or philosophy, macrocurricular design of the school, selection of content, or over some perception of failure in design or practice. Where group deliberation prevails, the curriculum is necessarily kept connected to the particularities of the local situation.

direct instruction   an instructional method that helps students achieve mastery of key ideas, facts, or skills. Direct instruction starts with a teacher presentation (lecture or demonstration), is followed by some experience in guided practice, and then shifts to the provision of feedback and corrections. Independent practice activities and ultimately demonstrations of mastery complete the procedure.

discretionary space   the degree of freedom accorded to a teacher in the design of the curriculum. The idea is to give the teacher enough freedom in the curriculum to make emergent classroom judgments.

discussion-based instruction   an instructional method that uses teacher facilitation and student discovery. Discussion-based instruction obviously requires smaller student groups. This naturally enhances the prospects for discussion.

evaluation   the sum effort of data collected to determine whether key purposes and objectives have been met at a school-wide or classroom-wide level. Testing mechanisms, observations, surveys, samples of student work, and interviews could all be used in evaluation.

extra-classroom experiences   the feature of the school curriculum that goes beyond the physical limits of the classroom. Learning occurs beyond the classroom and the activities that the school chooses to sponsor outside of the classroom are no less important than those justified within the classroom. These activities are referred to as extra classroom experiences.

expressive goals   the exercise of microcurricular judgments that was not part of the pre-planned sequence of instructional events. Expressive goals are important to the curriculum development process because they give the school experience important flexibility while also honoring the professional judgment of the teacher. They are the main ways that teachers can honestly respond to the particularities of their classroom situation.

fidelity perspective, on curriculum implementation   a view of curriculum implementation concerned with the degree of exactitude that exists between the planned curriculum and the implemented experience. The fidelity perspective implies that the curriculum is a script for teachers to follow, one that could even include instructional prescriptions.

fusion, as a pattern of content organization   a pattern of content organization that seeks to bring two or more subject fields (or subfields) together in a way that erases all distinctive lines and essentially merges or blends them into one synthesized subject.

general education   the macrocurricular feature of the curriculum that refers to the educational experiences common to all youth in the school. This can be contemplated as common requirements, which might include being taught common knowledge, common skills sets, and common values, with or without common experiences.

horizontal articulation   how all school experiences fit together within a grade level, usually over the course of an academic year. If we think about scope and sequence as a horizontal articulation concern, we are thinking about how school work done early in the academic year will logically flow into work done later in the year. Whenever we think about the order of educational events and the range of expansion on key ideas, concepts, and content taught within a grade level, we are working on the horizontal axis.

independent and individualized instruction   school work done by students that is accomplished without the direct assistance of the teacher. Independent work in the classroom is associated with individualizing causes. It should account for pacing differences and other forms of differentiation related to aptitude, achievement, and interest levels. In this way, independent instruction represents an important procedure for individualization in the curriculum.

inquiry-based instruction   an orientation to teaching that tries to put the student into the role of a researcher.

integrated core, as a pattern of content organization   a pattern of content organization that looks to core values and core problems in the living experience of the learner. The organizational center of the core curriculum transcends subject matter lines and is built around topical focal points of inquiry.

instruction   a planned course of learning experiences, designed and justified by the teacher, which aims to fulfill the purposes of the school curriculum.

item discrimination   a metric used to tell us how well a test item on an exam does with the highest performing students on the exam. A positive discrimination, which is desirable, means that the students who got the item right were, generally speaking, the students who had the highest overall scores on the exam. Item discriminations apply to norm-referenced exams and indicate how effectively the items are discriminating between the relative performances of the students.

latent curriculum   that aspect of the curriculum experience that teaches implicit lessons about important values and attitudes. Latent messages accompany all manifestly rationalized experiences in the school in both positive (learning to love to read) and negative (learning to hate school) ways.

learner, as a theoretical factor in curriculum development   knowledge of which provides all kinds of benefits to the curriculum. The nature of the learner accounts for at least four main factors: (1) developmental issues in learning; (2) individual aptitudes and deficiencies; (3) home and community cultures; and (4) individual interest levels. Each of these has a role in making important procedural decisions.

macrocurriculum   refers to the all-school experience. It is most concerned with building-level design factors, including the organization of courses across and within grade levels, school-wide mission features, and school-wide (extra-classroom) experiences.

microcurriculum   development and operation of classroom-based activities. Curriculum development in the microcurriculum is conducted through an articulation between classroom actions and macropurposes, and includes any number of actions pertaining to instructional change, such as the development of classroom units, the design of lessons, the application of various teaching models, and the design of classroom-based assessments.

mutual adaptation perspective, on curriculum implementation   perspective on curriculum implementation that is modeled on the notion that curriculum development is an interplay between the design of the curriculum and the practice of the curriculum. Under mutual adaptation, the teacher has an obligation to the design of the school experience, meaning that she must account for the normative features of the school mandate, but the design of the school experience also has an obligation to teachers, meaning that it provides direction to them while also acceding to their emergent professional judgments.

norm-referenced tests   exams that feature what is known as relative measures, which means that an individual's score on the exam is relative to the scores of other individuals. In this way, the norm-referenced test is designed to produce a distribution of different scores that allows the school to judge higher and lower performers.

pedagogy   what actually happens when teachers begin to teach, when they begin to interact with students and conduct or implement the planned instructional experience. Pedagogy is what we might view as the emergent or expressive side of teaching. We witness it in the spontaneous and situationally bound behaviors of teachers.

pervasive skills values   cut across or bridge virtually all content areas of the curriculum. Because they have no particularized place in any one realm of inquiry or subject matter, pervasive skills/values play an important role in giving some unity and focus to the curriculum.

portfolio assessment   medium for appraisal of the actual work accomplished by students during their time in school. This could be done by the teachers—who would keep an ongoing folder or record (from September to June) of the work accomplished by the students—or by the students themselves. The intention is to provide object examples of just how far the students have grown in an academic year.

reliability   refers to the consistency of response witnessed on an appraisal instrument. One form of reliability, known as stability consistency, concerns the consistency of a test over a period of time. Alternate-form reliability refers to the consistency between alternate forms of the same exam. Internal consistency refers to the extent to which an appraisal instrument consistently represents a single construct or outcome. Obviously, in all the cases discussed, good clarity in the questioning routines, the criteria used to score the tests, and the directions and administration of the test help the cause of reliability.

rubrics   scoring guides for the appraisal of constructed responses. Rubrics describe the things we are looking to find in a response. If these descriptors are clear and unambiguous, they are less likely to give us reliability problems. The orientation of the rubric can be holistic, meaning that it simply aims to give a general assessment of quality without specifically aiming to judge any of the constituent elements of the response or it can be analytic, which aims to offer some judgment of quality against named specifics.

society, as a theoretical factor in curriculum development   a theoretical factor in the curriculum that obliges the school to reflect the key skills, values, principles, and attitudes of society. This essentially means that democratic skills and values must be contemplated in the curriculum. So, we think about the school experience from the standpoint of encouraging the skills and values central to effective participation in democratic life.

specialized education   refers to individualized educational experiences in the school. Specialized education encompasses several different functions, including what we traditionally label as exploratory education (educational experiences that respond to and broaden the individual interest levels of students), enrichment education (educational experiences that respond to high aptitude, achievement, and interest levels), remedial education (educational experiences designed to assist with lower performing students) and career education (educational experiences, such as vocational education, designed to fulfill particular career needs).

subject matter, as a theoretical factor in curriculum development   a theoretical factor in the curriculum that asks what content or knowledge is deemed to be most worthwhile in the experience of the school. The factor of subject matter forces us to make a case for some organized sense of useful and worthy content in the curriculum.

Tyler's rationale   a three-part continuum designed by Ralph Tyler for the curriculum development process, represented by a movement from purposes to experiences to evaluation.

two-dimensionality in the formation of objectives   refers to the kind of behavior or skill expected students to learn and the content to which it applies. Thus, we can say that the formation of objectives must seek to integrate some conception of content knowledge with some conception of skill development.

validity   the extent to which our appraisal instrument can be trusted to yield truthful results. Various forms of validity apply to curriculum evaluation. Content validity refers to the linkage between what is taught in the school experience and what is actually appraised in the evaluation or assessment. Predictive validity refers to the capacity of an appraisal instrument to predict future behaviors or effects. And construct validity refers to the capacity of an appraisal instrument to effectively represent a particular characteristic (such as thinking skills, self-esteem, or democratic attitudes).

vertical articulation   how the analytical elements of the curriculum fit together across grade levels. In other words, how is the teaching of math in seventh grade related to the teaching of math in eighth grade? Vertical articulation is the tool we use to build coherence in the educational experience of children over the course of their entire school career. Using vertical articulation, we build prerequisites into courses and we see scope and sequence as a matter that goes across grade levels.

SUBJECT INDEX